WAKING THE SLEEPING GIANT

March 2022

WAKING THE SLEEPING
GIANT

Unlocking the Hidden Power of
Business to Save the Planet

JAKE KHEEL

LIONCREST
PUBLISHING

WAKING THE SLEEPING GIANT
Unlocking the Hidden Power of Business to Save the Planet

ISBN   978-1-5445-2012-4   *Hardcover*
       978-1-5445-0391-2   *Paperback*
       978-1-5445-0390-5   *Ebook*

Dedicated to two sustainability pioneers—

Ted Kheel and Frank Rainieri

CONTENTS

FOREWORD

IF YOU VISIT PUNTA CANA IN THE DOMINICAN REPUBLIC, you can have a lovely time enjoying all the tropical vacation classics: swimming, sunbathing, snorkeling, hammocks, golf, piña coladas, you name it.

But if you have a little curiosity and an extra hour or two, you can also get a peek at a lesser-known side of Punta Cana. This is a side that you won't get at your average resort—and it's fascinating.

You can see an innovative laboratory where scientists are farming coral to save the reef ecosystem. You'll see thousands of wriggly worms composting garbage. You'll see endangered hawks that have made the resort grounds their new home.

That's what this book's author Jake Kheel spends his days creating. Jake and his boss Frank Rainieri, along with Rainieri's wife and kids, have created a unique resort, Grupo Puntacana, that combines environmental activism with good business. It's a model that proves you can both make green and be green. *Waking the Sleeping Giant* is an important guide to how other businesses can do the same. It's a vital message.

Now admittedly, I'm a bit biased. I have a long history with

Punta Cana. My grandfather Ted Kheel, who died ten years ago, was a New York-based labor lawyer and civil rights activist who represented Martin Luther King Jr., among others. He was also an environmental advocate long before it was trendy.

In 1969, on a bit of a lark, he invested in an undeveloped patch of jungle in the Dominican Republic. Everyone thought it would be a bottomless money pit. But my grandfather made a smart decision: He teamed up with a then 24-year-old Dominican businessman named Frank Rainieri.

The two of them started slow. In the early 70s, they built a resort of just ten thatched-roof huts. I remember going as a kid. There was barely phone service. There was a single fuzzy black-and-white TV in the rec room. It was an adventure to even get there. Punta Cana International Airport didn't exist. The trip included a seven-hour jeep ride over dirt roads from the DR's capital, Santo Domingo, with the driver occasionally hopping out to chop branches with a machete.

But over the next decades, Frank and his family (his wife Haydee, and his kids Frank Elias, Francesca and Paola) have done a remarkable thing. They've built this area into a huge tourist mecca, providing thousands of jobs and an international airport. And, inspired by my grandfather, they've been on a mission to make it a sustainable resort.

To that end, my grandfather and Frank had the foresight to hire Jake fifteen years ago to be Grupo Puntacana's environmental guru. Jake is my second cousin, the great-grandnephew of Ted Kheel. Ted saw in Jake that key combination: entrepreneurial spirit and social conscience.

Here, Jake tells the stories of how he's done it, while feeding tourists at the same time. You'll read about how to make a golf course that doesn't soak up a lot of water (it uses a special type of desert-bred grass and recycled water). You'll read about how to deal with the environmental crisis of invasive lionfish that were devouring the coral.

It's a great book. And I say that with some amount of annoyance. I'm a professional writer who has spent years attempting to hone my craft. Jake created this book without seeming to break a sweat. (Not to mention, he's a triathlete, has a beautiful wife and son, and lives in a gorgeous part of the world, so that's also kind of maddening). But Jake also happens to be a wonderful and thoughtful guy who is helping the world in big ways, so it's hard to hold a grudge. Especially after a couple of piña coladas in a hammock.

AJ JACOBS

JOURNALIST, LECTURER, HUMAN GUINEA PIG, AND

AUTHOR OF FOUR *NEW YORK TIMES* BESTSELLERS

INTRODUCTION

I WAS SIX YEARS OLD WHEN MY MOM HAD AN ALLIGATOR shot on our front lawn. It was 1983 and the American alligator had nearly been wiped out in the United States from poaching. Under strict protection by the Endangered Species Act, you could get arrested or pay a big fine for simply bothering an alligator, much less blasting one with a shotgun.

The Endangered Species Act, however, wasn't working for my family. My mom called the local authorities and she was told the animal had to bite someone to be removed. She had no choice but to take matters into her own hands. She had two kids and four dogs running around the house all day. A ten-foot dinosaur with a mouth full of sharp teeth on her lawn was not an option. If pest control wouldn't remove the critter, our neighbor Johnny Shultz would happily take care of it.

Riddled with buckshot, the dead gator sank, but soon its body bloated with air and gas. Like a reptile zombie, it floated back to the surface. Under instructions from our mom to hide the endangered contraband from the authorities, my brother and I lassoed the corpse and stashed it in a nearby ditch, proudly showing it off to our friends as our "pet" 'gator.

I was still pretty young, but even then it struck me that any law that forced people to do the opposite of what it intended was flawed. Instead of protecting the alligator, we were forced to kill it. There had to be a better way.

My brother and I grew up on a six-acre plant nursery surrounded by still-wild southern Florida swamp, horse farms, and backwoods characters blasting country music from their pickup trucks. We roamed the nearby woods, mucked around in canals, fished in man-made ponds, and chased our dogs around the neighborhood.

Animals were a big part of our childhood. My mother was an animal-lover—she raised tropical birds and fish, dogs, cats, guinea pigs, and even a couple of miniature horses. But she also would not hesitate to take out any dangerous wildlife that made its way onto the farm, like the poor alligator. Once, my mom pulled over on our way home from school and stoned a poisonous water moccasin snake to death in the middle of the road. My brother and I watched in stunned silence from the backseat.

We later moved to Massachusetts and while there were no snakes or alligators, we spent most of our time splashing around in the marshes and ponds of our rural town. I had no idea at the time that my childhood adventures in Nature would lead to the field of sustainability. All I knew was I liked to play outside. (Note: Throughout this book I spell Nature with a capital N as is typically done in the life sciences and also to emphasize the profound uniqueness and importance of the natural world.)

The idea of environmental protection came into clearer focus for me when my elementary school designed an environmental crash course for our seventh-grade class. For several weeks, all of our classes were taught through the prism of the environment. We measured tree heights in math class. We read Rachel Carson's *Silent Spring* in English class. We studied the environmental movement in history class. We learned about acid rain, pollution, global warming, and, of course, the Endangered Species Act.

Before then, it had never occurred to me that Nature, the thing I treasured the most, was so seriously threatened. The rainforest, a place I had never seen, was being mowed over and transformed into cow pastures by the second. Animals I had only seen on TV were being extinguished off the face of the Earth. Aerosol spray and leaky refrigerators created a growing hole in the ozone layer. Our entire planet was warming. Yet no one was talking about it. How could I be so oblivious to such a serious situation? This really got my attention.

I decided I had two options. I could continue to blissfully enjoy Nature while it was steadily demolished, or I could try to do something about it. I was the kind of kid that made drastic decisions, so at age twelve I chose to dedicate my life to protecting the environment.

FROM SPIDER MONKEYS TO DON QUIXOTE

As a Wesleyan University undergraduate, I began by studying all the "ology's": conservation biology, geology, ecology. I understood that science was inextricably linked to environmental protection, but I also knew I didn't want to be a scientist. In fact, I wasn't even sure I wanted to go college. I dropped out before my sophomore year and moved to Costa Rica. Sitting in a classroom felt too far removed from saving the rainforest, so I went to the country that I had heard was synonymous with Nature. I signed up to build trails as a volunteer at the Monteverde Cloud Forest Reserve.

My first day on the job, we spent eight hours hauling bags of cement and dragging bundles of fifteen-foot long metal rebar through the lush forest trails. Our task was to build a bridge over a stream in one of the most remote and least visited areas in the park. With no roads or motorized vehicles allowed, it took back-breaking labor to build even a simple bridge.

At lunch, I sat exhausted, dripping wet from the rain and sweat, eating a "gallo pinto" (rice and bean) sandwich. What the hell I was doing? I wondered. What did building a bridge have to do with protecting the cloud forest?

I contemplated quitting on my first day, when suddenly we heard a crashing sound in the canopy above. Our work crew watched a family of spider monkeys noisily making their way towards us, pausing long enough to observe and throw some fruit our way, before moving on. We spent only a few moments with them, but I was hooked. One surprise visit by wild monkeys was enough to convince me to stick out four incredible months in Costa Rica, immersed in its rich ecological diversity.

Building trails also helped me realize that there are a lot of ways to contribute to helping wildlife, like those monkeys. Building bridges made the cloud forest more accessible to visitors. Our bridge allowed more people to have the experience of spontaneously connecting with animals in the wild. It didn't take a scientist to do that. I discovered there was a role for all types of people in environmental protection.

Refreshed and focused after my Costa Rican sojourn, I returned to Wesleyan intent on completing my degree. Though still convinced my future was in the environment, I settled on a Spanish Literature major, moonlighting in environmental studies. College would be about reading Don Quixote and Gabriel García Márquez, not memorizing plant taxonomy.

After college, I bounced around the US and abroad, jumping between environmental internships and restaurant jobs, until I decided to get serious about my career. I spent two years sharpening my eco-credentials at Cornell, earning a master's in environmental management.

My breakthrough came after grad school, when I found a job working for my great uncle Ted Kheel, at his environmental foundation in New York City. Already into his 80s, Ted was a late convert to environmentalism but he had developed a deep passion for the issue. After a long and celebrated career as a labor lawyer and mediator, Ted dedicated his golden years to launching a collection of not-for-profit foundations undertaking environmental initiatives in and around New York City. Ted took me under his wing and I became his trusty sidekick.

For three years, we worked closely together on his foundations' efforts. For me, it was a total immersion in running a not-for-profit. I got to wear half a dozen different hats working on fundraising, selling sponsorships, organizing conferences, managing websites, publishing books, even writing the curriculum for a university ecology class. Far more important than Ted's assortment of quirky projects, I had the opportunity to absorb lessons directly from one of the country's most renowned problem-solvers. I was like a young apprentice learning under the conflict resolution master, sharpening my skills for future challenges.

One day at the office, Ted's Dominican business partner, Frank Rainieri, approached me about working for their resort in the Dominican Republic. Frank and Ted had been in business together for decades. I had met Frank before and had even done an internship at the resort, helping his foundation for a few months after college. Despite this, I never imagined working for the resort full time. Frank was a businessman and a developer, not an environmentalist.

Frank persisted. The foundation director had gone back to school and Frank was in a tough spot. He needed a new director and sensed that, though inexperienced, I had potential. He believed the resort's environmental efforts would be energized from some fresh blood. Ted was disappointed I was leaving, but he also recognized a big opportunity for my career.

I packed my bags and moved to Punta Cana, Dominican Republic. Almost immediately, I started questioning my decision. I had set out to save Nature and here I was taking a job for a private company. Grupo Puntacana, it turned out, is not just a resort. It's an expansive group of tourism-related businesses, including hotels, an international airport, golf courses, real estate development, an electricity and water utility, a security company, and even an industrial laundry facility. This sure didn't seem like saving the rainforest. In fact, my new employer was more like a fast-growing city than a national park.

It had also never occurred to me to work in tourism. I always imagined I would work as a national park ranger or in a conservation organization saving monkeys, like I had done in Costa Rica. I took the job to get some useful real-world experience. At the very least, I could pad my resume and live by the beach for a year or two.

This turned out to be my first taste on the sustainability frontlines and it changed my life and career. Fifteen years later, I am still working for Frank and Grupo Puntacana. I can't imagine a more effective platform for protecting the environment than working for a company. But I wasn't always so convinced.

THE ENVIRONMENT VS. DEVELOPMENT

What had I gotten myself into? The Punta Cana region is a thriving, rapidly growing tourism destination. Grupo Puntacana is one of its most important promoters, and the motor driving the region's growth is tourism.

Yet I was an eco guy. I had never studied hospitality and had no particular interest in the travel industry. I knew nothing about airports or real estate. I hate golf. I am a proud environmentalist, first and foremost. What could I possibly contribute to conservation working for a company whose objective, it seemed, was to steamroll Nature to make money? Wasn't the very idea of constructing hotels and golf courses completely at odds with saving the planet? Surely my classmates at Cornell would be horrified by my new job at a Nature-extinguishing resort.

I soon discovered that despite its money-making veneer, Grupo Puntacana (GPC) had a long trajectory in sustainability, long before it was in vogue. GPC had voluntarily created an environmental division that self-policed its assorted businesses, keeping them in line *without* impeding the growth of the company. It had formed the Grupo Puntacana Foundation, a not-for-profit funded by the company, that got its hands dirty confronting messy social and environmental challenges, while functioning like an extension of the business. The Foundation was tasked with minimizing the resort's impact on the environment but, more intriguing, to help devise creative solutions to different ecological challenges facing the entire Punta Cana region. Now I would be leading those efforts.

My new position posed an intellectual challenge: How to achieve the two equally important, but often adversarial goals of economic growth and environmental protection. While I was working for Ted, he repeatedly lectured that the conflict between Nature and development was the biggest challenge facing mankind. He was convinced that sustainable development was the best way to resolve this conflict. Ted's insights were prescient, but at the time it was still just theory to me. Grupo Puntacana gave me a chance to try it out in the real world.

I soon discovered that the private sector could have a profoundly positive impact on society if its power and energy were channeled properly. Companies, I learned, could be induced not only to improve their own practices but also to make valuable, far-reaching contributions to environmental protection. In fact, it didn't take long to convince me that thoughtful businesspeople are the key to reversing our current planetary crisis.

However, changing the way businesses like Grupo Puntacana operate would require embedding my personal passion for protecting Nature within the reality of the private sector. My single-minded focus on conservation had to be adjusted to a more versatile, flexible goal of achieving this ideal called "sustainable development." Rather than sacrificing my values, I would have to figure out how to protect the environment from the inside of a company out. I was forced to consider new ways to protect Nature *and* the bottom line. Convincing businesses to somehow help protect the environment meant mastering the subtle art of sustainability. I quickly became a disciple.

STUMBLING INTO SUSTAINABILITY

Grupo Puntacana discovered sustainability by necessity. Founded fifty years ago by Ted Kheel and Frank Rainieri, a pair of unsuspecting visionaries, the company had evolved from a fledgling hotel made up of a few rustic cabañas in a remote corner of the Dominican Republic into a major tourist destination.

In Grupo Puntacana's early days in the late 1960s, the term *sustainable development* hadn't yet been coined. Instead, the partners used a mix of resourcefulness and ingenuity to confront their most pressing day-to-day problems. Often the practical solutions they encountered turned out to be cheaper, while simultaneously (and often inadvertently) reducing their environmental footprint. With little income from the fledgling resort, Frank and Ted needed to be creative to keep the operation afloat. They discovered they could save money by taking advantage of local conditions and available materials, consuming less water and energy.

GPC's environmental practices matured gradually over the years, transforming from a strategy to survive bankruptcy into a legitimate part of the company's operating philosophy. The environment and the local community were integrated into the company's decision-making process. As it became a leader in Caribbean tourism, GPC's sensitivity towards the local people and concern for the environment were a key piece of its winning formula.

Tourism, as it turns out, is a significant driver of the global economy and a highly relevant slice of the sustainability conversation. Today, over a billion people travel around the world on a yearly basis. Travel produces a profound impact on people, places, and local environments, sometimes positive and sometimes not. Too many visitors can put immense pressure on local habitats and communities. As tourism expands throughout the world, it has brought increasingly complex challenges with it.

In developing countries like the Dominican Republic, the government often doesn't have the resources or foresight to adequately safeguard its natural and cultural resources. Governments enthusiastically seek to attract investment and create new jobs. Too often, this short-circuits preventative environmental measures. Long-term planning gets steam-rolled by aggressive developers. The burden of protecting sensitive destinations often falls on the companies developing them. This can present conflicts of interest even the most thoughtful and ethical companies have trouble avoiding. The world, in particular the Caribbean, is littered with tourism destinations that have been spoiled by lax government oversight and overzealous developers.

Sustainable tourism, on the other hand, seeks to attract visitors to new destinations without degrading the natural and cultural assets that drew them there in the first place. The need to safeguard a destination seems obvious. In fact, the global tourism industry has often treated the planet and its people poorly, with devastating effects. How to get sustainable tourism done, where the rubber meets the road, is a lot harder than it sounds.

How can a company reduce its environmental footprint, create improved conditions for local people, and simultaneously make money? Is it even possible to make a stronger, more competitive yet sustainable business? I have spent the past fifteen years of my career trying to figure out how to transform the theory of sustainable tourism into reality. If sustainability can make at least one tourism business more successful, perhaps it can create a domino effect of positive impact for other businesses in the Dominican Republic and throughout the Caribbean. With enough positive examples, just maybe, sustainability can go viral throughout the global tourism industry.

HURRICANES FUEL INNOVATION

In 2017, Hurricanes Irma and Maria barreled through the Caribbean, battering Puerto Rico, British Virgin Islands, Saint Maarten, and other islands. The same year, Hurricane Harvey smashed Houston and southern Texas. Combined, the three storms affected tens of thousands of people (causing close to four thousand casualties), demolished entire cities and countries, and left untold destruction in their wake. It was the costliest hurricane season in history, causing an estimated quarter of a trillion dollars in damage.

We nervously tracked the storms from Punta Cana. After flattening Puerto Rico, both Irma and Maria took last-minute turns to the north, barely missing Punta Cana. Grupo Puntacana was spared, receiving only limited impact. We experienced a couple hours of wind, a few days of rain, and some fallen leaves and branches. The power stayed on and life went on too.

Despite our near miss with Irma and Maria, it's clear that the planet is rapidly changing. Storms and natural disasters are increasingly impacting our business. We were fortunate to have the resort up and running after only a few hours. But we have experienced the devastation of hurricanes before and in all likelihood, we will again in the future. The increasing frequency and severity of the storms has made it critical to have a strategy to confront them.

In our case, Frank took the lead. Throughout the storm prep, he emphasized the importance of responding quickly once the storms passed, no matter if their impact was severe or minor. The faster we could get the resort open for business, the better off everyone would be. The best way to help our people recover from a disaster, he reasoned, would be putting them to work quickly to generate income for their families. Frank pushed us to prepare for the worst, but above all to get up and running as fast as possible. Nowadays, sustainability experts call the ability to respond and recover rapidly from disasters "resilience." Frank calls it good business.

Tourism increasingly must confront more than just extreme weather. A barrage of new threats confronts destinations, especially small islands: emerging diseases and viruses, massive coral degradation, drug-related crime, invasive species, terrorism, and even seaweed invasions, just to name a few. Is there a clearer example of how precarious the tourism industry is than what it is struggling through with the new coronavirus? A virus that originated in China has shuttered tourism worldwide for months, including the entire Caribbean. It will be more months, possibly years, before travel recovers.

Rapid change is the new normal. If we want to stay profitable, we had better be ready to deal with it. Businesses as a whole, and especially tourism destinations, must be dialed in to adapt to new threats and become resilient.

Quickly adapting to change, ironically, creates all kinds of competitive advantages. For example, the Punta Cana destination fiercely competes with other tourism destinations in our region, such as Mexico and Jamaica. When disaster strikes, the country and companies that can demonstrate they have the situation under control the quickest will have a competitive advantage over their rivals. To Frank's point, getting the resort back online after a storm not only helps local people, it attracts visitors who are unable to visit other destinations that are slower to open. Companies that respond quickly and effectively put themselves in a position to prosper.

My experience at Grupo Puntacana has convinced me that our commitment to sustainability has made us a stronger, more resilient company. Confronting myriad new challenges forces our company to adapt and innovate. As we will see in these pages, it helps maximize our creativity. This constant adaptation helps sharpen our collective skills in response to fresh challenges, but also trains us to exploit our ability to innovate to gain competitive advantages.

Being an innovator offers another valuable benefit: it attracts fellow problem-solvers. Over the years, Grupo Puntacana has become a magnet for inventors, pioneers, and creators thinking outside the box. Every time we face a new problem, whether it be what to do with our garbage or how to use bacteria to break down sewage, we are the first stop for entrepreneurs, scientists, and companies looking to test new ideas, products, and theories. All they need is a company daring enough to experiment, and often that's Grupo Puntacana. This has its pros and cons, of course, but in the long run, we benefit from exposure to new, and sometimes wacky, ideas. Overall, being approached by mad scientists has been useful to our company in the face of constantly evolving problems.

Similarly, our employees and collaborators know our quirky

history and willingness to use our resort for R&D. Some of our best ideas and most effective solutions have come from in-house. Our own employees have become part of a learning community that enthusiastically confronts challenges with fresh ideas. When I get approached by a consultant or expert with a new idea, my first stop is almost always one of the company's different departments. I use our internal experts not only to determine whether a product or solution is feasible, but whether we need the consultant at all. The question becomes, "Can we do it ourselves?" More often than not, we can.

WAKING THE SLEEPING GIANT

This book re-examines business as usual. Unfortunately, there is no standardized sustainability textbook. Like the challenges we face, sustainability is dynamic and evolving. It's often more art than science—no model, checklist, framework or certification will magically make a company sustainable. No amount of charitable donations will offset a company's bad deeds. True change will only happen when companies integrate sustainability into their business model.

But what that looks like is different for each company, industry, and place. Sustainability is like a good recipe; it requires thoughtful ingredients, practice, and a bit of failure. Nonetheless, even the best recipes will produce different final results depending on the ingredients.

In these chapters, we will learn the basic elements that make a solid sustainability recipe for companies. We will explore how to transform corporations into a positive force for change in society. By awakening this long-dormant sleeping giant, we will discover how companies can have a lasting, positive impact on communities, local ecosystems, and entire industries. Done right, sustainability can be a tremendous asset to the bottom line of businesses, while also producing tangible, enduring value for society and the planet. It will take some prodding, but there is a sleeping giant within every company.

Sustainability requires creative ingenuity, a positive attitude, and some good luck. But it doesn't necessarily require hiring a sustainability guru. In fact, it is critical that up-and-coming professionals can be convinced to become well-placed sustainability guerillas *inside* of companies, whether it is their expertise or not. The way to move the needle is to embed sustainability soldiers in diverse professional disciplines and infiltrate companies. We need sustainable programmers, lawyers, architects, engineers, accountants, human resource executives, and so on. Young professionals need to take their concern for the future of the planet and make it their job.

No offense to my many friends promoting eco-lifestyles, but we will need more than eliminating plastic straws and buying local veggies to make a dent in the planetary crisis we face. As prominent author Bill McKibben puts it, "Go ahead and screw in that energy efficient light bulb, but screw in a new congressman while you're at it." I would add, "And change the chip in your CEO." Promoting good individual habits is useful, but transforming corporate decision-making and culture from within can translate into major sustainability victories.

Today's companies have unprecedented power and reach. Corporate leaders need to see that sustainability is not an obstacle to their financial success, but often the key to achieving it. Environmentalists have long used lawsuits and inflicting bad publicity on wrong-doers to achieve their goals, but a better bet is figuring out how to make a positive example of companies themselves. Businesses already invested in sustainability can offer invaluable insights to their peers. If there's one thing that convinces a CEO to do something, it's talking to a fellow company that got rich doing it. Waking the Sleeping Giant means persistently altering corporate leaders' mindsets until sustainability becomes the default.

In these pages, the unexpected and inspirational history of Grupo Puntacana sets the stage. For fifty years the company has embarked on a highly unusual experiment in sustainable development that, though not always successful, can provide important lessons for other businesses. The tourism industry in the developing Dominican Republic is the backdrop to demonstrate the art of Waking the Sleeping Giant. Lessons herein are applicable to nearly all industries. By sharing them, I hope to help other companies integrate sustainability into their businesses and harness the power of companies to secure an enduring and profitable future.

CHAPTER ONE

THE BIRTH OF A PIONEER

PUNTA CANA WAS BORN OF MISTAKES, THE FIRST AND biggest made by my great uncle, Ted Kheel. Ted was a renowned labor lawyer, negotiator and master of conflict resolution in New York City. He worked with numerous US presidents, mayors, unions, and business leaders, mediating some of America's thorniest labor disputes. But Ted didn't know a thing about the Dominican Republic.

At a labor meeting in Florida in the late 1960s, an acquaintance from a maritime union talked up the DR as a land of opportunity, encouraging Ted to buy property there. Despite a three-decade rough patch under one of the western hemisphere's most notorious and cruelest dictators, Rafael Trujillo, the Dominican Republic's prospects had begun to improve since his assassination. More importantly, the country had abundant and cheap land.

Intrigued by the prospect of a good deal and never one to shy away from adventure, Ted thought it over and decided to buy a couple of acres "on a lark." His contact sweetened the deal. "I can get you thirty square miles of beachfront property." Too good to pass up, Ted assembled a group of friends and associates and acquired an exquisite tract of white-sand beach and dense jungle. The group believed they had bought a slice of paradise, but in reality, it was a mosquito-infested outpost.

Worse, it was in the middle of nowhere. Anchoring the far eastern edge of the Dominican Republic, the trip to the new plot of land required a full day of arduous travel from the nearest airport in Santo Domingo. Family members that Ted forced to make the trip remarked, "We had to take a jeep over dirt roads and the driver used a machete to cut down trees and branches that blocked the road."

The remote area was inhabited only by scattered communities of fishermen, wood charcoal farmers, and coconut trees. Though blessed with stunning ocean views and turquoise seas, there was little else: no houses, electricity, paved roads, or drinking water. The land may have seemed like a bargain, but unless they could figure out what to do with it, it would become a lesson in bad investing.

THE RAINIERI REVELATION

After numerous missteps, the investors met with an ambitious 24-year-old Dominican named Frank Rainieri who would radically change their fortunes, and eventually the trajectory of the entire country. Frank had a vivid imagination and he immediately developed a rudimentary plan for the property. "We need to buy a tractor and clear some land so we can build bungalows and attract visitors," he told Ted. Frank worked for an agricultural company and planned to become a rice farmer, but when the investors asked for his recommendation for the project, he didn't hesitate. Frank proposed tourism.

Given the Dominican Republic's reputation today, tourism

seems like an obvious choice. In 1969, however, it was a dicey proposition. The entire country had less than one thousand hotel rooms. Besides the CIA and other US government officials, it attracted only sporadic foreign tourists. Neighboring Haiti was the popular destination at the time. The DR still brimmed with leftover political turmoil from its post-dictatorship years. In fact, as recently as 1965, the country had been occupied by the US military as part of geo-political wrangling during the Cold War.

With no alternative plan, Ted and his partners trusted Frank Rainieri's instincts. They approved the construction of a few simple beach cabañas. Remote and simple, Grupo Puntacana's first "hotel" could accommodate no more than forty people, though it was not exactly a hotspot. As Ted joked, "Our highest occupancy never exceeded my wife, children, and any relatives or friends I could convince to join us."

The original beach casitas of Puntacana Resort & Club

The project faced an uphill climb to get off the ground. To make the trek in safari trucks, Frank often had to carve out new roads and fill in potholes as he went. As they got closer to the coast, they had to wait for the tide to recede to expose the existing road. It often took seven hours to get there.

Through it all, Frank was driven by a dogged determination and a knack for making things work. He took on half a dozen other odd jobs and business schemes to make ends meet, all the while struggling to keep the lagging project alive. He hustled to keep squatters off the unoccupied land. He convinced local politicians to let him carve out new access roads. He even set up a small school to attract scattered locals and their families to come work at the new beach "resort."

The undertaking clawed forward with only modest progress through the 1970s, until *Club Méditerranée* (as Club Med was then known) approached the group about building a hotel. At the time, Club Med was expanding their all-inclusive resort concept and wanted to try their hand in the Dominican Republic. Gilbert Trigano, the president of Club Med, a tourism pioneer in his own right, needed land.

In preparation for Trigano's initial visit, Frank cleared some land on the coast and took him to see the ideal location for the future Club Med. When they bounced up to the beach in an old, weathered Jeep, Trigano stripped down to his bathing suit and jumped in the water. He picked up the sand and smelled it. He rubbed it on his skin and looked at it closely. Then he got out of the water and told the group, "Let's go."

They continued along the coast sampling different beaches and testing the sand until they arrived precisely where Ted and Frank had built their beach cottages. Trigano was decided. This was his spot.

"But Gilbert," Ted protested, "this is our resort." Despite the fact that they were losing money by the minute with a handful of rustic and mostly unoccupied cabins in one of the most isolated regions in the country, Ted and Frank were reluctant to part with the lot. After some haggling, the deal went through and three years later, Club Med had a shiny, new resort—but no way to get tourists there.

Their first problem—a viable resort—was solved. But their second problem—viable transportation—also needed solving.

DRUNKARDS POINT BECOMES PUNTA CANA

Difficult access wasn't their only issue. The place didn't have a name. What is today known as Punta Cana originally had two unofficial names: Punto Borrachón (Drunkards Point) or Yauya, a Taino Indian word. Punto Borrachón, while perhaps accurate for future resort-goers' penchant for unlimited, all-inclusive alcohol, was too hard to say in English. Yauya was a confusing tongue-twister for gringos. The region needed an appealing calling card. Rainieri looked to his surroundings for inspiration. He found it in the trees. He took the name of the native palm tree called the Cana palm and combined it with the site being the farthest point on the island. The intrepid developers adopted the name "Punta Cana" for the region. Their company became Grupo Puntacana.

Access was more complicated. Recognizing that getting Club Med off the ground would require air travel, Grupo Puntacana approached the Dominican government about building an airport in Punta Cana. At the time, the notion of Punta Cana as a tourism superpower was preposterous. The region had one hotel and a few beach cabins, but little else. At the time, the government was planning a new tourism destination on the north coast. The president, believing Punta Cana's future was pure fantasy, turned down the airport request.

With their bid for an airport denied, Grupo Puntacana made a counterproposal: Would the government give them authorization to build their own private airport? This idea was so outlandish that the Dominican government, probably assuming it would never happen, gave them the go-ahead.

Club Med, the first all-inclusive resort in Punta Cana

After working out some creative financing, the group built a rudimentary runway and a simple airport terminal. Everything was done on the cheap, using local materials. Eventually they secured a few flights, beginning a steady trickle of small planes full of Europeans looking for adventure, sun, and sand.

With Club Med ramping up, Grupo Puntacana decided it was time to upgrade its cabanas and built a bigger and better hotel. The region's potential came into clearer focus. Beyond the eight kilometers of white-sand beach on GPC's property, there were vast expanses of untouched beach to the south and north. The majority of the country's eastern region was divided into large landholdings of dry forest, beachfront, and mangrove swamp owned by locals, most of whom hadn't given a thought to tourism. If Frank and Ted could entice some courageous hoteliers to build a few hotels in the region, the tourism spark could be lit.

Gradually, a few Spanish hotel chains followed Club Med's lead, purchasing land to the north of Grupo Puntacana, in what today is known as Bavaro. Resorts sprouted along the coast, with growth picking up in the 1980s and exploding in the 1990s. Tiny villages ballooned to dense but disorganized peri-urban towns. As the number of hotels expanded, Punta Cana caught the attention of more hotel chains. Air traffic increased, which encouraged more hotel and real estate development. From that point forward, the Punta Cana region grew exponentially.

Fast forward to today, and the Punta Cana region is closing in on fifty thousand hotel rooms, by far the most potent tourism destination in the Caribbean. The original dirt landing strip has transformed into Punta Cana International Airport, one of the busiest airports in the Caribbean and Central America, receiving four million arriving passengers a year and growing. In many ways, the tourism industry has become the economic driver of the entire country, stimulating agriculture, construction, exports and a vast array of new businesses.

Ted Kheel and Frank Rainieri put the Punta Cana International Airport on the map

Frank Rainieri went on to become president and CEO of Grupo Puntacana and an icon in tourism. He is one of the most successful, self-made businessmen in the Dominican Republic and known around the world as the pioneer of Dominican tourism. While both Rainieri and Kheel deserve the credit for Punta Cana's unanticipated rise, both downplay their reputation as visionaries. From the beginning, they both admitted there was no way to predict just how successful the region would become.

"Every time someone would say how visionary we were," Ted once told me, "I just had to laugh. We weren't visionary at all. We made a mistake buying the land in the first place. Club Med made the second mistake in buying land from us."

The project had hemorrhaged money for years. Family, friends, and business partners urged Ted to throw in the towel. Frank meanwhile had been mocked in the DR for his quixotic pursuit of building a resort in the middle of nowhere. No one had ever owned and operated their own airport before. Most people thought the two of them were delusional.

Yet they kept at it, due in large part to their unique relationship. Frank and Ted had developed a solid rapport and strong level of trust. Ted was a problem-solver with a knack for coming up with creative solutions to difficult problems. Frank was tenacious about getting things done. "We were just trying to survive and not lose our shirts," Ted recalled. "I had a local partner on the ground who was working hard. There wasn't a whole lot I could do but keep going."

Frank Rainieri recognized the arrival of Ted Kheel and the slice of land in the eastern Dominican Republic as the opportunity of a lifetime.

NECESSITY IS THE MOTHER OF INVENTION

Early Grupo Puntacana could be summarized simply: they had no money. After several early investors gave up on the project, Ted was forced to buy them out, making him the primary stockholder. With Ted alone bankrolling the operation, Grupo Puntacana had a meager budget for construction, salaries, and materials. They were on the hook to build an airport, though, so they needed to devise an inexpensive way to get it done.

In the late 1970s, Frank approached family friend and aspiring architect, Oscar Imbert, to design and build the airport. Imbert was a recent architecture graduate at the time with little practical building experience. He was fascinated with the houses built by native Taino and Arawack Indians in pre-colonial times. They relied on local materials, like thatch and wood, and dealt with the heat by allowing the coastal breezes to cool their huts.

Imbert decided to borrow these native concepts for the airport. Since GPC had neither constant electricity nor the money to install air-conditioning, he designed open spaces with low walls to maximize air flow from the nearby ocean breezes. He repurposed limestone coral rock that had been removed from the first runway to construct walls and walkways. The building itself was built using arrow-straight, locally grown eucalyptus trees. The roofing was made from locally abundant Cana palm thatch, threaded together much like the Tainos had done.

Imbert left space in the thatch to let in natural sunlight, decreasing the need for lighting and reducing electricity demands. He was militant about sparing as many native trees as possible, in many cases building around them instead of cutting them down. The airport was an early example of green architecture without even knowing it: extremely low energy consumption, use of local materials, and preservation of local vegetation.

Punta Cana International Airport under construction using local materials

This type of eco-friendly design may seem unremarkable for an airport today, but this was the early 1980s. There was no handy manual for green architecture. There was no LEED certification. Besides a handful of American hippies building teepees, sustainable architecture was practically nonexistent. The Punta Cana International Airport, in its earliest iteration, was a case study in adaptive design. Innovation driven by necessity.

The airport turned out to produce a substantial environmental upside—sustainability became a priority.

DESTINATION STEWARDS

Following Grupo Puntacana's fortuitous discovery of green architecture, the company slowly graduated to a more deliberate focus on the stewardship of the entire Punta Cana region. This enlightened approach has a simple explanation: self-interest. GPC's principal revenue stream depends on the arrival of airplanes and passengers. By collecting landing fees, selling services to the airlines, and taking advantage of other revenue-generating opportunities, the Punta Cana International Airport is Grupo Puntacana's most valuable business asset.

However, the vast majority of Punta Cana tourists stay at hotels in Bavaro. A relatively small percentage of the four million passengers actually visit Grupo Puntacana's resort. As a result, the company has a vested interest in the success of the entire region, not just the success of its resort property alone. If the many hotels in the region are unoccupied, that means fewer passengers arriving to the airport. If the number of hotels in the regions ceases to grow, that affects the growth of the airport. The financial success of Grupo Puntacana is intimately linked to the ongoing success of the region as a whole.

This unique interdependency creates a strong argument for sustainability. The growth and expansion of a destination like Punta Cana inevitably leads to both environmental and social impacts. In order to have growth, you need drinking water, electricity, waste management, housing, health, education, and many other basic services. These utilities are normally the purview of the government. Yet even in the earliest stages of Punta Cana's development, beginning with the construction of the airport, the Dominican government abdicated that role. Grupo Puntacana was forced to prioritize solutions for regional issues as part of its corporate decision-making, effectively filling the void left by the government.

Unquestionably, Grupo Puntacana believes in helping the Dominican people and protecting the environment, but its quasi-governmental role originated from an instinct for self-preservation. If the company didn't intervene and find ways to form a functioning community with basic services, while protecting the local environment, it was doomed to fail. In practice, this meant that Grupo Puntacana assumed a stewardship role for the entire eastern Dominican Republic beginning in its earliest days.

It took me some time to understand this fundamental connection. In 2009, we applied for the prestigious World Tourism Travel Council (WTTC) "Tourism for Tomorrow" award. The awards are divided into numerous categories for entities with specialization in community, cultural, environmental, and wildlife conservation. We applied in the category of Destination Stewardship, believing that Grupo Puntacana's work on a regional scale qualified us for the most expansive category. Applying in any single category would shortchange the breadth of our programs. After the first round of reviews, the award organizers called me, wondering if we were confused.

"Destination stewardship normally refers not to companies but to cities, governments, or tourism boards that work on behalf of an entire destination," they told me. I went back and pored over our application to find a more suitable individual category. Stumped, I insisted that our impact couldn't be described by any one of the individual categories. After an inspection visit to Punta Cana by a WTTC award judge, a few months later we received the WTTC award for Destination Stewardship in Brazil. Not even the WTTC could ignore our position in the region.

A PRIVATE GOVERNMENT

With only meager support from the Dominican government, the Punta Cana region has been developed almost entirely by the private sector. Government neglect has led the private sector to fill the vacuum left by the government, for better or worse. This began with the construction of the Punta Cana airport but has continued for decades. Until recently, nearly all roads and highways were built or paid for by the hotels. There are no municipal drinking water or water treatment facilities; what exists has also been built privately. Most of the businesses in the region rely on private security companies, as opposed to a local police force. The hotel association has even equipped a privately funded fire department.

Development driven exclusively by the private sector, unencumbered by government intervention, has many advantages. Businesses innovate, act efficiently, compete, and drive growth. We've seen this unfold right outside our resort doors, as the Punta Cana region has grown at a breathtaking clip since the 1990s. Tourism has created tens of thousands of jobs and immense economic opportunity that is the envy of much of Latin America.

But the region's success is also one of its greatest threats. As tourism swells, Punta Cana continues to attract many thousands of people from throughout the island, including nearby Haiti, in search of jobs and opportunity. The lack of government presence means the destination has grown explosively over the last several decades with little planning, and even less investment in public infrastructure. This puts considerable stress on local resources. It has also led to the establishment of improvised communities in sub-standard living conditions.

The private sector has had to fill the void left by the government absence. The results have been mixed. For example, nearly all hotels in Punta Cana have private wells for drinking water. Each hotel builds its individual system to cover its needs but there is no formal drinking water system for local communities surrounding the hotels. Those communities rely on a patchwork mosaic of private wells, water trucks, or tap illegally into private aqueducts built by the hotels. The local government issues permits to drill wells but they are rarely backed by an understanding of the capacity of the freshwater source.

Similarly, each hotel has a private water treatment facility for sewage. Yet the largest nearby community, Verón, with some eighty thousand residents, is not connected to any type of water treatment. In the best case, each building has at least a rudimentary septic system that partially treats sewage. In the worst case, and by far the norm, sewage filters untreated underground.

This haphazard water system leads to serious risks. Without regional oversight of water, each hotel operates in autonomy. Individual hotel properties take into account their own water needs, without contemplating the needs or consumption of their neighbors. In Verón, water is a free-for-all, with no consideration of the big picture. In some small neighborhoods, there are as many as fifty private, individual water wells. On a regional level, that is a lot of wells pulling from one limited water source; an underground aquifer that supports all of Punta Cana.

As growing volumes of partially treated or untreated sewage from Verón leak underground, the aquifer is not only at risk of over-exploitation, but also of contamination. Unfortunately, the local government doesn't have the resources or capacity to manage water on a regional scale. The federal government, on the other hand, hasn't gotten its hands dirty organizing the chaos. The result is increasing exploitation of underground water and serious risks to existing water resources.

This situation is known as a "tragedy of the commons," where individuals (or hotels) act according to their own self-interest, but not necessarily in favor of the common good. Each well that taps into the aquifer represents the interests of one party, but not all of Punta Cana.

Similarly, the way garbage is handled in the region is precarious. There is no environmentally safe option for landfilling. The current landfill is an unregulated dump overwhelmed daily with thousands of tons of waste from hotels and nearby communities. Hundreds of informal pickers sort through the waste. Heavy machinery moves the garbage around to make way for more.

The proliferation of clandestine dump sites is also a problem, as waste haulers look to shortcut their transportation costs by illegally dumping in vacant lots. Similar to the water situation, the local municipal government is overwhelmed by the garbage problem. The national government has put its head in the sand rather than confront the threat.

In addition to critically fragile public infrastructure, enforcement of environmental laws and permitting is also limited. While companies tend to act aggressively in order to grow, they will often comply with laws only to the degree they are enforced. In other words, most companies will spend as little as possible to protect the environment, unless someone forces them to. With limited government regulation, most environmental regulations in Punta Cana are essentially voluntary. Compliance for formal permitting processes for building and operating hotels has been mixed—some resorts and businesses strictly comply with environmental laws, while others simply wait to be fined. Enforcement is even weaker. The Punta Cana destination, with close to forty-five thousand hotel rooms and growing, has just one government environmental inspector assigned to it.

Grupo Puntacana, on the other hand, has made good environmental practice a virtue, not just out of a sense of social responsibility, but also out of need to keep its business alive. Drinking water, sewage, and solid waste are threats that could slow down the growth of tourism in Punta Cana. Because of the airport, this would impact our business more than any other resort. The company leads by example because ultimately, environmental degradation could affect its bottom line.

As we will see, Grupo Puntacana has pioneered solutions to many of the region's most critical environmental threats, including waste management, not only because it's the right thing to do, but because it's a real part of protecting its business.

THE COCONUT RULE

While he was beginning to build his first hotel, Frank Rainieri often traveled to other tourism destinations, such as Miami and Cancún, for business meetings. On one trip, while waiting in the lobby for an elevator to his twelfth-floor room, he found himself staring at the sandy feet of a barefoot tourist. The image of a bathing suit-clad tourist in a skyscraper elevator was jarring. Frank had a revelation. People living in cities don't come to the Caribbean to ride elevators. Building towers belonged in cities, not by the beach.

Beachfront towers cause more than aesthetic problems. In late afternoon, the tall hotel towers block the sun from the beach, leaving visitors in the shade. This restricts sunny beach time to a few hours in the morning. Most tourists travel to the Caribbean to sit beneath a coconut tree, not in the shade of a large building.

As he walked around, Rainieri also noticed the hotel pools and patios were filled with sand. The hotels had eliminated the natural coastal vegetation to provide access from the high-rises to the beach, so the exposed sand was blown off the beach towards the hotel. With the soft sand swept away by the wind, the beaches were compacted and hard, as opposed to the fluffy, powdery sand tourists had come to expect.

While building vertical hotels made it possible to pack more visitors into one property, it also damaged the visitors' beach experience. Towers provide more rooms, but the available beach is finite. Building skyscrapers causes serious overcrowding of beaches. Today, this phenomenon is known as "overtourism," one of the biggest challenges facing the global tourism industry. Too many people trying to access a single place inflicts heavy stress, often robbing it of its original allure.

When Frank returned to the DR, he urged his fellow hoteliers in Punta Cana to adopt a voluntary building code. His idea was to limit the height of construction to four stories, the height of a coconut tree. Frank convinced the hotels not only to limit the height of the buildings, but to self-impose rules on density to limit overcrowding on the beach, like he saw in Mexico. Punta Cana's earliest hotels agreed to put a limit on rooms per square meter. They also left large expanses between the pools, hotel buildings, and the high-tide mark on the beach, all to protect the beach from losing sand. Frank had foreseen the threat of overtourism long before it became a global threat. He led Punta Cana's hoteliers to a creative solution.

Lower buildings have had a dramatic impact in Punta Cana. To date, there are still no hotels taller than four stories, though money-hungry, recent entrants in the hotel market are threatening to upend this code. Many hotels manage to fit thousands of rooms on their property but preserve vast expanses of green area. One of the most commonly cited attractions by guests of Punta Cana is that despite huge volumes of visitors, the beach doesn't feel overcrowded. There is enough unoccupied beach for guests to lounge in the shade of a coconut tree.

In 2000, the first comprehensive environmental law in the DR began to regulate hotel construction. New construction would need to be at least sixty meters (almost two hundred feet) from the high-tide mark, to protect both the beaches and the buildings. The vast majority of Punta Cana's hotels, built long before the law was conceived, were already in compliance. Though Punta Cana suffers from other issues related to lack of planning, maintaining a relatively low level of density (compared to similar destinations) is not one of them.

Interestingly, the company that would seemingly benefit the most from cramming as many high-rise towers into the region as possible is Grupo Puntacana. Increased density would, in theory, allow the region to receive many more visitors. This would increase air traffic and GPC's revenue. If high-rise hotels were all they were cracked up to be, Frank surely would have promoted the idea. Instead, he convinced the hoteliers to do the opposite, voluntarily limiting the height of their buildings because he felt it would be better for the destination over the long term. Over time, the region has continued to grow and attract new investment. It's clear that Frank saw the beach for the trees.

THE ACCIDENTAL ENVIRONMENTALIST

In 1991 at a New York City bistro, Ted Kheel was enjoying lunch with his friend Maurice Strong, the acting secretary general of the Earth Summit in Rio de Janeiro, Brazil. Known formally as the United Nations Conference on Environment and Development, Strong encouraged Ted to attend. Ted replied that he knew nothing about environmental matters and didn't have much to contribute in Rio.

However, after lunch he looked into the conference to see if he could help his friend as a favor. He quickly concluded that the conference had a problem: nobody had heard of it. The Earth Summit wasn't getting any news coverage. Ted didn't know anything about protecting the environment, but after years as a labor mediator in New York City, he knew how to leverage his media savvy and relationships to generate publicity. He offered to help promote the "Earth Pledge," a symbolic commitment by participants to "make the Earth a more secure and hospitable place for present and future generations."

At the time, Ted represented the renowned American artist, Robert Rauschenberg. Figuring the artist could help raise the meeting's profile, Ted recruited Rauschenberg to make an original work of art for the conference. The piece, "Last Turn, Your Turn," was reproduced as signed posters and sold to raise money for the *Earth Times*, a newspaper that reported on the summit and climate change. The Earth Pledge became the iconic image of the summit and helped launched a brand-new concept: sustainable development. The term "sustainable development" was popularized at the Earth Summit. Hundreds of individuals and world leaders signed the Earth Pledge, including US President George H.W. Bush.

One chance encounter had catapulted Ted, who admittedly had no previous interest in the environmental cause, into a second career. He proceeded to spend the next decades looking for solutions to what he called, "the most urgent conflict facing humanity today: the conflict between economic development and environmental protection." Over the course of twenty-five years, Ted became an environmental activist, philanthropist, and thought leader engaged in environmental protection. He leveraged a diverse cadre of friends, artists, business associates, and quirky characters to support his cause in all kinds of unique ways.

Undoubtedly though, his most important contribution to environmental protection was his insistence on using Grupo Puntacana as a laboratory to test sustainability-based solutions in a real-world situation. Ted recognized that the "green" airport he and Frank had built was just the beginning of what they could accomplish.

SUSTAINABLE DEVELOPMENT = CONFLICT RESOLUTION

Ted Kheel's distinguished career was built on his profound mastery of conflict resolution. He was a world-class expert in solving difficult disputes. He took on newspapers, railroads, and teacher strikes and successfully brought adversaries to agreements. Ted's system for conflict resolution was simple, yet devastatingly effective. He distilled complex problems down to their component parts, allowing the solutions to bubble to the surface. Ted's secret for resolving labor disputes also serves as a primer for getting sustainability done.

In his book, *The Keys to Conflict Resolution*, Ted proposes that in order to truly understand the source of a conflict, you must first strip it down to its core questions. What does each side want? What outcome is each party looking for? What issues can they agree on? In fact, much of Ted's philosophy for resolving disputes depends on removing the superfluous issues that neither side is fixated on, instead focusing on the central areas of interest of each party causing the friction. When you clarify what issues are at the core of the disagreement, it makes the path to finding solutions that much easier.

Once you have the issues clear, it is important to start by identifying points of common interest among the parties. Rather than getting bogged down in their differences, Ted got each side warmed up by starting with the safe space of agreement. Were there any issues they already agree on?

At the end of any negotiation, each side must be able to walk away from the bargaining table with a win for their side. Reaching agreements, even on minor issues, allows each side to feel they are getting something they want, and therefore winning the negotiation. Ted would subtly massage each aggrieved party's ego to identify commonalities, gradually working towards confronting their stickier differences.

Ted used a beautiful metaphor to describe his process. The best way to carve a sculpture of an elephant, he would say, is to begin chipping away at a block of stone, eliminating everything that is *not* an elephant. What you have left is a sculpture of an elephant.

A central tenet of conflict resolution is that most disputes arise over a disregard for other parties' *interests*. In environmental disputes, developers feel their business interests are being unnecessarily impeded by environmentalists. Environmentalists, they believe, want to save every tree and endangered snail at the expense of the bottom line.

Environmentalists, on the other hand, are suspicious of businesspeople, whom they believe only care about making money, with no regard for the environment. Businesses could care less about tree frogs and old growth forests; they would just as soon steamroll entire ecosystems to make a buck.

From his background in conflict resolution, Ted made a simple but profound realization. Interest disputes cause the vast majority of environmental damage in the world today. What we need, Ted discerned, are outcomes that are good for both the environment and business. That's where the Earth Summit and sustainable development came into the picture. The solution to the conflict between economic development and environmental protection is sustainable development. This seemingly obvious statement, that environmental protection must be good both for the planet and business, has become conventional sustainability wisdom. In 1992, it was way ahead of its time.

When I arrived at Punta Cana in 2005, I was just like the tree-huggers that so annoy developers. I was focused solely on environmental protection. Yet I was going to work for the guys driving the bulldozer, so I would need strategies to slow growth and limit the impact of development. That seemed to be the only way to keep the trees standing.

Yet I quickly learned that the environment is a critical piece of a much larger puzzle, particularly in the tourism industry. There are many other stakeholders with their own interests and aspirations. Many local communities are afflicted by poverty, lack of education, and poor health conditions. Improving their lot can cause environmental degradation. But the people from these communities deserve the right to dream of a better future, too.

Similarly, businesses exist to grow and generate value for

their stockholders. Businesspeople are not necessarily opposed to Nature, but they need to generate profits or they will cease to exist. Prioritizing the environment or the local community over financial success may drive them out of business. As we will see, environmental protection can certainly improve a company's profitability, but it can also impede its growth.

The art of sustainability is to find a balance between three core interests: business, environment, and people. Gradually, I adopted Ted's sustainable development philosophy as my professional mission. My passion was for the environment, but I wouldn't be successful if I didn't also recognize the need for improved education, health, housing, security, and even the arts. Likewise, I would need to learn how to help business *and* Nature.

In Punta Cana, I became determined to confront the often-competing ideals of environment and development. Where are the points of compatibility? When we peel away the posturing and politics, what are the underlying issues? What can each side agree on? Once we can see the big picture, it is often a matter of gaining concessions to reach an agreement. In other words, revealing the sculpture of the elephant.

Grupo Puntacana had a clear vision of the need to balance Nature, community, and the bottom line, at least in theory. Achieving it, however, was in a nascent stage. It would take time and practice to get sustainability ingrained in the company. By deploying Ted's conflict resolution process, GPC learned that when used effectively, sustainability could become a powerful tool.

SUSTAINABLE TOURISM, NOT ECOTOURISM

Over the last decade and half, I have accompanied CEO Frank Rainieri to dozens of tourism and sustainability conferences. Frank makes a great keynote speaker because there is no one like him: a businessman that built a country-transforming, unimaginably successful tourism destination, but is also decorated with fifty years of sustainability credibility.

More often than not, Frank surprises the audience by proudly declaring, "I am not an environmentalist. I'm a businessman. I don't believe in ecotourism. I believe in development. Sustained and sustainable development."

At first, I wanted to hide under my seat when I heard him. The conferences brought us there to share how we managed to protect the environment, but Frank seemed ready to bash the environmentalists. I was afraid he'd get booed off stage.

Eventually though, I understood what he meant. *Sustained* development is a destination that keeps growing, however gradually, without losing its attractiveness over time. It's a model built to last and produce value over the long term.

The Caribbean is littered with failed resorts, abandoned airports and destinations that had their day, but eventually went belly up or became white elephants. Every island has at least a few. A project might have operated at one time, but eventually tourists stopped showing up. More often than not, their failure had something to do with the how they treated the local people or environment. Frank was talking about how to build a destination that stands the test of time.

Similarly, he objected to the term "ecotourism" because it seems to subvert the importance of the business. Most people associate ecotourism with *nature-only* tourism, where visitors are taken to a remote outpost with rustic accommodations, where a few visitors can commune with nature. Ecotourism often means sacrificing comfort or convenience in order to minimize impact. As one of my sustainability friends put it, "Ecotourism means pooping in a composting toilet."

While this is certainly an exaggeration (I know of many outstanding ecotourism experiences that offer flushing toilets), there is an important distinction between sustainable tourism and ecotourism. Sustainability encompasses environmental, social, and *economic* success. It includes the "eco," but provides greater flexibility in the types of experiences, locations, activities, and tourism models. Ecotourism is a more rigid model that favors the environment over all other factors. Ecotourism seems to apologize for having brought humans in the first place. Sustainable tourism celebrates it.

Ironically, being small and off the beaten path doesn't guarantee environmental protection. Often the isolation and remoteness of ecotourism destinations demands increased travel distance for guests and a greater carbon footprint. Food has to be brought in, usually from far away. Bringing visitors to previously inaccessible places can be an energy-intensive undertaking.

Similarly, the emphasis on "eco" means building near or within protected areas and fragile habitats. Building hotels, even lodges, in sensitive habitats can place undue pressure on them. Construction can be a messy process, impacting ecologically important places with construction waste, housing of workers, and the creation of roads and infrastructure. Ecotourism often serves as the tip of the spear that opens up protected areas for more high impact types of tourism. Though there are lots of great examples of low impact ecotourism, there is an equal number of eco-endeavors that lead to overtourism in previously pristine places.

This is not meant to take potshots at ecotourism's fixation on ecological protection, but to highlight what it's missing. Namely, a compatibility with financial and social goals. Strict ecotourism, in turns out, has proven to be a difficult business model to sustain. Many projects have had to evolve or disappear. No one will remember a company that is incredibly effective in minimizing its environmental footprint if it goes out of business. What sustainable tourism seeks to achieve is a dynamic, adaptable formula that can be applied to different circumstances and realities.

Grupo Puntacana's relationship with Nature wasn't always so eco-friendly. Back when Punta Cana was still a seldom visited outpost, Frank was an avid diver. One of his favorite pastimes was hunting sea turtles. The decline of sea turtles today makes this behavior seem barbaric, but at the time, sea turtles seemed like an inexhaustible resource. Frank collected turtle shells to decorate the hotel dining room, and locals ate the meat. He even named the restaurant "La Tortuga" based on his trophies.

However, each year he saw fewer turtles near the resort. Hotel guests and resort staff also noticed fewer sea turtle heads periscoping out of the water. Frank became concerned. If he was already seeing fewer turtles, would his children, and eventually their children, see *any* sea turtles in the wild? He quit turtle hunting cold turkey. Protecting turtles became a priority for the resort. La Tortuga was renamed "La Cana." Later, the resort's fanciest hotel was named "Tortuga Bay," where in some seasons guests can watch recently hatched baby turtles hustling towards the sea.

Frank's moment of enlightenment coincided with Ted's circuitous journey into environmental protection, which had been awakened at the Earth Summit. Together they formed a unique vision, pushing Grupo Puntacana to launch a wide range of project efforts to safeguard two of its most important natural assets: the people and the environment.

SIN PRISA, PERO SIN PAUSA

When Frank refers to "sustained and sustainable" development, he is referring to one of his favorite Spanish phrases: "*Sin prisa, pero sin pausa.*" This translates roughly as "slow but steady." Frank's corporate philosophy is to make the best possible decisions for the company, the community, and the local environment so that Punta Cana and Grupo Puntacana continue to flourish now and in the future. Development creates jobs, growth, and upward mobility for local communities. When done right, sustained development can create businesses that produce value over the long haul.

Just as businesses demand perseverance, so does sustainability. Most businesses take time to become truly profitable. Likewise, sustainability shouldn't be expected to have immediate success; it takes time to mature. In Grupo Puntacana's case, it took almost three decades to produce real value.

Companies normally plan for down years, though they do their best to avoid them. The same is true for sustainability. It may take time to fully appreciate the benefit companies can receive from a commitment to sustainability. The programs will face obstacles. They may even implode. However, the companies that demonstrate perseverance and grit will eventually be rewarded.

CHAPTER TWO

FINE-TUNING THE SUSTAINABILITY ORCHESTRA

A FEW YEARS AGO I WAS INVITED TO SPEAK AT THE COR-
nell Hotel School. It was my first return to campus since
graduating. Though armed with a master's degree from a university, I hadn't studied hospitality or tourism. Ironically, I
would be presenting at a part of campus I had never visited, dis-
cussing a subject I hadn't formally studied: sustainable tourism.

The students, though, were hungry to hear examples of
sustainability in action. They had researched academic papers
and books that examine ecotourism or green tourism, but they
rarely heard from professionals working in the field. There just
aren't that many sustainability veterans in the travel industry.
Even for students studying it, sustainable tourism is still something of a mystery.

Though the term "sustainable development" was formally
defined at the 1992 Earth Summit in Rio, in the ensuing twenty-
five years sustainability has remained an abstract concept for the

general public. Even more so for companies. Plenty of magazine articles and a handful of books theorize about what sustainable development can and should be. Yet there are surprisingly few companies that have made a deep dive into sustainability, leaning on lots of reasons why it doesn't fit within their particular business or industry. Many companies don't know even where to begin. The travel industry, in particular, has been especially slow to adapt.

The constant cycle of name changes for the same idea hasn't helped the confusion—corporate social responsibility (CSR), environmental social governance (ESG), corporate accountability, and shared value to name a few. Though useful, the moving target of names often serves to confuse corporate boards and busy executives deciding whether sustainability has a place in their company. Experts pumping out new names for the same basic idea could take a page from Ted Kheel's book, *The Keys to Conflict Resolution*, and simplify what sustainability is.

On campus, I was introduced to the cutting-edge work of Dr. Stuart Hart, professor of business management at Cornell University. His book, *Capitalism at the Crossroads*, attempts to unclutter some of the confusion and create a road map for companies to embrace sustainability. (Though unhelpfully, he uses the term "global enterprise" as yet another term for sustainability). Hart makes a clear case for how sustainability can benefit a company, producing value for a wide variety of industries in a number of important ways.

GREENING

"Image is everything," as world famous tennis player Andre Agassi famously put it. For companies, a strong public image is important in nearly all industries. Brand reputation can influence a customer's purchasing decision, encourage them to recommend a company or product to their friends, and determine whether they become loyal, repeat customers. Image may not be everything but having a good one sure can help.

Improving a business's image for acting responsibly is sustainability's low-hanging fruit. Hart refers to this as "greening." By embracing sustainability, companies can gain reputational benefits that become potent marketing tools. This is typically the benefit that companies understand best. Being sustainable can strengthen a company's brand, helping to drive profits.

Hart's greening principle, however, is not to be confused with "greenwashing." Greenwashing is disinformation used to present an environmentally favorable image, usually for companies that don't deserve one. In sustainability's early days, companies realized the power of being eco-friendly and tried to fake it, selling themselves as sustainable, even if they weren't. Greenwashing gave companies the appearance of being conscientious, fooling consumers into choosing their products, in spite of a less than stellar record. Greening is hard-earned recognition; greenwashing involves scamming customers.

For a time, greenwashing watered down the public relations benefit of good environmental practices. Consumers became rightfully suspicious of a company's intentions as brands made superficial green gestures but made no measurable sustainability effort. Consumers had little way to discern real from greenwash. Virtually anything could be called "eco."

Greenwashing had a wide impact. The term "organic," for example, was nearly meaningless in its early days. With no guidelines to define what organic meant, companies could manipulate ads, labels, and marketing to steal some eco-goodwill from consumers. Eventually the term "organic" was clearly defined and companies using it had to certify their products to prove they were, in fact, following organic practices.

Even today, companies continue to push for more stringent definitions of organic, raising the bar to entry even higher.

At one time, you could get away with talking a good green game without actually doing anything. Nowadays it is increasingly difficult to pull off greenwashing. Consumers have an array of tools at their fingertips to find out what companies are really up to. In fact, conscientious customers can research how and where products are made, the impact they generate, and the treatment of individuals, animals and ecosystems that helped make them. Reporting and verification programs, barcodes that determine a product's chain of custody, certificates of origin, and third-party certifications have forced companies to sharpen their green skills. Today, you can find out the exercise habits of the chicken you're about to eat and whether a farmer received a fair shake in selling his coffee beans. This type of transparency-based purchasing is only going to increase.

Furthermore, customers have never been more empowered to voice their concerns. They can not only explore a company's practices, but share what they learn publicly. Social media and user-generated review sites have given consumers a platform to expose the fakers publicly. From the point of view of companies, it has become far too risky to be debunked as a fraud for disingenuous or downright false advertising. Nothing scares a company more, reputationally-speaking, than having its dirty secrets exposed and gone viral.

Ultimately, transparency is generally a good thing for the environment, especially when companies undertake legitimate positive action. Authentic sustainability boosts a company's integrity with consumers and can project a positive public image. Companies that green up can and should reap the reputational benefits.

WHEN THE ROOSTER CROWS

I had only been working for Grupo Puntacana for a couple of weeks in 2005 when Frank Rainieri's secretary called to inform me that my new boss was waiting for me in my office. Brand new to the company and admittedly spooked by the call, I was about to get my first taste of the importance of greening.

When I got there, Frank described my challenge. He explained that he fully supported protecting the environment, he was all in on helping the community, understood why it was important to our business, and proclaimed that he would always support sustainability as long as he was CEO. So far, so good.

But Frank wasn't concerned with convincing *himself* of the importance of protecting the environment; he was already committed. I needed to help him convince Grupo Puntacana's board of directors and top executives, who weren't necessarily true believers, that this investment made sense. I had to preach beyond the converted.

"We spend a fortune every year protecting Nature, but no one knows it," Frank said. "Do you know what a rooster does when its hen has eggs? It crows. That way everyone knows it has eggs!" Frank continued, "We're doing more than most companies on social and environmental programs, but no one knows it. We need to start getting publicity for our programs to show our own executives and shareholders that sustainability is good for us. They won't question our programs anymore because it will be clear they are good for our reputation. So start crowing."

Sustainability, Frank insisted, had to become an inseparable part of the company's image. By demonstrating how valuable it was to our brand, we would effectively safeguard our programs into the future. He needed me to make a strong case to the board of directors and the future leaders of the company, starting now. When we were no longer around to defend our sustainability programs, they would have already proven their value. Rather than an *expense*, it would become an *investment*. By getting publicity for our work, we would be future-proofing the company's philosophical and *financial* commitment to sustainability. It wouldn't make sense to eliminate it.

Frank's point was spot on. At the time, Grupo Puntacana was fully bought into sustainability, long before it was in fashion. (In fact, before the term even existed.) But we didn't do a good job of telling our story. We were doing good work but weren't getting credit for it. If our programs didn't produce any appreciable value, the company board, while not necessarily unhappy with them, would see sustainability as just another expense. When the going got tough and profits dipped, it would be the first thing to get cut.

Frank's instructions to start crowing were clear enough, but equally important is what he *didn't* say. He never demanded starting a greenwashing campaign to cover our environmental flaws. He didn't ask me to start a sexy new program to garner attention. There would be no paid advertising to launch a media blitz. Frank wanted us to promote what we were *already* doing. We didn't need to add new programs; we needed to do a better job of promoting them. If it went well, eventually we could justify doing more. Like the rooster with eggs, he wanted us to make some noise. *Crowing* was Frank's way of saying *greening*.

SELLING PARADISE

For tourism businesses, survival depends on image. Savvy travelers do their homework and search for information about countries, destinations, and hotels. What they read and hear can influence whether they decide to travel to a place like Punta Cana. If a Google search reveals a destination is unsafe or polluted, it can literally make or break its tourism future. Tourism businesses need to make an impression *before* a guest ever steps foot on site.

After that first impression and once a booking is made, guest perceptions continue to be paramount. It will impact how they talk about a place, online reviews they write, photos they post on social media, and whether they recommend it to their friends. Word of mouth advertising is one of the most sought-after types of marketing in tourism. It is harder to get, more authentic, more influential than paid advertising, and can decide the long-term viability of a destination.

To inspire customers to sell paradise for us, we need all the ammunition we can get. The way a hotel treats the environment, its employees, and surrounding communities has become a central part of how travelers perceive it. Good environmental practices can create a positive narrative about the place. In fact, some research shows travelers are willing to make booking choices based on a company's social and environmental programs. Though hard to quantify, sustainability can be at least one of the reasons travelers choose one place or hotel over another.

After the chat with Frank, I went to work. I hit Dominican television stations and hosted media tours in Punta Cana. I wrote press releases and applied for sustainability awards. I began writing articles in the DR and the US about sustainable tourism, appeared on radio programs and even did an appearance on Fox News. I became a regular at international conferences and meetings and networked with travel writers and journalists. I made myself available for articles and interviews. We invited schools, universities, companies, and even a few celebrities to see what we were doing firsthand. Frank made it clear that my job wasn't just to make sustainability happen, but I had to be able to communicate it to the public. I became the Crower-in-Chief.

SAVING IS GOOD FOR YOU

When a customer finishes a transaction at an ATM machine at the Banco Popular Bank in the Dominican Republic, they are given odd advice. "Please don't print your receipt. By doing so you will be saving a tree from becoming paper." The bank's campaign went beyond their ATM machines. Online, radio, TV, print, and billboard advertisements around the country encouraged Dominicans to save electricity, water, and paper. They promoted recycling.

The campaign simultaneously encouraged the public to think about saving its money, presumably by opening a Banco Popular checking account. "Ahorrar Nos Hace Bien" ("Saving is Good for You") was an award-winning marketing campaign that linked good environmental practices with simple financial advice. The bank bathed its corporate brand in eco-friendliness, but with the intention of attracting more customers.

Banco Popular went further than that. The bank implemented sweeping efficiency measures in their banks around the country. They installed solar panels at each of their locations (dozens around the DR), using their financial acumen to bankroll the investment while taking advantage of a tax incentive program for renewable energy. The bank then set up a sophisticated centralized monitoring center to measure the performance of each branch. All of these measures positively impacted the bank's operating costs and ultimately its bottom line.

Banco Popular used its in-house capability and existing marketing budget to plant a flag as the first environmentally-minded bank in the country. It reached its customers with a positive environmental message in a way that few foundations could. Not-for-profits rarely have the resources to pull off a national marketing campaign at the scale of Banco Popular. The bank was promoting itself and its services, while using its marketing capability to influence environmental practices.

For months, Ahorrar Nos Hace Bien was everywhere. Banco Popular scored big by not only promoting its eco-credentials, but by backing it up with an efficiency and renewal energy program. By getting ahead of the competition, Popular defined the terms of the conversation among their competitors, forcing other banks to react. Today, every bank in the country makes significant investments in social and environmental programs, in most cases nudged by Popular. Saving turned out to be good not just for customers, it was good for Banco Popular too, a textbook case of greening.

ECO-EFFICIENCY

Greening is often sustainability's easy win. But there is more benefit to be gained beyond reputational value: cost-savings. Hart coined the term "eco-efficiency" for his second principle, which describes a company's ability to maximize financial savings gained by more efficient use of its resources. If a building, for example, uses less water or energy, it not only helps the planet, it saves money on its monthly bills. If you can manufacture your product with less raw materials, that efficiency saves money. Few companies, whether they care about the environment or not, think wasting resources is a good thing. If they can save money while helping the environment, it can be a valuable windfall.

There are a lot of ways to become eco-efficient. Good old-fashioned training and employee awareness programs encourage employees to shut down their computers, turn off lights, or adjust the A/C or heat. Employees can be convinced, prodded, or penalized into saving the company money (and saving the planet), by reducing consumption on the job.

Beyond behavioral change, there is an ever-growing arsenal of new and sophisticated technologies that help companies monitor and reduce their consumption. Efficient and automated lighting, heating and cooling controls, improved insulation, remote monitoring systems, and innumerable improvements in building design save companies money while doing right by the planet. Not only do we have smartphones, now we have smart appliances. Our washing machines, refrigerators, and dishwashers are capable of producing savings by performing more efficiently. Renewable energies like wind, solar and biomass have also become viable means to squeeze greater efficiency out of a company's operations.

In the hospitality industry, the average hotel dedicates between twenty-five to forty percent of operating costs to energy use. With such a large drain on a company's bottom line, investing in efficient energy use and renewable energy can significantly reduce operating costs. This is especially true on small, sunny, wind-swept islands where fossil fuels have to be imported. Energy tends to be extremely expensive. For example, as the cost of solar energy has decreased, the fast return on investment has made adopting cleaner energy a simple decision. Eco-efficiency is a no-brainer for a lot of companies.

The cost of water in developing countries is another reason why eco-efficiency makes financial sense. In the Caribbean, companies are rarely tied onto a municipal water system. Most rely on private wells. On some islands, without available underground aquifers, the water must be purified at a costly desalinization plant. This is a significant capital investment and makes water use expensive.

The water then needs to be pumped long distances to reach end users. Combining high energy costs needed to pump the water from one place to another, with high water costs, makes eco-efficiency an even more potent money-saver. Consuming less water means not only saving a limited resource like drinking water, it means consuming less energy to treat and pump the water in the first place. Efficiently managing water means substantial, long-term savings providing a positive impact for the environment and significant business gains.

Few executives would promote wastefulness within their company. Making a habit of efficiency is a matter of necessity in order to compete in most industries. Eco-efficiency can simultaneously help reduce a company's ecological footprint along the way. When forming part of a coordinated greening strategy, saving energy can provide both savings and improved public relations.

Grupo Puntacana has been particularly adept at building eco-efficiency into its master planning and infrastructure, even in the early days. In ensuing chapters, we'll look at different big picture water- and energy-saving strategies the company deployed to bring down costs and consumption at the same time.

LEAPFROG TECHNOLOGIES

Hart's third principle is again inspired by Nature. In the business world, a breakthrough technology or radical new process can vault a company far ahead of its competition. Instead of incremental improvements in routine processes, a "leapfrog technology" drastically changes the face of an established business. These technologies can catapult a company into competitive advantage. Increasingly, leapfrog technologies take aim at a company's negative social and environmental impacts.

Most of us are familiar with the idea of leapfrog technologies. Technology companies have spent the last decade swallowing up established industries. Uber, the world's largest taxi transportation company, doesn't own a single vehicle. Airbnb is one of the largest hotel operators and real estate corporations and doesn't own a home. Amazon started as a bookseller but has revolutionized the idea of commerce entirely. Most of us take advantage of these new businesses on a cell phone we carry around in our pocket. The way these companies rallied behind a new idea shattered what everyone else was doing and has changed our lives.

What then does an environmental or social leapfrog technology look like? It is an innovation that not only transforms a business but also simultaneously protects the environment and helps people.

CRADLE-TO-CRADLE CARPET

Desso, a Netherlands-based company, illustrates leapfrogging within an unsuspecting part of their business: carpeting. Traditionally, Desso's clients looking for carpeting would purchase wall-to-wall carpet for office or residential spaces. They owned the product for life. Eventually, the carpets would become worn down and need replacement. This meant the customer not only had to buy a whole new carpet, but also had to dispose of vast quantities of used carpeting. According to industry estimates, approximately 4.7 billion pounds of carpet are discarded in the United States every year. Most years, waste carpet accounts for close to one percent of all municipal solid waste by weight, or about two percent by volume. That's a lot of carpet in the trash.

Desso made a simple observation related to their conventional carpet business that would have profound consequences. When replacing carpeting in an entire office building, Desso's clients were forced to change entire offices' worth of carpet, when in fact only a small portion of the material had actually worn out. Carpeting in busy hallways, meeting areas, and heavy traffic corridors was more prone to wear, tear, and spills. Once it started to look shabby, it needed replacing. But what about the carpet under desks, tables or furniture that received virtually no foot traffic? This flooring rarely wears out but was torn out with the rest of the beat-up carpet. Desso's clients paid huge sums to replace massive quantities of perfectly intact carpet, inadvertently contributing massive amounts of garbage to landfills.

Desso decided to offer clients a new model. Rather than owning the carpet, they could lease it. Desso would sell their clients the new concept of floor coverage instead of selling carpet by the square foot. Using a specialized carpet comprised of removable tiles, Desso would remove the worn pieces of carpet and replace them as part of a lease agreement. If the idea of leasing carpets sounds odd, so did the idea of short-term leasing of cars and houses before Uber and Airbnb made it commonplace. Desso was onto this new form of leasing long before the tech giants took over.

By employing a lease model, Desso induced their customers to become long-term clients that paid for an ongoing service, rather than a one-time purchase. For customers, it was more economical and attractive to replace sections of carpet and comprised a lower initial investment. This also meant that only sections needed to be removed, as opposed to entire rooms.

Desso then redesigned their carpet composition using a "cradle-to-cradle" concept. The authors of the book, "Cradle to Cradle," William McDonough and Dr. Michael Braungart, invented the idea of cradle-to-cradle products to model human industry on nature's processes. Instead of "cradle-to-grave" products that need to be disposed of when they are no longer useful, cradle-to-cradle products are designed with the express intention of being reinvented after their original useful lifespan ends. Like Nature, cradle to cradle doesn't produce waste at all.

Cradle-to-cradle is an upgrade over traditional recycling, or what McDonough calls "downcycling." In recycling, the original material is transformed into something it was never intended to be and the material is downgraded into something of lesser value. "Upcycling," on the other hand, is the process of transforming by-products, waste materials, or unwanted products into new materials of equal or better quality than the original product.

Desso's new carpet material was upcycled through a process whereby damaged sections were refurbished and transformed back into new carpeting. The "new" carpet tiles were then redeployed to their clients. Rather than recycling used carpet into another unrelated product, Desso built carpet that could be repaired and reused perpetually.

Cradle-to-cradle design makes perfect sense for a carpet lease program. Desso transformed its business with the goal of generating toxin-free products that are specially designed to be taken back and converted into new, high grade products. Their profits climbed while drastically reducing their contribution to landfills. This leapfrog technology gave them an advantage over many of their competitors and transformed their business.

THE GRASS IS ALWAYS GREENER

Leapfrogging can take different shapes and sizes. Though often associated primarily with technical breakthroughs, leapfrogging also happens in agricultural. Golf course design, for example, is a good example of how new agricultural technologies have transformed golf courses throughout the southern United States and Caribbean. A big part of this change is due to a super grass seed and a new way to water it.

Golf has a complicated story. Though golf's popularity has been waning for years, new courses continue to be built around the world. The reason is simple. Though fewer and fewer people are playing the game, golf courses remain a highly effective tool for selling real estate. In fact, the primary motivation for building a golf course has surprisingly little to do with golfers.

Golf courses are typically designed to create attractive suburban communities. They are like manicured movie sets with the sole purpose of enticing home construction.

In reality, most people living on golf courses don't actually play golf at all. Many of the homeowners living on Grupo Puntacana's golf courses, for example, enjoy the ocean views, tidy scenery, and vast green landscapes. They are, however, more than happy to let someone else mow the lawns. While looking out on a golf course every day, they rarely if ever pick up a set of clubs. Worldwide, total golf rounds played on a given course seldom cover the actual cost of maintaining it. Maintenance is more often subsidized by real estate sales and homeowner maintenance fees.

This arrangement means the design of a course is critical to its future economic viability. Since home sales and fees are the primary source of funds for upkeep, the more it costs to maintain a course, the less profitable real estate will be. At the same time, a course that is outrageously expensive to maintain eats into sales revenue. Golf courses need to be eco-efficient, but that is not always the case.

Paradoxically, many high-end golf courses are designed by big-name architects that could care less about future operating costs. They get their fee whether or not the course is economical to maintain. It's not cheap to groom holes, water grass, upkeep landscaping, and fight off pests with synthetic chemicals. The more prominent the course, the more it costs to keep it looking pristine. Yet big-name golf courses are often built with little foresight into maintenance, dooming the course to a life of massive overhead costs.

A thoughtful design, however, can not only reduce overhead, but also minimize a course's environmental impact.

To many environmentalists, golf courses are antithetical to the local ecology. They criticize the use of synthetic fertilizers and herbicides, intensive water usage, threats to nearby water bodies, and loss of forest and natural spaces. For a long time, environmentalists took aim at golf and their criticisms were often more than justified.

However, not all golf courses are created equal. The determining factor of whether a golf course is an ecological nightmare or benign, are the ingredients that go into building it. If a course is thoughtfully designed, carefully constructed, and maintained in an environmentally conscientious way, there is no reason it has to be destructive. Thoughtful design can not only provide economic growth, but also the creation of new wildlife habitat. Vegetation and turfgrass on golf courses can also provide a buffer between other sources of contamination and critical water bodies. Locating a well-made golf course between a mall parking lot, with all of its oil and gas runoff into storm drains, and a lake can actually be a good thing. Environmental groups have increasingly begun to see the value of golf courses, *if* they are designed to minimize their ecological footprint.

In the early 1990s, Grupo Puntacana began to plan its first golf course to jumpstart sluggish real estate sales. The resort had a hotel and an airport but few residences. As it continued to grow, Frank and Ted were convinced the company would need to diversify. The future of Grupo Puntacana was in selling land, building residential communities and then offering services to homeowners.

At the time, the company's finances were precarious, even in the best years. With little cash on hand, it would require real ingenuity to spur real estate development while keeping golf course construction costs down. By deploying a few unique leapfrog technologies, Grupo Puntacana not only launched its nascent real estate program, it produced far-reaching changes in the Caribbean golf industry.

WATER SAVERS

In environments like Punta Cana, building a golf course means using water, and lots of it. The eastern Dominican Republic, though certainly not a desert, has limited annual rainfall. Drinking water in Punta Cana is obtained from wells that drill into underground freshwater aquifers. The aquifers are a limited reserve that recharge slowly. They have to be managed carefully so water-intensive activities and resort hotels won't deplete the available drinking water. If the Punta Cana region wanted to continue building hotels in the future, it couldn't afford to waste a drop of this vital resource.

The key to guaranteeing the future availability of freshwater, Frank concluded, was to safeguard the aquifer in as many ways as possible from the outset. Better to be safe than sorry, Grupo Puntacana needed to be thoughtful about water consumption. To that end, conserving water has become an ongoing theme throughout the company's history.

Equally important, it was critical to avoid contaminating existing groundwater. One way to do this was sewage treatment. Frank had seen other destinations build hotels first and decided what to do with sewage later, only to later fall victim to contaminated drinking water. Resorts without proper sewage systems had contaminated groundwater and coastal waters, requiring costly interventions to undo the damage, spoiling their own future prospects.

The new golf course would need to be irrigated. Before breaking ground on his first golf course, Frank took the unusual step, especially for a resort without a lot of cash, of building a water treatment facility. The facility was unique; it was designed to not only clean sewage, but treated water would then be used as irrigation for the golf course. Rather than injecting treated or untreated sewage into the ground, the most common practice at the time, Grupo Puntacana recycled it. By doubling the use of every drop of water, the aquifer would have a chance to recharge naturally. The treatment plant was a buffer against contaminating *and* over-stressing the aquifer.

Hell-bent on keeping costs down, Frank stumbled across a low-tech but highly effective treatment technology. An anaerobic system, the sewage first passes through a reactor devoid of oxygen. Mimicking natural processes, the anaerobic environment produced microorganisms that do the heavy lifting of breaking down organic material. The anaerobic technology helps avoid an energy-intensive aeration system, which would require near constant electricity to mechanically agitate the sewer water. Using few moving parts and no sophisticated technology, the system doesn't require difficult-to-find replacement parts. It also eliminated the use of imported, synthetic chemicals to treat the water.

From there, the semi-treated water flows into several large, shallow ponds that are exposed to direct sunlight. The sunshine puts the final touches on purifying the water. The suspended solids settle out of the sewage to the bottom of the ponds. Using this pioneering method, the recycled water achieved tertiary treatment, clean enough for irrigation on the golf course.

GPC's treatment plant was designed to collect wastewater from all of the resort's current and future homes, buildings, hotels and even the airport, powered principally by gravity. It relied on few pumps and comparably little energy consumption. The water flows from the resort's bathrooms to the reactor, then to the ponds, and finally is pumped to different irrigation ponds for use on the golf course. Over time, this has led to massive savings, producing a lower energy bill for water treatment, even as the resort has grown.

For a struggling resort to make an investment in sewage treatment before it had sufficient buildings or homes to merit it is truly remarkable. In the modern developed world, sewage treatment is usually a minimum requirement when planning a city. It would be unthinkable, for example, for a new hotel in the US to dump raw sewage into nearby water bodies or inject it into the ground.

In developing countries like the Dominican Republic, however, entire metropolitan cities with millions of residents, such as Santo Domingo, are built without a single functioning water treatment plant. Building a water treatment plant for a non-existing resort was almost as outlandish as building a private airport. But that was just the beginning.

GRASS GOES NATIVE

Grupo Puntacana later deployed another leapfrog technology that would make its golf courses even more cutting edge: the use of a specialized grass seed, paspalum. The new turfgrass was adapted from a native Caribbean grass variety that had evolved the unique ability to withstand continuous salt spray from the ocean. Paspalum is hardy and thrives despite being irrigated with brackish (salty) and treated water. Its ability to subsist on lower quality water meant that paspalum required significantly less consumption of fresh drinking water.

The new grass also requires little topsoil. Normally when constructing new courses, particularly in soil deficient environments like Punta Cana, developers need to truck in massive quantities of topsoil. Paspalum made it possible to rely primarily on local crushed limestone covered with thin layers of local soil and sand. Considering golf courses occupy hundreds of acres, relying on local materials produces huge cost savings, not to mention reducing the environmental footprint from trucking.

The color of the grass, it turns out, is a critical element of selling golf and golf course-based real estate. Golfers and homeowners alike want to see vast expanses of green. They don't care if it's the dead of winter or if they are in an arid desert. They demand vibrant, green grass year-round. Critically, paspalum stays electric green throughout the year.

Golfers are also connoisseurs of the *feel* of grass. Paspalum, it turns out, is tough as nails but also silky smooth. It recovers quickly from heavy foot traffic, golf cart tires, and tough coastal weather without losing its "playability."

Frank, as usual seeing the big picture, deduced that Grupo Puntacana's primary competition for its golf course would be destinations that have seasonal weather, where the grass goes dormant and turns brown in the winter. Having year-round green grass turns out to be another advantage over other golf courses. Taking advantage of its lack of seasonality, GPC pioneered "wall to wall" use of paspalum, seeding it on all greens, tee boxes, and fairways. This strategy keeps the entire course green, allowing it to pop out in photos in magazines, advertisements, and eventually on the Golf Channel, in spite of lower operating costs than competitor courses. Paspalum allowed a newcomer golf course to compete with more famous and better financed courses in the region. Its verdant color stood out, while lowering construction and maintenance costs.

The advantages of using paspalum became so obvious that today it is the standard for courses throughout the Caribbean. It's not only a highly effective product, but it produces cost savings in water, energy, topsoil and chemical inputs. Beyond financial savings, paspalum makes a substantial contribution to protecting the local groundwater. Now it can be found on dozens of courses in the Caribbean, southern United States and even Egypt.

The adoption of anaerobic sewage treatment and a turfgrass are not technologies we typically associate with industry-altering innovations. Paspalum is no Uber. Nonetheless, a super grass and poop-consuming microorganisms can be equally transformative leapfrog technologies. The more essential point is that pursuing innovation can be a game-changer for business *and* the environment. GPC's first golf course ignited private residence sales within the resort, diversifying its airport and hotel businesses to include a potent real estate component. The financial impact for the company was a game-changer.

GETTING TO GREEN

Stuart Hart cites some powerful reasons to motivate companies and CEOs to take the plunge into sustainability. Often, it takes blending a little of each for companies to become proactive about injecting environmental and social considerations in their corporate mission. Whether the goal is to squeeze a little public relations benefit, produce some cost-savings, or take a chance on a new innovation that could revolutionize the business, there are numerous ways to make the case for sustainability.

Yet probably the most powerful argument to pursue sustainability is learning from examples of highly profitable companies that have already fully embraced it. There is a growing class of companies that are born with sustainability in their DNA, making it not only a virtue, but a key to explaining their success. These corporations consider each component of their business and how it impacts society: where they get their water and how they use it, their carbon footprint, the impact of their product on local communities and ecology, the treatment of their employees, the raw materials they use and where and how they source them, among other considerations.

Not all sustainable companies are newcomers, however. In fact, many established companies have extensive histories in the sustainability space. Patagonia, the venerable outdoor clothing and gear company, made protecting the planet part of its mission from its inception. An American company, Patagonia was started by a scraggly crew of rock-climbers that depended on climbing gear made by European manufacturers. Avid adventurers, they traveled constantly in search of new rocks to climb.

Along the way, they noticed that the traditional pitons used to secure their ropes were impacting the places they loved to climb. Once virgin rockfaces were pockmarked with left-over metal, defacing the natural facade. The pitons not only made the mountains look disfigured from an aesthetic perspective, over time the integrity of the rock was compromised, making it more dangerous to ascend.

The group went to work, teaching themselves to be black-smiths to design and make their own gear. More than a business, the primary motive was to make a product they wanted to use that left no trace on the rocks they climbed. The climbers began to forge a homemade design of removable pitons.

Soon, their DIY pitons became so became so popular that the makeshift blacksmiths were forced to sell them and they inadvertently became businessmen. Later they expanded into making other climbing and outdoor gear, predominantly equipment they themselves preferred over existing gear. Over the ensuing forty years, Patagonia evolved into a highly profitable global brand, transforming its CEO, Yvon Chouinard, into an implausible billionaire and a prophet for the virtues of building companies that do good.

Patagonia's mission describes Chouinard's philosophy: "Build the best product, cause no unnecessary harm, use business to inspire and implement solutions to the environmental crisis." The world would be a different place if all companies assumed a version of this mission statement!

Today Patagonia has a vast array of environmental programs, from investing to preserve wild lands, leading activist advocacy campaigns for environmental causes, designing their own eco-friendly products, and making environmental documentaries.

Patagonia has been in the forefront of childcare programs for employees, pioneering advertising that encourages their customers to reduce their environmental impact, and a half-dozen other initiatives worthy of business school cases studies. All the while, they have made their financial success a formidable argument for getting other companies to join them.

In his book, *Let My People Go Surfing*, Yvon Chouinard summarizes: "If we wish to lead corporate America by example, we have to be profitable. No company will respect us, no matter how much money we give away or how much publicity we receive for being one of the '100 Best Companies,' if we are not profitable. It's ok to be eccentric, as long as you are rich; otherwise, you're just crazy."

Much like the Cornell Hotel Schools students I visited, we have heard a lot of talk about what sustainability can and should be, but tangible examples of companies deeply committed are still quite rare. Even more scarce are companies that take the time and risk to share their experiences publicly in order to provide an authentic perspective of how initiated companies can inject sustainability into their veins. Chouinard's book is a valuable resource that should be required reading for all CEOs. (I gave Frank a copy.)

Patagonia has become an inspiration to many businesses. It is an example of a company that exploits its creative capacity to innovate and solve societal problems, all while making money. Until they tap their hidden power to leverage their resources as a force for good, companies will remain Sleeping Giants. In the next chapter, we'll look at how this can happen in an industry that has a profound impact on the planet and people: tourism.

CHAPTER THREE

WHEN THE PRODUCT IS THE PLACE

IN EARLY 2008, JAMAICANS IN THE TRELAWNY PARISH woke up to discover their beach had vanished overnight. There was no hurricane. The beach had not eroded naturally. It had mysteriously disappeared. The enigma of the missing beach led to an international criminal investigation, forensic sand analysis, and eventually the discovery that thieves had dug up hundreds of tons of sand and sold it to local hotel owners. The sand burglars hauled away close to 1,500 feet of beach in the middle of the night to avoid detection, making more than five hundred clandestine trips in dump trucks. Hoteliers who bought the sand claimed to have no idea of its origin. The white, powdery, Caribbean sand was worth approximately a million dollars.

Sand, it turns out, is one of the most widely exploited resources in the world. It is a key ingredient in concrete, glass, and many electronics. According to a United Nations Environment Program, "sand and gravel represent the highest volume of raw material used on Earth after water." By some estimates, 80 percent of everything built on our planet is built out of concrete, which requires enormous quantities of sand. The global sand trade, which includes mining, dredging, extracting, and shipping enough raw material to meet the explosive demand for urban housing, is estimated to be worth $70 billion a year.

Sand, however, is a finite resource. It takes decades to regenerate in the rivers, beaches, floodplains and mines where it naturally occurs. Desert sand is unfortunately not a viable substitute and can't be used in construction. As the global demand for sand skyrockets, decreasing supply has made it an increasingly valuable commodity. In fact, illegal sand mining is now a global issue. Sand mafias like the one that stole the beach in Jamaica are spreading, at times provoking serious violence, and this unassuming but precious mineral is indeed becoming one of the world's most prized minerals.

Sand is an equally important economic driver in the Caribbean, though less for its use in construction and electronics than for its aesthetic value. For many people, a Caribbean vacation is the ultimate escape from their day-to-day cold to a palm tree-lined fantasy. The Caribbean is a collection of island nations in the same sea, but more than a geographic region, it has come to epitomize transparent turquoise seas, stunning sugary white-sand beaches and exquisite postcard sunsets. The Caribbean means paradise.

The majority of Caribbean islands depend on tourism for their livelihood. Yet it would be impossible to sell this vision of paradise if the ocean were a murky, contaminated soup, if beaches were littered with trash, or the palm trees were falling into the ocean because the sand had eroded away. There is no faking paradise.

In tourism, the product is the place. Unlike other industries, tourism, particularly coastal tourism, depends on two primary resources: people and Nature. More people than ever are traveling to see new places, try new things, immerse themselves in different cultures, and appreciate the world's natural attractions. They may want some comforts of home, but most travelers seek a unique escape from the daily grind. They want new experiences. As much as the Caribbean is a vacation destination, the diverse Caribbean islands also offer the opportunity to dip a toe into an entirely unique culture, with the benefit of some of the best beaches in the world.

For businesses that operate in tourism, the relationship between the business and the local environment and people could not be clearer. Tourism businesses must protect their natural and human resources because that is what drives their bottom line—at least that's the way it should be.

Unfortunately, this doesn't always happen. Tourism businesses are often so focused on customer service and meeting revenue targets that they neglect the natural assets that draw their guests in the first place. In the Caribbean, one of the most neglected assets we have is the humble parrotfish.

THE FISH THAT LAYS THE GOLDEN EGG

Beaches are not what we think they are. We imagine a beach as a fixed location that will always be there; a place we can visit any time. In reality, natural coastal beaches are only snapshots in geologic time, dynamic and constantly evolving. A sandy beach is a collection of weathered, pulverized rock mixed with fragments of shelled creatures that have been deposited temporarily on the shore. The sand moves and migrates along the shoreline and the beach continually changes. The tropical beach on which we sip a piña colada today didn't look the same twenty years ago, and it won't look the same in another twenty.

Similarly, not all beaches are the same. Beaches are made

up of a wide variety of sands and are created by diverse environmental conditions. Beach sand can come from sediments of rivers, volcanic eruptions and ensuing lava flows, or organisms that inhabit nearby ecosystems. There are black-sand beaches, pink beaches, rocky beaches, and of course, white-sand beaches. Surprisingly, Caribbean white-sand beaches are produced, in large part, from the guts of reef-dwelling parrotfish.

Parrotfish are brilliantly colored fish that inhabit coral reefs, attracting divers, snorkelers, and underwater photographers. If you have ever laid eyes on a coral reef coffee table book or a David Attenborough film on reefs, parrotfish were likely one of the most eye-catching creatures there.

Beyond their kaleidoscope of bright colors, parrotfish are bizarre creatures. They travel in schools of several dozen fish, led by a dominant super-male who earned his place in the pecking order by changing genders. In fact, parrotfish jump genders multiple times throughout their lives.

Besides sexual dexterity, parrotfish have odd sleeping habits. They sleep in a self-made mucus cocoon believed to disguise them from predators such as eels and sharks. Unfortunately, its slimy nightgown doesn't protect them from spearfishermen.

Besides being striking to look at, scientists have begun to appreciate the important role parrotfish play in supporting coral reef health. Parrotfish are herbivores and a critical part of their diet comes from grazing algae that grows on the reef. When too abundant, algae can be damaging to corals, denying the corals sunlight and space to grow, eventually suffocating them. Parrotfish are natural grazers that protect the corals from destructive overgrowth of macroalgae.

More relevant to the tourism industry, parrotfish are sand-producing machines. Parrotfish have rows of tightly packed teeth that take the shape of a parrot's beak, which they use to grind up pieces of rock and coral. Their teeth, comprised of fluorapatite, are one of the hardest minerals in the world, stronger than copper, gold, and silver. Perfect tools for making sand.

Like cows that inadvertently suck up dirt and pebbles while grazing a grassy pasture, parrotfish accidentally bite off chunks of rock and coral while nibbling for algae. Unable to completely digest the hard substrate, their teeth and stomachs grind it up before excreting it. Over time, the parrotfish's feces, made up of finely digested calcium carbonate, becomes picturesque white sand. Parrotfish literally poop out much of the white sand that adorns Caribbean beaches.

Parrotfish are such prodigious poopers, scientists estimate that one adult parrotfish has the capacity to produce up to two hundred pounds of white sand a year. The larger and healthier the local parrotfish population, the bigger the underwater sand banks for local beaches. Considering Caribbean coral reefs generate an estimated $3 billion dollars a year in tourism and fisheries, the parrotfish is literally worth its weight in gold to the Caribbean economy.

REEFS IN PERIL

Unfortunately, humans still haven't fully grasped the importance of parrotfish, or that of other reef fish. Severe overfishing of commercially important species such as grouper, sea bass, and red snapper has led artisanal fishermen in many islands to target less economically valuable species, like parrotfish. Known by experts as "fishing down the food web," this phenomenon means that parrotfish, though not widely considered a delicacy, have become an increasingly common sight on the plates of local restaurants. This comes at a direct cost to the health of the coral reef.

When I arrived in Punta Cana, protecting parrotfish was definitely not on my radar. As a scuba diver, I am fascinated by coral reefs and the creatures that inhabit them. I knew a few of the underwater hand signals for different creatures I had been taught as a scuba diver. I had read that coral reefs were the "the rainforests of the sea" and learned about some of the key services reefs provide to coastal communities: seafood, recreational activities, and even protecting homes and people during storm events. Yet I didn't know anything about parrotfish or what they had to do with sustainable tourism.

As I began to look into the situation of the eight-kilometer coral reef in front of Grupo Puntacana's property, the role of parrotfish became much clearer. Like most Caribbean reefs, the Punta Cana reef was in bad shape. A rapid assessment conducted by coral experts confirmed that our reef had some of the lowest densities of fish in the Dominican Republic and even lower densities of living coral. The reef still had world-class reef structure—complex underwater worlds made up of caves, cliffs and shallow fringe reefs—but our reef was largely empty of fish and consisted of far more dead rock than live coral.

Importantly, the reef had suffered what the scientists call a "phase shift," meaning that instead of corals, the reef had a greater coverage of macroalgae than coral. The algae was so abundant that it was outcompeting the corals, the opposite of what you need for a healthy coral reef. Our reef was in deep trouble.

At the same time, we studied possible reasons for so few fish. We knew there was a small but active fishermen community nearby in Juanillo, but it didn't seem plausible that a few dozen guys in battered fiberglass boats with rudimentary fishing gear could deplete eight kilometers' worth of reef fish. But that's exactly what was happening.

Our research proved they were in fact making more than a dent. Fishing day in and day out, with no government oversight or catch limits, the fishermen had managed to clean out the majority of the valuable reef species. Having decimated the local population of groupers, snappers, conch, and lobster, the local fishermen were fishing down the food web. Our surveys indicated that sixty percent of the local fishermen's haul was parrotfish.

Despite a critical ecological importance when alive, parrotfish have a relatively low market value as seafood; they fetch a lower price compared to other species. Yet if the fishermen caught enough of them, the larger parrotfish hauls could make up for their low price. Instead of catching fewer pricy fish, the fishermen speared vast numbers of easy-to-spear parrotfish. Despite making less money per pound, fishermen had a perverse incentive to aggressively pursue even more of them. This of course put added pressure on local parrotfish populations.

It was a worst-case scenario for the reef. It was overgrown with algae and not enough coral. Simultaneously, one of the most prodigious tools to control that algae, herbivorous parrotfish, was being systematically wiped out. Fishermen pursued less valuable parrotfish because there was little else available. Eventually the reef would become so degraded it would be unrecoverable.

This sequence of bad news was troubling, not just from an environmental perspective but a business perspective too. Without healthy corals, the reef ecosystem would ultimately become so degraded that it could no longer provide any of the ecological services that benefit the local tourism economy. For example, without healthy coral reefs, our hotels, homes and other infrastructure would become more susceptible to storms, hurricanes, and flooding. Eventually, our beaches would erode from increased impact from the sea and storms.

Research by The Nature Conservancy assigned a value on the protection of human infrastructure provided by coral reefs against flooding in storm events. In the Dominican Republic, like many islands, healthy coral reefs are worth hundreds of millions of dollars in avoided storm and flood damage. This is not a trivial matter for a resort selling real estate and building golf courses and hotels right along the coast.

Worse, as we lost parrotfish, we lost production of vital white sand. As beaches eroded, we wouldn't have sandbank reserves available to replace them. The fishermen were putting a dent in our local sand factory.

With depleted reefs, tourists wouldn't have colorful fish to look at when they went diving or snorkeling, which directly impacts our ability to sell excursions to visitors. Combined with lost beaches, it is difficult to imagine millions of tourists a year visiting Punta Cana without its showcase beaches or dazzling reef fish.

As complicated as this problem seemed, there was a huge upside in terms of efficiency. If we could rebuild the parrotfish population on the reef, we could create a positive chain reaction to help rebuild the coral reef. Parrotfish would be able to graze overabundant algae growth and help the reef recover, subsequently restarting the sand production process. If we could restore some balance on the reef ecosystem, we had a chance to protect our balance sheet in the future. But where to start?

THE CORAL WHISPERER

Austin Bowden-Kerby is a coral reef champion. Sporting a long gray beard and a PhD in marine biology, he is part scientist and part coral whisperer. In 2003, Austin, working with the international foundation Counterpart International, visited the Dominican Republic and used his charm and enthusiasm to convince us to do something entirely new: replant the reef.

The premise was simple. Based on his experience in Fiji and Puerto Rico, Austin proposed we grow corals in underwater nurseries made of homemade metal frames affixed to the ocean bottom. He helped us situate the frames in a spot with ideal water quality, lots of light, and plenty of sand. The metal frames were bent in an A shape and anchored to the sandy sea bottom.

Austin collected small pieces of fast-growing but highly endangered staghorn corals (*Acropora cervicornis*) that had naturally fallen off the reef from storms or waves. He then secured the coral fragments to the frames with plastic tie-wraps. Free from natural predators on the reef and situated in ideal growing conditions, the corals would grow just like plants on a farm.

At first, the frames looked empty with only a few dozen lonely fragments cinched in place. But if the conditions in the nursery were right, after six to eight months the corals would double or triple in size. And it worked—spiky coral fragments soon covered the frames with dense, almost impenetrable branches of coral. In a matter of months, we could barely make out the metal frames at all. Once the frames were overgrown with coral tissue, Austin would trim the coral growth from the nurseries and plant them back on the reef.

Resembling traditional plant gardening, this new restoration technique was nicknamed "coral gardening." Austin had pioneered some of the early techniques for growing corals in underwater nurseries and subsequently made it his life's mission to share his faith in coral gardening around the planet. Fortunately for us, his evangelizing mission brought him to Punta Cana, just in time.

Staghorn coral is a species historically common to the Caribbean, but its populations have been decimated from disease, storms, and predators. At one time, staghorn was the spiny yellow carpet that covered large tracts of reef throughout the Caribbean. It grows in dense thickets of coral fingers that reach out like tiny tree branches. When healthy, staghorn and other corals provide habitat for many reef species and help grow the structure of coral reefs. Today, over 80 percent of staghorn has been lost in the Caribbean and its future hangs by a delicate thread.

The goal of the project was to create staghorn coral nurseries as a life support system. If we could keep enough genetic diversity alive in nurseries, we could then transplant the coral tissue back on to the reef. Eventually they could reproduce sexually on their own on a much larger scale, without our help. The end game was not to transplant corals indefinitely or to rebuild the entire coral reef. On the contrary, if we were successful, the replanted coral population would become abundant and healthy enough to put us out of the coral gardening business altogether. It seems counterintuitive, but the goal of coral restoration is to make it obsolete.

Worst case, we could keep remaining staghorn colonies in managed nurseries before they became extinct in the wild. Coral gardening alone wouldn't solve our overfishing problem, but we preferred taking a proactive approach to rehabilitating the reef over waiting for the staghorns to disappear. When we started in 2005, this was a real possibility. Months of surveying only turned up a handful of surviving wild staghorn coral populations. Without our intervention, it's likely they would have gone locally extinct.

Austin's passion for coral restoration was not shared by all coral scientists at the time. Though he had legitimate scientific credentials, many coral specialists believed restoration was mere eco-fantasy. Rather than a realistic methodology for conservation, coral gardening, they believed, was a pseudo-science that held little promise to reverse the dire state of the world's reefs.

Up to that point, the scientific community's traditional answer to the coral reef crisis seemed to be the same: continually monitor declining reefs and publish the depressing results in academic journals. Conservation organizations advocated solving the coral decline through public awareness campaigns and environmental education. Divers were encouraged to take care not to touch corals while underwater. Boaters were taught to avoid tossing their anchors on fragile reefs. Damaging fishing practices, like dynamiting reefs or the use of chlorine to extract certain creatures, were banned in certain areas.

Years later, governments were encouraged to create marine protected areas and designate no-fishing zones. All of these methods were essential, but also insufficient. Coral restoration held promise to recover damaged reefs, but it had not yet become a proven piece of the reef conservation toolkit.

CORAL GARDENING GOES 'UNDERGROUND'

Poised to install our first coral nursery, the entire project was nearly derailed before it ever got started. Several coral reef foundations, led by Reef Check, spoke out publicly against different techniques of coral restoration at the world's biggest annual coral reef science conference. In a widely disseminated publication, they cautioned against deploying significant resources to "engineered construction" of coral reefs, including coral gardening. They concluded that investing in restoration would misuse valuable financial resources that could be better spent pursuing more traditional conservation strategies. In short, they advised international donors and foundations to steer clear, since the new field of restoration was overrated and over-hyped.

Despite widespread skepticism towards this experimental field, we disagreed with the scientists that favored a wait and see attitude. For one, we were driven by a private sector impatience that prefers action over exhaustive analysis. Second, we knew that no foundation or government was coming to our reef's rescue. Following conventional coral wisdom, we had been diligently documenting the decline of our reef without doing anything. We were convinced that following the status quo meant watching the slow-motion demise of staghorn, and probably many other coral species, right in front of our eyes. If the experts thought it foolhardy and the donors were unwilling to take a risk on restoration, the private sector would have to step in and get it done.

As newcomers to the world of reef conservation, we decided to proceed without fanfare, quietly trying our hand at growing corals. With guidance from Austin and later backed by the scientific know-how of a few brave restoration pioneers at the University of Miami Rosenstiel School of Marine and Atmospheric Science, we began our experimental project by surveying the coastal area in front of our property and neighboring resorts. We identified a few remaining colonies of staghorn and collected as many "genotypes," or genetically different corals, as we could. The goal was to ensure our staghorn gene pool was as diverse as possible. We set up a half-dozen frames in a shallow, protected area of the reef with crystal clear water known as the "Aquarium." We periodically visited the nursery to clean off algae, dust off sand from the corals, and measure the growth rates.

Then we waited to see what the corals would tell us.

RESUSCITATED REEFS

The corals responded. Slowly at first, but after the first few years more emphatically. Soon we had explosive growth in our underwater nurseries and as much staghorn corals as we could handle. In 2010, University of Miami scientists conducted the first regional survey of restoration projects, which at that time consisted of a half-dozen or so nurseries scattered around the Caribbean and Central America. To our surprise, we had one of the largest and most productive staghorn nurseries in the Caribbean. Equally important, our constant presence at our nursery site kept local spearfishermen at bay. The Aquarium dive site, where the nursery was installed, had become an ad hoc, no-take fish refuge. Reef fish populations recovered and soon the site had the highest fish densities of any site in the Dominican Republic. This was a direct but inadvertent result of the restoration work.

Like everyone else doing coral restoration at that time, we learned while doing. Coral gardening was the ultimate do-it-yourself project. It was a new technique with few scientifically proven methods. Restoration meant accumulating practical know-how from experimentation. We learned about "outplanting corals," transplanting nursery-grown fragments of coral back onto the reef, through trial and error. We took tiny samples of nursery-grown coral tissue and transplanted them to the reef using epoxy or cement to hold the fragments in place. Over time and with careful documentation, these experiments gave us a clear idea of where, how, and when to transplant corals to achieve the best survival rates. In the ensuing fifteen years since those early trials, we have transplanted close to eight kilometers of coral tissue back to the reef and continue to use new technology and techniques to improve our success.

At every step of the project, the corals' growth encouraged us to keep pushing ahead. The more we invested in coral restoration, the more Nature rewarded us, whether it was directly linked to our restoration efforts or not. We saw the return of nesting sea turtles to our beaches for the first time in years. We documented the appearance of a family of local manatee, a species that had been locally extinguished decades before. We even had the occasional visit from passing dolphins and humpback whales. The video of the unsuspecting diver that filmed a passing twenty-foot whale shark became an instant classic. The divers' eyes nearly bugged out of his scuba mask as the shark's enormous shadow blocked out the sunlight above. Our reef was still in tough shape, but we were getting clear signals from Nature that we were on the right track.

Grupo Puntacana Foundation also benefitted from being a pioneer in coral restoration. With exposure in several scientific publications and some international publicity, we began to attract the financial support of international donors, including the Interamerican Development Bank, the United Nations Development Agency, the European Union, and German Development Agency (GIZ). Interestingly, whereas few donors had expressed interest in working with us before, suddenly they saw value in working with the private sector.

With continued support from the resort and newfound donor funding, we expanded our efforts. Soon we were helping other organizations in different regions of the Dominican Republic, Haiti, and a half-dozen other Caribbean islands try their hand at coral restoration. We helped create nurseries in many other sites, training other institutions, individuals, and even government officials in coral restoration. Our Foundation developed a PADI specialty dive certification in "Coral First Aid," allowing visiting tourists and dive enthusiasts to contribute to restoration efforts as volunteers. Our humble beginnings had transformed into a hub for coral restoration knowledge-sharing. In 2019, we received a prestigious award from the Ecosystem-based Adaptation Facility that funded the expansion of our work into new techniques and new geographies in the Dominican Republic.

The general skepticism towards coral reef restoration gradually softened as well. Today, coral restoration is a growing discipline widely accepted by the scientific community. Projects have sprouted throughout the Caribbean, Pacific, and Australia's Great Barrier Reef as more and more resources are dedicated to the worldwide plight of reefs. In 2018, the first large conference dedicated to restoration, Coral Futures, was held with scientists, practitioners, and donors advancing the field of restoration. Even Reef Check has begun advocating coral restoration.

Restoration techniques also continue to evolve. Scientists and practitioners are deploying new methods to make restoration more efficient while propagating greater varieties of coral species. Restoration science has begun to recruit the help of tech entrepreneurs, engineers, materials scientists, and governments to eventually bring the work to a much larger scale. New tools like sexual reproduction, micro-fragmentation, and genetic engineering are all expanding the boundaries of coral reef restoration.

Coral gardening went from Austin Bowden-Kerby's kooky hobby to a serious conservation tool. A few small experiments like ours have transformed into a virtual tidal wave of effort to save coral reefs from mass extinction. We now employ a small army of reef gardeners including scientists, interns, dive enthusiasts and even fishermen (more on this later). We have expanded our partnerships to include a half-dozen restoration organizations around the Caribbean and formed a consortium to track progress of nurseries throughout the Dominican Republic and Haiti. Our Foundation now works with various international experts to master new ways of successfully reproducing corals and introducing new reef organisms to help accelerate coral propagation.

We learned a key lesson from this project: The private sector can play an important role in conservation. We took a calculated risk when many conservation organizations, donors, or scientists wouldn't. Since we are not your typical environmental not-for-profit, we could take risks they weren't willing to.

Furthermore, we learned that the private sector is capable

of acting in its own best interest (in this case, protecting our reef and our beach), while contributing to environmental protection. By increasing the amount of coral tissue, improving water quality, and generally doing a better job protecting the reef, we bet that we could help staghorns and other species of corals recover. Eventually the corals would return to reproducing sexually without our help and this investment would also benefit our beaches.

This sort of enlightened self-interest should be attractive to other hotels as well. If we could get more developers to do the same, our impact would be magnified. Now we just needed a way to convince local fishermen to lay off the reef fish.

DANGEROUS CATCH

One year I was asked to give a talk to the largest hotel association in the northern Dominican Republic. Before my speech, I talked with a few members about the challenges of collaborating with local fishermen. I was surprised when one hotelier commented, "For us, the fishermen are little more than a pest."

There is no doubt that artisanal fishermen can be a complicated lot. Convincing them to comply with fishing regulations can be a dicey proposition. Fishermen associations, meanwhile, seem to dedicate more time to bickering, staking out territories, and quarrelling amongst each other than catching fish. Subsistence fishermen are generally as law-abiding as a Hell's Angels motorcycle gang.

Still, the hotelier's conclusion was too harsh. What about coastal developers? Resort owners are usually the new arrivals to a beachfront property, not the fishermen. After purchasing their land and beginning their project, most hoteliers invest little time and effort establishing relationships with local fishermen. The goal is to keep them off their property, out of sight, and as far as possible from guests. For many hoteliers, the fishermen are like rats, roaches, and mosquitoes. Just another "pest," as the hotelier said, to be dealt with.

My experience, however, has shown that more than a nuisance, fishermen are often an under-utilized asset in coastal tourism. Surprisingly to some people, fishermen have unique skill sets that if channeled correctly, can be valuable to resort developers. At the same time, they can be converted from a menace that overexploits reef fish to a viable conservation ally. The challenge is how to corral the fishermen's unique talents and harness them to benefit tourism. This has been the key to confronting overfishing in Punta Cana.

In Punta Cana, there are half a dozen types of artisanal fishing, but the majority of fishermen can typically be divided into two general factions: deep-water fishers and reef fishermen. The deep-water fishermen navigate miles offshore in small boats called *yolas*, connect to improvised breathing gear attached to an air compressor on-board, before plunging hundreds of feet below the surface. Once at the ocean's bottom they swim or walk along the ocean floor, breaking and collecting conch, spearing fish, octopus, lobster, and sea cucumbers.

While this type of fishing can lead to greater rewards by capturing larger and more valuable species, it comes with considerable risk. If the makeshift breathing apparatus fails at two hundred feet underwater, there is no getting back up. In fact, many fishermen perish at sea. Equally common are fishermen that spend too much time at great depths with no safety procedures, suffering from physical ailments associated with decompression sickness, known as "the bends." In most fishing communities, there are at least a handful of former fishermen with hearing issues, a damaged arm or worse, caused by the bends.

Free-swimming spearfishermen, on the other hand, float along in the shallower water near shore with snorkels and spear guns. These fishermen work the coral reef day and night. Often, they don't even have boats. Instead, they launch themselves off cliffs or simply walk in from a beach, spear guns in hand. They swim determinedly along the reef, methodically harpooning everything in their path. The size and species they gaff matters less than bringing in as much prey as possible.

The fish are skewered and attached to floating plastic bottles bobbing along behind the fishermen, attached by nylon strings. The fishermen continue swimming along the coast, dragging their catch behind them, until they get to a boat launch, sometimes several miles away. (All of this bloody, floating bait might create a different predator problem, if the local shark populations hadn't already been decimated too.) Near shore, spearfishermen typically sell their wares to a waiting merchant at the landing. Though far less dangerous than deep-water compressor fishing, it's still not an easy day job.

FISHING DOWN THE FOOD WEB

Ironically, Punta Cana fishermen largely ignore the massive tourism market to sell their wares. Very little of their catch is consumed locally. Instead, local fish buyers spend the day camped out near the fishermen's dock, waiting to be the first in line to buy their catch. When the fishermen arrive, the fish buyer opens an ice-packed cooler and purchases virtually everything they bring in, paying cash on the spot.

The higher quality or "A grade" fish fetch the highest prices. Low grade fish, like parrotfish, are sold for peanuts. The stocked coolers then disappear into the back of the buyer's truck and off he goes to sell the day's catch, often in nearby towns, cities or vendors in other regions of the country. All told, the majority of local catch is sold far from the hotels and restaurants of the tourism economy.

The fishermen's finances make it difficult to sell to formal businesses, even if they wanted to. Fishermen don't get a regular paycheck; they earn what they catch. They have good days and bad days, which means they are often in debt or in need of quick cash. They live day to day and usually can't endure the glacial pace of payments by supermarkets, hotels, and restaurants. Thus, they become dependent on fish buyers to purchase everything they bring in and to pay immediately.

This fish buyer system, whereby an intermediary fish purchaser controls much of the market, triggers a number of important problems for the coral reef. The worst of these is the practice encourages fishermen to capture any and all species, even the ones with relatively low market values. Instead of leaving these fish on the reef, fishermen are encouraged to capture more of them by volume to make the low price worth their time.

Since the fish are sold far from the tourism area, local hotels and restaurants don't have buying power to incentivize better, more sustainable fishing practices. With no government oversight or fishing limits, the health of the local fishery is in the hands of the fish buyer. More often than not, this is bad news for the coral reef.

The catch-all fishing model is the way fishermen offset their decreasing returns as overfished populations shrink. In other words, the fewer fish they find, the more fishermen are forced to *increase* their pursuit of the remaining fish. Fishermen also target new fish species traditionally left alone. The practice of "fishing down the food web" limits the diversity of the fish on the reef and creates markets for species that didn't exist previously. Fishermen are caught in a vicious cycle and can rarely get ahead of declining species populations.

Decimating one species usually means pursuing a new one instead. If you don't remember seeing Chilean sea bass on a menu until a few years ago, it is likely because it wasn't previously considered seafood. A deep-water species found in southern waters near Antarctica, Chilean sea bass was once known as Patagonian toothfish. It got rebranded, giving it a new and more appetizing name. Soon it began showing up on more and more menus, making it one of the most sought-after new fish in the world. Today, Chilean sea bass is in serious trouble due to overfishing.

Even when fishing rules do enforce minimum size limits, such as in the United States, these regulations can have a destructive impact on fish stocks. The larger fish are typically more prolific reproducers, accounting for a larger percentage of offspring. Minimum size limits actually remove the larger fish from the ecosystem first, reducing the amount of juvenile fish. Intensive spearfishing not only gives fish populations no time to recover, but there are also fewer productive egg-layers to speed up a potential recovery. The result, of course, is dwindling fish stocks.

FISHERMEN GARDENERS

This complex dynamic coincided with a dilemma we faced with our coral restoration work. Coral restoration is a low-tech but labor-intensive endeavor. Underwater coral nurseries need constant cleaning and maintenance. Sand on the corals must be cleaned off and pesky predators like fire worms need to be removed from the frames. After storms, divers have to go out and reposition the frames and recover broken coral fragments.

Once the corals begin to grow, they can quickly overrun the frames with fresh coral tissue, requiring out-planting. All of this has to be done while underwater, meaning coral gardeners need to be proficient divers accustomed to spending long hours laboring underwater.

While our corals continued to grow like gangbusters in the nurseries, our efforts to transplant the coral tissue lagged behind. With limited resources to pay experienced professional divers and scientists, we depended on volunteers, interns, and our limited staff to transplant the corals back onto the reef. Soon we had too much coral and not enough bodies to plant · it on the reef.

Frustrated by too few fish and too much coral in our nurseries, we stumbled onto a crazy idea. What if we hired and trained a few spearfishermen to work on our coral nurseries? If it worked, we could solve two problems at once: reduce fishing pressure and speed up our restoration efforts. It was a long shot, but in theory it made sense.

When we approached the fishermen, they were understandably suspicious. While we had maintained a respectful relationship with them over the years, it was more of a truce than a partnership. Our foundation had undertaken programs for years educating fishermen about the importance of protecting critical species. We worked with them to carve out no-fish zones and encouraged them to get organized into an association so they could more easily sell directly to the resort.

Grupo Puntacana pioneers coral restoration in the Caribbean

But in terms of reducing overfishing, the national fishing authority, CODOPESCA, was nowhere to be found. Without government oversight, local compliance with fishing laws was voluntary and mostly ineffective. For years, Grupo Puntacana had allowed the fishermen do their thing as long as it didn't impact our guests. But our company had no formal authority to limit fish catch. Though we knew overfishing had a tremendous impact on the reef, we were powerless to stop it.

Now we brought them a different kind of proposal. Backed by a grant from the Interamerican Development Bank, we offered to hire the fishermen as coral gardeners. We would pay for their dive certification, train them in coral restoration, and pay them to help restore the reef. We didn't have enough money to hire them full time, but we could at least try an experiment with a few willing guys to get things in motion.

Many of the fisherman, however, hadn't finished grade school. They had little practice in reading and writing. The idea of taking a diving class with written exams was intimidating. Moreover, any time they spent studying and taking classes was time spent away from making money. How would they feed their families in the meantime? The fishermen were skeptical.

With considerable persistence, we convinced a few brave fishermen to get certified as PADI Open Water Divers. We trained them in our coral restoration specialty dive course. We hired them a few days a week to help maintain the coral nurseries. Most of our new coral gardeners continued to fish, but they were making consistent cash with us on the side, so they stuck with it. The fishermen proved to be adept in the water and efficient at transplanting corals (often more effective than our interns). They were unfazed by rough weather, choppy seas, and long hours. Coral gardening, it turns out, is easier than spearfishing. We were making progress.

ASSOCIATION OF ARTISANS AND MARINE SERVICES

While it was easy to hire local spearfishermen, we soon ran into trouble paying them. Using funds from an international donor meant we had to keep careful accounting of the project. We couldn't make under-the-table payments. We had to pay our new coral gardeners with real checks and that included tax withholdings. The fishermen wanted cash. We had to figure out how to pay them or our ingenious scheme would flop.

It turned out the only way to pay the fishermen was to get them organized, or more specifically, incorporated. We thought about using an existing fishermen association as the formal vehicle to pay them, but we needed to change their own self-perception. It was no longer only about fishing. We wanted the fishermen, and hopefully their families, to rebrand themselves and become part of the tourism economy. The fishermen proposed a new entity called The Association of Artisans and

Marine Services (ARSEMAR, the Spanish acronym). Once ARSEMAR was formally incorporated, we opened a bank account and the once-destructive spearfishermen were soon getting paid to restore the reef.

Local fishermen become coral gardeners

Initially, ARSEMAR consisted of no more than three part-time coral gardeners, not exactly a reef revolution. Yet we had started something important: unifying an unruly, independent group of individuals into small business owners. We had managed to create a business relationship with the fishermen, as opposed to a charitable one.

Importantly, we demonstrated the first inklings of a viable alternative to spearfishing that we could build on. The fishermen were motivated workers when they got paid. In the next few years, we provided formal training to several dozen local fishermen in different ocean-related skills: boat captains, scuba divers, and coral gardeners. A half-dozen fishermen abandoned fishing altogether in favor of regular paychecks and steady work with ARSEMAR. Carlos, one of the original pioneers to try his hand as a coral gardener, became the president of ARSEMAR and turned it into a full-time gig.

During my talk to the hotel association, I mentioned the comment by the hotelier about fishermen being "pests." I told them, "We used to think the fishermen were pests too. But now we think of them like we do any other trade. They are like just like a plumber, but they happen to be fixing the reef instead of a leaky toilet. We just needed to figure out how to take advantage of their unique skills."

ARSEMAR's former fishermen are no longer voracious poachers, exterminating the local fish population and ruining the reef health. We discovered that while some of the newfound coral gardeners couldn't care less about the actual corals, many do. Once they began to replant corals, they became like their kids. They worried about their survival. This was a significant change.

Importantly, we learned that fishermen have skills that can contribute to the tourism industry, *if we let them*. We had laid the groundwork and persuaded fishermen to lay off reef fish by encouraging them to migrate to other work. Rebuilding an entire parrotfish population would not be an overnight job, but we had taken some important steps.

In 2017, in a rare display of coherence, the Dominican Ministry of Environment declared the capture and commercialization of parrotfish illegal. While the new law was mostly symbolic, due to the government's inability to consistently enforce it, the ban gave us some bargaining power. It provided a unique opportunity for the tourism sector to use its purchasing power and its contact with visitors to support an initiative that directly benefits its beaches. We got behind the movement to ban parrotfishing in Punta Cana.

Early studies demonstrate that the density of parrotfish near our resort is improving. Similarly, the reef has shown signs of recovering corals and other species. Yet as soon as we make progress on one front, it seems another one opens up behind it. Soon we were forced to discover that the fishermen weren't the only ones with unique talents that we would have to engage. We would have to involve their families as well.

LIONFISH INVASION

Some of the most beautiful animals in the sea are also the most dangerous. Lionfish, also known as zebrafish or firefish, are a hand-sized reef fish with long, ornate feathery fins, and zebra-like stripes. Besides looking elegant, the fins are highly venomous and produce an excruciating sting. Despite being dangerous, lionfish are prized by saltwater aquarium enthusiasts. In aquaria, they float harmlessly around the tank, eyeing their tank-mates and waiting to be fed.

Similarly, swimming in their native waters in the Indo-Pacific, lionfish populations are kept in check naturally. Predators such as sharks, moray eels, and grouper consume enough lionfish to maintain a balanced population. These competitors also limit lionfish from exploring and expanding to new territories. Lionfish populations also depend on available prey, consisting of small fish and invertebrates. These species know lionfish habits and hunting techniques and can hide and avoid them. Lionfish have to work hard to get a meal and in their natural environments, they are just one among many reef species.

In the mid-1990's, however, lionfish were spotted in South Florida, where they are decidedly less benign. Experts suspect that the first lionfish were released from saltwater aquaria into the ocean off the coast of Florida, either during a storm or by accident. Lionfish quickly made themselves at home in the greater Atlantic, soon migrating as far north as the Carolinas and as far south as Brazil. This new invader, at no fault of its own, soon became a serious environmental threat to Caribbean coral reefs.

Skilled and efficient hunters, lionfish feasted voraciously on unsuspecting Caribbean fish, which had never seen them before. In no time, they began overpowering native coral fish populations. Gorging on easy prey, Caribbean lionfish grow to sizes not seen in the Pacific.

Lionfish also compete with local species for space on the reef, driving their rivals off to look for new habitat. Studies have shown that a single lionfish in non-native waters can reduce the presence of native species by 80 percent. Once established, it's possible to see dozens of lionfish occupying a small area of reef and few other species.

Equally problematic, in foreign environs lionfish become shapeshifters, adapting to a wide range of conditions. They can live near and far from the shore, at great depths and in shallow water, on and off coral reefs. Roving to different underwater habitats, lionfish become new competitors to local species throughout the Caribbean.

LIONFISH FILETS

By 2007, we had heard the warnings of the impending arrival of lionfish to the Dominican Republic yet hadn't actually laid eyes on one in Punta Cana. One day I got a call from the general manager of Tortuga Bay, our most luxurious hotel, who had caught wind of the lionfish invasion. Vincenzo wasn't at all interested in their ecological impact; he was worried about their excruciating sting. "If I have to take one of my guests to the emergency room because they get stung by a lionfish," he warned, "we are going to have a big problem. We have to do something."

Just like that, reported lionfish sightings began pouring in. We found them hovering around dock pilings near the shore and saw them near the coral reef. But I knew we really had a problem when lionfish turned up on local fishermen's spears. Lionfish, they told us, were beginning to crowd out local species. It was time to dive into a search for solutions.

According to most conservation organizations, the best way to control lionfish was to unleash the power of the market on them. It turns out that beneath their venomous spines, lionfish offer a tasty white filet that, when properly prepared, can be an attractive option for restaurants. In Florida, activists began holding "lionfish roundups," competitions where people armed with spear guns compete to harpoon as many lionfish as possible. The roundups were followed by barbeques and fish fries, giving people a firsthand taste of the fish. One solution to the lionfish invasion was to put them on the menu.

In Punta Cana, we had all the necessary ingredients to make this work: numerous restaurants, a growing population of lionfish, and a group that had proven to be equally as insatiable hunters as the lionfish themselves—spearfishermen. After studying the Punta Cana lionfish population, we decided that an occasional roundup might stir some publicity, but it wouldn't be enough to control the problem. We needed a more consistent approach.

First, we needed to create demand for this new commodity. We started with the chefs. Though initially incredulous, they warmed up to using lionfish filets after we brought in chefs from other restaurants to demonstrate how to safely remove their spines and properly prepare filets. Speaking the same language, the visiting chefs convinced GPC's chefs that serving lionfish, despite the scheme having been dreamt up by a bunch of tree-huggers, wasn't a terrible idea after all. Lionfish were cheaper than better-known species and made a more interesting story. Guests could eat an exotic but delicious filet and simultaneously help protect the coral reef.

It was an equitable solution. If Tortuga Bay was worried

about lionfish stinging their guests, the least they could do was pitch in by consuming them. We recruited local fishermen to bring in a few dozen fish and held a couple of tastings to get the chefs on board. I got a photographer friend to take some sexy foodie pics of lionfish dishes and convinced a glossy Dominican food magazine to feature Tortuga Bay's new menu item. The guests took to it. Lionfish quickly became a signature dish.

We made a dent in the local lionfish population, but the macabre satisfaction of slaughtering lionfish faded fast. Our chefs were frustrated when they couldn't get enough lionfish. If we wanted it on the menu, they needed a consistent supply and that wasn't happening. During bad weather, rough seas or following bouts of rum drinking, the fishermen were too inconsistent about bringing in lionfish. Worse, a few fishermen had been stung by lionfish, an agonizing experience that made it more attractive to pursue less hazardous species.

The fishermen also couldn't withstand the hotel's similarly painful payment process. Even if they earned less money fishing other species, they preferred quick cash over the sluggish pace of the hotel's accounts payable. Fishermen can't wait weeks at a time to get paid. Our two principal partners, the chefs and the fishermen, were losing patience with the whole lionfish enterprise.

FROM THE MENU TO THE MANTELPIECE

With our lionfish program on the rocks, we came across a breakthrough. While presenting at a conference in Cuba, our manager Susanne spotted a lionfish, though it was neither in the ocean or on a restaurant menu—she discovered a stuffed lionfish at tourist gift shop. The Cubans' solution to controlling lionfish was to turn them into souvenirs. Like stuffed piranhas sold to visiting tourists in the Amazon, they sold lionfish as quirky keepsakes. As soon as I saw the photo, I wanted a stuffed lionfish for my office. More relevant, I was convinced lionfish could become a curious memento that would help control lionfish in Punta Cana.

We set out to learn how to do taxidermy, the art of stuffing and preserving dead animals. We found taxidermists in the Dominican Republic, but none that worked with dead fish. If we wanted stuffed lionfish, we would had to bring in a professor from Cuba to teach us how.

The visa process took over a year, but finally our Cuban fish taxidermist made his way to Punta Cana. We held a workshop for the fishermen's wives where they learned how to carefully gut the fish without damaging their delicate skin. They studied how to fill the hollowed fish carcasses with sawdust and which chemicals to use to keep them from decomposing. Finally, the women learned how to paint the prepared specimens so they looked as lifelike as possible.

Armed with a handful of lionfish souvenirs, we started selling to local gift shops, with the proceeds of forty-five to sixty-five dollars going straight to the artisans. The women, who previously had low-wage jobs or didn't work at all, suddenly could make a couple hundred bucks a month selling lionfish. Motivated by the extra income, the women did something we hadn't been able to: convince their husbands to round up lionfish. The demand for lionfish souvenirs in turn created a more reliable supply for our restaurants.

Fisher family members make lionfish souvenirs

It had taken us a few tries but with the help of local artisans and their husbands, we now have a battle-tested strategy to confront the lionfish invasion. We adapted Florida's and Cuba's solutions to our reality in Punta Cana. Using the power of the local market, we helped local fishermen and their families bring in extra money while simultaneously tackling a serious environmental threat. Studies show that we have, in fact, slowed the spread of lionfish in our region.

A few years later I was chatting with a prominent conservationist and she informed me that our lionfish souvenirs also did something that conservation programs rarely do: empower women. Unbeknownst to me, there had been growing criticism of conservation programs as being sexist. The money for protecting Nature often goes exclusively to the men of the household, such as fishermen. This often doesn't benefit the entire family since the men control the resources and how they are utilized. By working directly with women, conservationists believe projects like ours can produce considerably more impact for fisher families.

STRANGE SEAWEED

We had gotten a handle on lionfish. Parrotfish were making a comeback. Our fishermen were becoming coral gardeners. The reef was still in tough shape, but we were making progress. There was much to be optimistic about, until we got blindsided by yet another unwelcome guest: sargassum seaweed.

In 2011, large waves of sargassum seaweed started showing up on our beaches. Sargassum forms masses of floating, reddish, stringy seaweed pushed along by ocean currents and waves. If it finds the right landing spot, it washes up on shore. This was the first time we had ever seen sargassum seaweed in such large quantities in Punta Cana and it wreaked havoc on our beaches. With each incoming wave of seaweed, the beaches became immersed in chest-high mounds of seaweed. Small armies of gardeners were deployed to remove the seaweed manually with rakes and wheelbarrows.

At first, it was an annoying but manageable problem. The beach cleaner teams simply scooped up the sargassum along with everything else that showed up on the beach including seagrass leaves, the occasional tree branch, and plastic. The volume of seaweed soon increased, however, washing up faster than our beachcombers could clean it up. Incoming seaweed stacked up behind already accumulated mountains of beached seaweed. The masses of material extended from shore back out to sea, making it challenging to even reach the water. Visitors had to climb over and wade through fresh waist-deep seaweed piles to get to the ocean. We had a serious problem.

We deployed mechanical beach-cleaning tractors to zigzag up and down the beach and rake up the sargassum. But it kept coming, like a nautical version of the Blob. We tried using front-loaders and tractors to scoop it off the beach, but using heavy equipment on a beach only makes the problem worse. The buckets of the front-loaders shovel up the seaweed, taking the beach sand with them. With heavy equipment driving all over the beach, the sand was compacted and filled with tire tracks. Not only did our visitors want no part of these beach-turned-construction-sites, we were at risk of inflicting serious erosion on our own pristine beaches.

The sargassum wasn't just a nuisance for beachgoers. The longer the seaweed mounds stay on the beach, the smellier it gets. Shrimp, fish, and small organisms happily stowed away within the seaweed mats in open water weren't built for dry land. When the whole floating ensemble hit the beach, the creatures dried up and died. The sargassum went from an eyesore into a rotten, decaying mess that stunk up the entire resort.

Our homeowners began to chime in, joining a growing chorus of complaints from hotel guests. They were understandably upset that their idyllic Caribbean vacation had been contaminated by seaweed. They didn't keep quiet about it either, peppering us with nasty reviews and harsh descriptions of ruined vacations on social media. We fielded equally loud complaints from our hotel managers, real estate vendors, and anyone else who had to look at beaches piled with rotting seaweed or torn apart by tractors. It was a complain-a-thon and we were pulling our hair out. We had no answer.

Worse, the problem cost us a fortune. Renting heavy equipment is expensive and the erosion it caused would eventually require a beach nourishment solution that wasn't likely to be cheap either. The impact on the hotels was also significant, with angry guests demanding refunds and even cancellations. If the cost to clean up sargassum wasn't bad enough, the damage to our reputation was becoming equally pricey.

Punta Cana wasn't the only destination suffering from sargassum. Islands throughout the Caribbean and the Cancún coast in Mexico were under siege by an onslaught of seaweed-related bad press. Articles in the *The Washington Post*, *The New*

York Times, New York Magazine, and Smithsonian documented the problem in Mexico and several Lesser Antilles islands. Journalists tried to determine the cause of the seaweed invasion, drawing even more negative attention to the crisis and further damaging tourism. The "Monster Seaweed" as it was known in Mexico had quickly become the greatest single threat to the Mexican tourism economy, forcing the government to declare a national emergency.

THE SECRET LIFE OF SARGASSUM

Theories attempting to explain the sargassum landings are almost as abundant as the seaweed itself. According to different sources, the recent presence of sargassum in Mexico and the Caribbean could be caused by global climate change, changing ocean currents, El Niño weather events, Saharan dust clouds, nutrients from Brazilian-Amazon farms, or dispersants used during the British Petroleum oil spill cleanup in the Gulf of Mexico. Each idea shares elements of modern science fiction but all are within the realm of scientific plausibility. In 2011, no one seemed to agree whether this was an exceptional event or if it represented a new paradigm shift in the region.

It was also not entirely clear where the seaweed originates in the first place. Large concentrations of sargassum seaweed occur naturally off the coast of South America, West Africa, and in its namesake Sargasso Sea off the Atlantic coast of the United States. Scientists have a general idea where the biggest seaweed patches form and grow, but they still had no clue where the point of origin lies or why its movement had changed to include the Caribbean.

Ironically, when contained in its normal range, sargassum is a unique and fascinating floating habitat with enormous economic, ecological, and even global benefits. At two million square miles, the Sargasso Sea is roughly the size of the United States and is an immensely productive habitat, serving as home and spawning area to several hundred invertebrates, fish, sea turtles, numerous migratory birds, and marine mammals such as sperm and humpback whales. The Sargasso plays a major role in commercial fisheries around the world as well, and in 2014, the Sargasso Sea Commission was formed to protect the sea as vital habitat of global importance.

The Sargasso Sea is also suspected to be an important player in retaining global carbon emissions. Sargassum is a carbon sink that may be a major factor in controlling the concentration of carbon dioxide in the lower atmosphere, impacting the global climate system. The floating mats of seaweed act as a giant carbon sponge, taking heat-trapping gases out of the atmosphere and storing them as seaweed. As human-caused climate change accelerates, sargassum could help humans combat climate change.

Nonetheless, when your CEO can't sleep at night due to bad press, messy beaches and exploding costs, sargassum is hard to love. I can admire sargassum's unique ecological contributions, provided it stays far from Punta Cana and doesn't ruin anyone's vacation.

As bad as 2011 came to be, it turned out that it was a light year for seaweed. The seaweed lasted a few months through the summer and then abruptly stopped arriving and was quickly forgotten. Yet if we thought this was a one-time problem, we were sorely mistaken. In 2013, 2015, and later in 2018, the arrival of sargassum in the Caribbean and Mexico got progressively worse, growing exponentially in size each year, while continuing for longer periods of time. The sargassum events were no longer a summertime phenomenon; the sargassum season of 2018 was an estimated three to five times greater than the initial landings in 2011 and lasted nearly the entire year. Scientists now believe a new Sargasso Sea has formed adjacent to the Caribbean and is here to stay.

SEAWEED BATTLEGROUND

The first few years we struggled through each seaweed season with our hands tied behind our backs. We were losing the battle badly. In 2013 we decided to take the fight directly to the sargassum, in the water.

I helped put together a crack team of in-house seaweed experts from Grupo Puntacana Foundation and our maintenance, landscaping, and engineering departments. We concluded that if we allowed the seaweed to reach the beach, we had lost the battle. Cleanup is expensive, the beach is unusable, our guests are unhappy, and ultimately the beach suffers erosion. If we waited for the beaches to get swamped in seaweed, we were done for.

What if, however, we could install floating barriers to deflect the seaweed offshore so it never made it to the beach? Desperate for a solution, the resort gave us a limited budget and some leeway to experiment. We imported several different models of commercial floating booms used to contain oil spills. The barriers helped but they weren't designed to deal with heavy seaweed and turned out to be flimsy under changing wind and waves. The sargassum washed over the top or forced the booms to flap upwards like a flag in a gale. The seaweed seemed to laugh at the barriers as it flowed by.

Our seaweed brain trust realized that if no barrier on the market would meet our specific anti-seaweed purpose—we had to make our own. We huddled in the maintenance department spit-balling barrier ideas on a whiteboard. The material had to be cheap and relatively accessible in our region. It had to float but couldn't capsize or collapse under the weight of the seaweed.

It had to resist harsh seas, waves, and wind but couldn't be so rigid that it would smash to pieces. We had to figure out how to anchor the barriers to the ocean floor and deploy them in front of long stretches of coast. Finally, the barriers couldn't entangle turtles or other marine life. We needed a breakthrough, bad.

After our brainstorm, we launched our first prototype consisting of two parallel PVC tubes and a network of smaller tubes supporting plastic netting hanging six to ten inches below the water surface. The barriers looked like a makeshift, DIY catamaran, but they proved to be stable and highly effective in repelling seaweed.

We had hit on a solution, now we had to deploy it at scale. After some experimentation, we determined the correct angle to deploy the barriers to block the seaweed, yet still allow it to drift naturally down the coast with the current. Once the sargassum collided with our barriers, it would eventually get pushed back into the natural currents without ever landing on the beach.

With a design in place and a concept for how to position the barriers, we prioritized beaches. With over six miles of coast, we knew it would be too expensive and difficult to deploy barriers along the front of the entire resort. Additionally, a good part of that coast was rough, rocky shore or golf holes. We concluded if it wasn't a beach, it didn't need a barrier. In addition, not all beaches were affected in the same way. Some got hit much worse than others. We mapped out priority beaches and got started.

Our maintenance warehouse soon became a seaweed barrier factory. In a matter of weeks, we had effectively protected close to a mile and a half of beach, with the barriers deflecting nearly ninety percent of the seaweed. The beaches could be cleaned manually or with beach-cleaning machines.

However, with tens of thousands of dollars' worth of floating barriers positioned offshore, the barriers couldn't just stay in the water unattended. We needed a strategy to maintain them.

The plastic mesh would break, the PVC joints would come apart, and eventually the ocean conditions would necessitate replacing barriers.

Once we again we turned to the fishermen. We recruited ARSEMAR, the association of ex-fishermen, to patrol the coast to fix and reposition broken barriers. We gave them spare parts to replace broken pieces, clean the netting, and change sections of damaged barrier. They used their own fishing boats and we provided gas. In addition to saving us the complicated task of buying a boat and assembling a crew, this approach allowed us to hire more local fishermen. Once again, their unique skillset as fishermen dovetailed perfectly with maintaining floating barriers. The fishermen were handy at solving problems at sea. In addition to restoring corals, the ex-fishermen became part of our Anti-Sargassum Team.

A SEAWEED CLEARINGHOUSE

The more proactive we were about confronting seaweed, the more others noticed. Without realizing it, we had become leaders in the anti-seaweed space. Resorts, companies, and Caribbean governments sought our advice. We advised the Dominican government on the best strategies for hotels and resorts and eventually formed part of the Presidential Commission on Sargassum Seaweed. The traditionally aloof Dominican government even began considering funding efforts to protect Punta Cana area beaches with our direct input.

Grupo Puntacana soon became a clearinghouse for any company, scientist, or university that had a proposed solution to the seaweed challenge. We received dozens of proposals, visits, and inquiries from people selling barriers, collection equipment, compost systems, biodigestors, and manufacturers of bioplastics. Having successfully protected our priority beaches from seaweed, we began working with partners to harvest it and convert it into something productive.

In 2018, the volume of invading seaweed once again broke all records. Like the rest of the Caribbean, we struggled through the summer and spent a fortune confronting the problem, but our barriers managed to help save the tourism season. Our proactivity quieted a lot of the complaints and the beach has rebounded faster and better than expected. Today we have close to eight kilometers of barriers installed and a contract with a new company to harvest the seaweed off the barriers with a specially designed floating harvesting barge.

As it is with much of life and in business, you often learn the most about yourself during crisis. From the trauma and stress of the seaweed battle (and the associated "Post Sargassum Stress Disorder") we learned some very important lessons.

The most eye-opening is that rapid environmental change is the new normal. We don't know for sure what caused the seaweed scourge. Potentially, it is related to climate change or large-scale, human-induced environmental changes occurring around the world. Regardless, no self-respecting scientist would have predicted that a second Sargasso Sea would form in the Caribbean Sea in less than a decade. Our planet is changing quickly and whether it is seaweed, storms, algae blooms, red tides, or something else, its oceans are changing too. If we want to have coastal tourism in the future, we must learn to innovate and adapt to these drastic changes.

Innovation, in turn, creates competitive advantages. The country, destination, or company that can adapt to rapid environmental change most efficiently and effectively will have a competitive advantage over others that don't. Punta Cana is competing with other tourism destinations like Jamaica, Mexico, and Aruba. The first destination that can say they have sargassum seaweed under control will be the winner of this particular battle. Though we can't say we have defeated sargassum, we are at least five years ahead of everyone else in the region in research and development, and undoubtedly better prepared and equipped to confront this challenge.

We also learned that being an innovator often attracts other innovators. If you are creative and groundbreaking in your approach to different challenges, you will likely draw other pioneers looking to solve problems. Whether we wanted to or not, Grupo Puntacana has become a magnet for seaweed contraptions and solutions, from the outlandish to the useful. Sorting through all the proposals can be time-consuming, but it also can be valuable exposure for a company. Having smart people give you good ideas for free is often worth its weight in boardroom meetings.

Ironically, private companies are uniquely equipped to confront new environmental challenges like rampant seaweed. Companies can respond quickly and with vast stores of creativity. In our case, the Dominican government realized the tourism industry was threatened by seaweed *seven years* after the problem had started! Our company already had a functioning seaweed response team, investment in R&D, and had been experimenting with solutions long before. By 2014, long before the government even considered the sargassum situation, I had already attended the International Sargassum Symposium in Texas, seeking information and ideas.

Today, the seaweed keeps coming. It hits new beaches and seems to evolve new ways to get through the barriers. Yet we continually match the seaweed's evolving strategies by adapting and evolving, as well. We have turned down the volume of the crisis from a 10 to a manageable 4 or 5. Eventually, someone will uncover a product or use for the seaweed, but for now we still have tourists on our beaches. Our product is still the place.

CHAPTER FOUR

TALES FROM THE SUSTAINABILITY FRONT LINES

AUDEN SCHENDLER DESCRIBES HIMSELF AS A SUSTAINABILITY "grunt." A few years ago, I heard Auden talk about his book *Getting Green Done: Hard Truths from the Front Lines of the Sustainability Revolution* and his work as vice president of sustainability at Aspen Skiing Company. Auden, it turns out, does the ski resort version of my job in Punta Cana. Sustainable tourism can be a lonely vocation, so it was uplifting to meet someone else slogging to make it mainstream in the travel industry.

Auden is a blond-haired, preppie-looking guy with a sports sunglass tan that looks right out of central casting for a ski instructor. Far from an elitist enviro, however, in his book Auden describes how he spent hours hanging around the maintenance department in pursuit of his green agenda. Making friends with the machinists and mechanics, he set out to find creative ways to make their lives easier, simultaneously solving key environmental problems at his resort. Most employees have enough headaches to solve on a daily basis without the high-minded eco guy telling them how to do their job. Instead of preaching only to high-level executives, Auden makes a blue-collar case for sustainability.

With years of experience in the field, his conclusion about the environmental movement can be summarized in one phrase: "Too many visionaries, too few grunts." In the real world, sustainability is not as easy as it sounds. It takes grit. According to Auden, there are too many philosophers preaching how sustainability is a slam-dunk proposition, thereby *underselling* how complex it is to actually achieve. At Aspen Ski Resorts, Auden is forced to face skeptical co-workers and bottom-line driven CFOs who challenge his green schemes.

In one example, he proposed a no-brainer energy-saving plan for Aspen's five-star hotel The Little Nell. Armed with a detailed business case, he recommended the hotel switch from wasteful incandescent light bulbs to highly efficient compact fluorescent bulbs. (Auden has been at this long enough that this story took place before the emergence of LED lights.) The energy and maintenance savings would pay for the newer, more expensive bulbs in a year. Yet when he presented his plan, The Little Nell's general manager schooled him on hospitality.

"When you go to Las Vegas and stay in a Motel 6, they have compact fluorescent bulbs. This isn't a Motel 6." The bulbs might save money, but the institutional lighting could also shed loyal customers, who were finicky about everything from the bed sheet thread count to the glow of the light bulbs. Even an obvious winner like energy efficiency, with its fast return on investment, can run smack into the unwritten laws of hotel illumination. He ended up implementing his efficiency program in a dingy basement garage, using money from a grant and no help from The Nell.

I can identify. In Punta Cana, I tried to convince the manager of Tortuga Bay, our boutique hotel, which hosts Hollywood stars and multi-millionaires in private jets, that they should install temperature sensors in each of the villas. The sensors trigger a switch, shutting down the air-conditioning when the guest either leaves the villa, or leaves the door open while admiring the ocean view. This device saves energy, money, and helps the environment. What guest would object to that? I was told flatly, "For what our guests pay per night, it's their cold air. They can let it out of their rooms if they want to." Motel 6, indeed.

While the attitude of my hotelier colleagues towards energy efficiency has softened over the years, one truth hasn't changed. Getting green done is not a given. Each situation requires a battle plan. Even when the CEO is squarely on board, there is still a considerable leap from getting high-level approval for a new program to actually *implementing* it on the ground.

Few CEO's have the time to micro-manage every new idea that comes across their desk. Sustainability, more than other areas, needs a champion to work around each successive roadblock, until the A/C sensor is installed or the wasteful light bulb is replaced. As Auden put it, "We need to recognize that it's one thing to watch a PowerPoint presentation on corporate sustainability, and another thing to make it real."

Sustainability is often more about engaging with the moving parts of your company and making a convincing case for your ideas to your co-workers, regardless of whether they are in the corner suite or the landscaping department. Sustainability requires hardheaded perseverance, a sense of humor, some creativity and occasionally some luck. Sometimes, finding the answer even requires digging through the trash.

NOT IN MY BACKYARD

When you own an airport, the more passengers you have, the

better. Punta Cana International Airport is the last stop for four million tourists every year. Each passenger represents revenue for our airport and the Punta Cana region. Naturally, we want our visitors to fall in love with Punta Cana, repeat their visit and, hopefully, tell their friends to come. As the destination grows, the airport grows, and Grupo Puntacana grows, too.

However, whether on a honeymoon or winter vacation, passengers never travel alone. They might pack a suitcase, some golf clubs, a few bathing suits, and perhaps their kids. Tourists also bring a whole lot of trash. Every time a plane lands in Punta Cana with a fresh load of tourists, it also discharges piles of their garbage. All of the leftover snacks, beverages, wine bottles, disposable food packages, discarded earphones, newspapers, used diapers, and assorted trash generated on a flight stays wherever that plane lands. Airports like ours are responsible for safely disposing of it.

It's not only the airplanes that make waste. Departing passengers generate garbage on their way out of town, as they buy last-minute gifts, munch airport fast food or throw back that last Presidente beer before boarding their flight. The airport terminal, meanwhile, includes several thousand staff from airlines, runway operations, government officials, and shops. These employees need to eat, producing vast quantities of food waste. A busy airport like Punta Cana can produce as much trash as a small city.

When you include the waste produced from its hotels, private homes, restaurants, stores, and office buildings, Grupo Puntacana is a resort that produces a lot of garbage. During peak seasons, the company, including the airport, generates over thirty tons of garbage a day.

The waste doesn't stop there. The Punta Cana region is home to hundreds of all-inclusive resorts, mostly north of GPC. Some of the resorts are like semi-enclosed cities, with two thousand to three thousand rooms on one property, hosting thousands of tourists at a time. Touting sprawling, seemingly endless all-you-can-eat buffets, the hotels in the region can generate hundreds of tons of garbage weekly.

In the US, the vast majority of garbage is sent to sanitary landfills. Only a tiny fraction is recycled, composted, or otherwise repurposed. Though not perfect, landfills at least have infrastructure in place to keep the trash from catching fire or causing widespread contamination. Impermeable liners keep harmful liquid leachates from seeping out into groundwater, rivers, or other water bodies. Inspectors visit landfills to analyze ground, air, and water quality. In fact, landfills, once closed, can be covered and turned into parks and recreation areas. When traveling in the US, if you have ever noticed a hilly park by the side of the highway, but far from any town, there is a good chance it was once a landfill.

Most developing countries, on the other hand, unfortunately haven't figured out what to do with their trash. Waste rarely ends up in a good place. It gets dumped in rivers or the ocean, burned in acrid trash fires, or tossed into giant unregulated garbage dumps. A dump, as we will find out, is not the same as a sanitary landfill. Some of the world's largest and most appalling dumps are found outside of Latin American cities.

In the Dominican Republic, responsibility for collecting and disposing of garbage falls primarily on overmatched local municipalities. Local governments in small towns and cities rarely have the experience or resources necessary to adequately cope with the garbage their citizens generate. Instead, informal waste haulers are sub-contracted and traipse around town in decrepit and leaking dump trucks, picking up garbage curbside. Whether in a massive mega-city or small town, garbage is normally sent to a sprawling dump somewhere on the outskirts of town.

Out of view of most of the population, a small army of "pickers" trailed by bands of pigs, cattle egrets, and dogs sort through a growing mountain of garbage in search of anything of value. Depending on the country, this means pickers search for valuable metals like copper and aluminum, some plastics, and perhaps cardboard and glass.

Despite the deadly serious health and environmental hazards posed by these dumps, most citizens have no idea where their garbage ends up. As long as it's "not in my backyard," a condition known as NIMBY, garbage ends up out of sight and out of mind.

In 2007, Grupo Puntacana was no exception. Despite its explosive growth, the Punta Cana region did not (and still doesn't) have a formal landfill. In its early years, the absence of a functioning local government forced pioneering hoteliers settling in the area to devise their own solution. One hotelier asked a local landowner, located about fifteen miles from the coast, to dispose of the hotels' trash in exchange for a moderate tipping fee. His land had once been a limestone quarry and possessed a large hollowed-out mine. The hotels offered to pay anyone with a dump truck to pick up their garbage and deposit it at the new "landfill," known as Gerom.

At the time, there was considerably less environmental awareness than nowadays. The Gerom dump had no protection to prevent contaminants from seeping out. It was an open pit with a couple of tractors that pushed the trash around to level it out. Gerom attracted a near constant parade of trucks dropping off the hotels' and local communities' garbage and an equally vibrant army of pickers sorting through it. Working without protective gear, they were exposed to whatever the trash contained, including viruses and infections.

The distance to the dump kept the garbage far from the hotels. Fifteen miles away surrounded by cow pastures, it seemed a world away from Punta Cana. However, the band of waste haulers soon realized they could save gas and tipping fees by dumping the waste closer to the coast. They made individual deals with dozens of local landowners willing to receive the garbage, without having to drive so far away. Other haulers simply found empty lots to dump the trash. Rather than one concentrated albeit unsightly dump far removed from tourists, now garbage was being dispersed across many unidentified, clandestine mini-dumps. There was no local government to stop it.

For close to twenty years, this was the Punta Cana region's waste management "system." With no local government and still relatively few hotels, garbage didn't seem like a pressing concern. The ad hoc arrangement wasn't ideal for the future, but in the short term it worked.

A TRASH TIME-BOMB

As development exploded in Punta Cana entering the 2000s, garbage could no longer be ignored. Mountains of waste posed a more immediate environmental threat. Besides being an eyesore (or more accurately, a fetid nose sore) and a health threat to pickers, the garbage was becoming a serious threat to local drinking water.

As I have already noted, Punta Cana gets its drinking water from underground aquifers. The ground is porous limestone rock. If a liquid gets discharged aboveground, eventually it filters through the rock underground. Leachates, the liquid substance that seeps out from common garbage, is a noxious soup filled with organic and inorganic substances in different stages of decay. It can be extremely hazardous. Without proper protective liners, the leachates can run off from the unregulated dump sites, potentially leaking into the aquifer. Punta Cana's drinking water, already threatened by untreated sewage, now had to confront pollution from garbage.

Garbage also creates a serious economic challenge for businesses. Formal businesses in the Dominican Republic pay considerable taxes to the national and local government. Yet those taxes haven't always covered the cost of municipal waste hauling. The local government picks up residential waste, but businesses are often on their own, duplicating their costs.

In the case of Punta Cana's hotels, the local government didn't even exist when they got started in the 1990s. The improvised waste hauling created in the early days became the norm. Even today, in the absence of public garbage service, most hotels and businesses pay private trash haulers to dispose of their waste. The waste-haulers, now organized into unions and acting more like cartels, can flex their monopolistic muscles when they feel like it, regularly raising their fees.

Sporadic price fluctuations made it difficult for hotels to budget for something as seemingly straightforward as getting rid of trash. Waste hauling fees were a moving target. I still keep a copy of the letter I got from our waste hauler in 2006, informing me that our monthly garbage fee would be increasing by ten percent effective immediately. For a company our size, this unexpected spike was worth tens of thousands of dollars.

Yet as prices soared, the quality of the waste service broke down. Our finely manicured property was littered with dozens of decrepit metal trash containers. Residents would leave trash bags scattered around the containers to avoid touching the smelly bin cover. Pickers, dogs, and cats would open the bags to sort through them to see what treasures they contained. As a result, each trash container devolved into a mini dump site. The company's transportation fleet consisted of a couple of battered, second-hand dump trucks. If one broke down, we could be stuck with rancid waste stinking on the curb for days.

This was certainly not the paradise we were selling. Saddled with high costs and terrible service, our trash situation was broken. No tourist came all the way to the Dominican Republic to look at piles of garbage. Worse, it was an environmental time-bomb waiting to go off, threatening the entire region. If we couldn't get a handle on trash, our business was in danger.

INSPIRATION THROUGH DUMPSTER DIVING

Worried about our water and fed up with the complaints and spiraling costs, Frank tasked me with taking on trash. The first step was to dive in, literally, and study our garbage. When your garbage is all mixed together in thousands of bags of unwanted human detritus, it can feel overwhelming and unmanageable. We had waste coming at us from every direction but no clear idea of its composition. How much food waste? What part was cardboard, plastic, or metal? If we could make sense of our waste, we might find clues of how best to dispose of it.

For two months, I was literally immersed in trash. With help from international consultant and garbage-ologist Victor Ojeda, we formed a trash team. We examined every garbage bag, at every location, at every point around the resort. We tore open the garbage from airplanes, the airport, hotels, restaurants, homes, and offices, dumping thousands of bags of waste in order to weigh, measure, and catalogue it. Waist deep in refuse, Ojeda helped us map our rubbish, determining who produced what and how much.

In order to make future projections, we compared passenger waste data in order to calculate the number of pounds each passenger produced based on their country of origin. This gave us estimates of how much more garbage we should expect for each additional future flight.

American travelers will be pleased to know they produce far

less garbage than passengers from France, though this has nothing to do with American eco-friendliness. Rather it describes how frugal US airlines are. While French passengers stretch their feet in free airline slippers while drinking wine and eating three course meals, Americans get a soft drink and if they are lucky a pack of peanuts. In Punta Cana, the long-haul Europeans are the undisputed champs of trash, producing as much as three times the garbage per passenger as shorter American flights.

ZERO WASTE TO THE RESCUE

After weeks of dumpster diving, we studied the data and noticed something curious. When the contents of each trash bag weren't mixed together like soup, it was no longer garbage. Some of the materials become valuable. Specifically, when food and organic waste was removed from soiling everything else, part of the refuse could be recycled. By classifying it rather than hauling off daily truckloads of trash, we could *sell* some of the materials. If it was clean, the plastic, cardboard, glass, paper, metal, and aluminum might have a market. The organic waste would need another approach.

Suddenly armed with information, our garbage problem seemed manageable. Ojeda encouraged us to become a Zero Waste International Alliance community. More of an aspirational goal than a specific target, Zero Waste seeks to minimize the amount of material sent to the dump to the absolute minimum. It is an ambitious integrated solution that seeks to reduce consumption, but also separates potentially useful materials from pure waste.

We knew it would be virtually impossible to eliminate all waste. We also knew that it would be difficult to get the members of such a diverse community to sort its garbage at each site. With hundreds of private residences and so many other moving parts, we could only expect a limited amount of waste separation before we collected it. Based on the experience of many cities, we learned that even if we were highly successful in educating different members of the resort, pre-sorting waste is a tall order.

Grupo Puntacana strives to become a Zero Waste resort

Instead, we designed the Puntacana Recycling Center, a centralized sorting facility based at the airport. Known as a materials recovery facility, or MRF in garbage parlance, our center would receive all of Grupo Puntacana's waste. Our design proposed a small army of sorters to open incoming garbage bags onto long tables and categorize different materials manually. Once separated, an industrial compactor would squash the materials into manageable bales that could be loaded onto trucks or into shipping containers. Packed in neat bails or plastic bins, the materials would then be trucked off to exporters.

After leaving our facility, each material would embark on its own recycling odyssey. Bales of cardboard could be trucked to Santo Domingo and transformed into low-grade packing material, like egg cartons and padded fruit trays. Compacted plastic bottles would be exported to countries like China and Malaysia that convert the plastic into carpet, fleece jackets, or back into bottles. Aluminum was exported to be melted back down into cans and aluminum foil. Glass bottles from local beers were collected and reused for new beer.

We had our plan. Now we just needed to pitch it to Frank to get the resources to execute it.

THE GARBAGE BIG PICTURE

Well aware of the importance of the bottom line, Victor and I had to make the financial case for Zero Waste. We estimated the income from selling recyclables and the reduction in waste-hauling fees. We budgeted staffing, transportation, and savings in hauling fees. Our budgeting bean-counters determined the all-important return on investment (ROI) for the project. Armed with spreadsheets and a spiffy presentation breaking down our plan, we took the scheme to Frank.

As we eagerly broke down the plan, Frank listened patiently. He nodded his head occasionally without asking questions. We began to sweat. Was Zero Waste dead on arrival?

When we finished, as usual Frank went straight to the core issue.

"Your plan is good. It has to make sense financially. But the real reason we need to do this is for our guests. We are competing with other resorts around the world, for vacations and real estate. We have to manage our garbage as well, or better, than our guests do at home. If not, they will go somewhere else."

In other words, if our resort is covered in garbage, visitors can always find somewhere else that is not. If they are used to clean streets and recycling bins at home, we had better offer a similar service. The only way to have our visitors imagine purchasing a home in Grupo Puntacana was to make our resort as close to home as possible. If we wanted visitors, we had better be able to deal with something as mundane as garbage. Being Zero Waste would be unique and create a competitive advantage for our hotel and real estate sales teams.

With Frank's blessing, we built our recycling plant. Since then, Zero Waste has become one of Grupo Puntacana's biggest environmental success stories. We now host hundreds of visits from students, researchers, politicians, business leaders, and foundations to see the first functioning MRF in the Dominican Republic. Zero Waste has also been featured in the national and international media and featured in academic journals. The Dominican Barna Business School wrote a business case study about the project. Through Zero Waste, we managed to perform sustainability jujitsu, converting an immense and very visible problem into a public relations windfall.

Nowadays, we classify materials at the recycling center and truck the recyclable materials to Santo Domingo, where they are either recycled locally or exported. All told, we divert close to 60 percent of all waste produced throughout the property for recycling or reuse.

The money generated from the sale of recyclables is donated to Grupo Puntacana Foundation to fund improvements in waste sorting around the resort. The foundation buys trashcans, builds recycling stations, and funds ongoing education programs. As the resort improves its separation of garbage before it reaches the recycling plant, we can truly push the boundaries of becoming Zero Waste.

While recycling has gotten us partway there, the resort has gone after our supply chains to avoid purchasing any and all disposable materials. By selectively choosing what we buy in the first place, we can minimize the amount of garbage that enters the resort. For example, instead of buying disposable takeout containers, our restaurants charge clients to purchase compostable or reusable containers. By prioritizing products and goods with less packaging, or those that can be transformed into new products, we are forcing vendors to rethink the products they sell. Rather than selling us milk in a whole lot of packaging garbage, we hope one day to receive nothing more than the milk itself.

Critically, we broke away from our dependence on the garbage mafia and their price gouging. Zero Waste reduced our contribution to the local landfill and slashed our waste-hauling fees, even while the amount of waste we receive increases each year. The project even forced some waste haulers to rethink their business and several pivoted into becoming recycling vendors.

More importantly, because of Grupo Puntacana's size, we made recycling viable for other nearby resorts. The volume of recyclables generated at our facility created a previously non-existent market in the Punta Cana region. Alone, each individual hotel wouldn't produce enough raw material to be interesting to recyclers. Grupo Puntacana, because of the airport, tipped the scale for recycling, making it economically feasible for others. Even smaller producers of recyclables can find buyers.

Over a decade later, Zero Waste is, and always will be, a work in progress. Garbage doesn't stop evolving and the amount of trash we generate continues to grow. We face new challenges all the time: volatile international markets for recyclables, complying with new international regulations, and confronting new materials to be disposed of. Though we have yet to achieve our mission of eliminating 100 percent of our waste, Grupo Puntacana planted a flag on the cutting edge of solid waste management. Scrapping the program and returning to our garbage-swamped past would be unthinkable.

But we weren't done. We still had to figure out what to do with all our food waste. That's where the worms came in.

WORMS: PUNTA CANA'S COMPOST CHEFS

During a visit to Punta Cana, journalist Victor Ozols of *Black-Book* produced a glowing review of our worm composting project that was one of my proudest professional achievements. The article, titled "The Latest in Luxury Resort Amenities: Worms" describes the unique eco-cache of our resort.

> "There were many things I enjoyed on our recent visit to Tortuga Bay at the Puntacana Resort & Club in the Dominican Republic. Our villa was luxurious. The food and drinks were divine. I loved the scuba diving, kayaking, and standup paddle boarding. Even the spa treatment was nice. But the thing that sticks in my mind now that I look back on our visit from a week's distance? The worms."

Worms have always been part of my life. Growing up in Florida, we used them to fish in our pond. Later, while living in New York City, I grossed out my friends by keeping a plastic "worm bin" under the kitchen sink. The worms consumed all of my household food waste. I would freeze fruit peels, coffee, eggshells and other organic garbage, eventually mixing it with newspapers and mounds of California red wiggler worms that shared my apartment. At Christmas, I would send friends and family homemade worm compost as a stocking stuffer.

Organic waste is transformed into worm compost and used on golf courses

To me, bringing worms to the Caribbean was as normal as bringing flip-flops and sunglasses. With their amazing gift for transforming smelly, undesirable organic waste into beautiful soil, worms provide an elegant solution to an intractable problem: How to get rid of food waste.

With Zero Waste, we managed to get a handle on a large part of Grupo Puntacana's garbage problem, separating the materials and selling the recyclables. However, we still needed a way to confront vast quantities of organic waste generated in our hotels, restaurants, homes, and in the sprawling landscaped areas around the resort. With over a dozen restaurants and hundreds of private homes, we produce mountains of food waste every day. Like most small cities, between 40 to 60 percent of our garbage is organic material. How could we turn food scraps into something useful?

In 2007, we launched an experimental worm composting project. Our first humble objective was simply to keep the worms alive in the hot, tropical climes of Punta Cana. No one had tried this before. Second, was to get rid of as much of our food waste as possible and transform it into something productive, in this case, compost. Finally, we wanted to test whether the project would be economically feasible and could be scaled up. Start small and then grow big. If we ever got to the point of churning out massive quantities of high-quality worm compost, we could sell it golf courses, landscapers, or homeowners to spruce up their gardens. Grupo Puntacana Foundation could make money selling the resort its own organic waste, transformed into compost. That was the plan, anyway.

In no time, we unearthed a Dominican worm whisperer that could supply us with the goods. Don Rafael had a knack for worm growing, producing masses of writhing indigo blue worms in a half-dozen improvised sheds in his backyard. He had developed a cottage industry selling worms to local farmers around the DR countryside. Goat and chicken farmers feed the worms their manure and then use the fresh soil to grow grass and hay to feed their cows. It's a tidy, closed loop. I hoped to apply the same idea to the hotel industry.

Before selling to us, Don Rafael insisted on visiting our facilities in Punta Cana. He wanted to ensure his offspring would be in good hands. After receiving his blessing, we made our way to his worm farm and drove off with a truckload of dark black soil laced with tens of thousands of pink, wriggling worms. I had previously convinced one of the resort kitchens to deliver a couple of fifty-gallon drums filled with ripe kitchen scraps. We were off and running. How different from feeding worms under my kitchen sink could this be?

A lot different, it turned out. Worm husbandry is a lot like beekeeping, another craft we would get to know later. The art is to keep the animals happy, healthy, and productive. In the case of bees, the primary product is honey. With worms, the goal is to produce rich, black soil. Unlike typical dirt, worm compost passes through their digestive system and comes out as worm castings or humus. This soil is embedded with a diverse, biologically active community of microorganisms, making it a potent medium for plants. Once again, we would be encouraging an animal to bless us with its poop.

To maximize production, the worms need a nice cool temperature, moist but not too wet surroundings, and a good, consistent mix of organic material. Their food needs to be fresh, can't contain meat or dairy, and shouldn't be too soggy. Worms turn their noses up at rotten food. This means the worm keepers need to find the right mix of food waste, manure, leaves and cuttings to make the perfect recipe. We needed to become compost chefs.

We failed. Repeatedly. First, our concrete-style worm bins were too small and too hot for the worms. Frantic to escape the hot soil, the worms climbed the walls of the bins, launching themselves overboard. To compensate, we began regularly watering the soil to cool them off. Overwatering the bins drowned the worms. We made some adjustments and finally got the temperature and moisture right. Then, we accidentally introduced a deadly worm parasite, *Planaria,* from local horse manure. It took a special oil concoction to eliminate the parasite, but we also lost a lot of worms.

We were flailing, the worms were suffering, and our guru was having second thoughts about entrusting us with his worms. Eventually, though, we worked out the kinks. After months of starts and stops, we not only avoided killing the worms, we produced what appeared to be beautiful, worm compost. Though not industrial quantities, we had our product. Now we needed our first customer.

EGGPLANTS ON THE FAIRWAY

In what turned out to be an overly ambitious decision, I

approached Julio, the golf course superintendent, to be our guinea pig. This was not an easy sell. A golf course superintendent is also a lot like a chef, but one with far more expertise and training than we had. Each superintendent has his own recipe for his course, consisting of a cocktail of synthetic fertilizers and chemicals that eliminate weeds, fungi, and other pests from his precious grass. With decades of experience, a university degree in soil science, and a well-tuned formula to keep GPC's golf courses in tip-top shape, Julio hardly needed a bunch of amateur worm-wranglers telling him how to run his multimillion-dollar golf course. He was rightfully skeptical of our proposal to use our compost on his course.

With much persistence on my part, Julio eventually relented. We proudly delivered a half-dozen bags of fresh worm compost to the Corales golf course. Corales is our fanciest and most expensive course, designed by the renowned golf course architect Tom Fazio. Corales is so well groomed, primped, and manicured that later it hosted the first and only PGA Championship tournament in the DR.

Giving us more leeway than we probably deserved, Julio liberally applied our experimental soil on the Corales course. At first, the worm compost appeared to work. It produced no burn spots and the grass continued to glow neon green. He enthusiastically added more worm fertilizer.

Within a few weeks, however, Julio gruffly returned what remained of our product. "I have eggplants on my fairway," he grumbled. The food waste we fed the worms was loaded with vegetable. As expected, the fruits and vegetables we fed the worms passed through their stomachs, churning out delicious compost. The fruit and vegetable *seeds*, however, remained imbedded in the compost, totally undigested. They passed the worms' stomachs and came out intact. When spread on the Corales fairway, it only took a nice tropical rainstorm for the seeds to sprout. Unfortunately, Julio's golfers were not at all interested in picking fresh eggplant. Golfers want green turfgrass.

We pressed onward, smartening up at a handful of professional soil conferences. I got connected to serious worm composters from the United States and Mexico and we slowly transformed our rinky-dink worm bins into a more professional compost factory.

International worm experts advised us to pre-compost the organic material in specialized bins that cook the food waste before feeding it to the worms. This killed the parasites, neutralized the seeds, and made the material easier to digest for the worms. We ordered a couple of commercial "aerated compost bins" from earthy Sonoma Valley Worm Farm in northern California. With the food waste getting cooked to 160 degrees Fahrenheit, we no longer had seeds or parasites. We scaled up from the Sonoma Valley starter kit and built a Dominicanized version of their commercial bins out of local materials, tripling the amount of organic waste we could process weekly. We were officially cooking up high quality worm compost, with no more veggies on the golf course.

Next, we recruited a soil scientist from California Polytechnic State University to run a proper scientific trial. With help from some of his graduate students, we compared our compost with some of the synthetic materials Julio used on the golf course. The trials laid out test plots on golf turfgrass. We applied different amounts and combinations of our soil on some squares, to be compared with the synthetic product on other squares. Julio and his team rated the color and health of the grass, without knowing which fertilizer had been added to each plot. The trials eventually demonstrated scientifically that our worm compost was of similar or better quality than the products Julio was already using.

Vindicated, now we knew our worm compost could compete. A less suspicious Julio wanted to know how much we could produce and at what price. Our resort has forty-five golf holes, covering hundreds of acres of land. We have miles of green space and hundreds of private villas with landscaping. Now that we had our recipe, we needed to transform our craft compost project into an industrial operation. In order to really compete, we needed Worm Power.

CONTINUOUS FLOW COMPOST

We brought in Worm Power, an innovative industrial worm farm in upstate New York. Worm Power built their business in concert with a concentrated dairy operation near Rochester. Pressured by local regulators to clean up their act, the dairy producers moved Worm Power onto the farm, promising them all the cow poop they could ever need to manufacture compost.

Nothing like the hippie communes that typically promote compost, Worm Power's operation was like the NASA space station of worm compost. With help from industrial engineers, Worm Power invented a special compost conveyor that pumped out a near-constant production of soil. The two-hundred-foot-long metal containers, dubbed "continuous flow beds," allow them to harvest compost without removing the worms from their habitat. This translates to an uninterrupted stockpile of humus (the fancy name for worm compost). Using tractors and front-loaders, workers fill flatbed trailers with thousands of bags of their golden dirt. Far from craft compost, Worm Power trucks their compost to commercial plant nurseries and farms around the United States.

Julio and his golf courses needed more compost and the only way to do it was to scale up. Worm Power made a short visit to Punta Cana, and with their technical advice we built our own

Dominicanized continuous flow bed. A forty-five-foot-long metal container allows millions of worms to sit undisturbed at the top of the bin, happily eating and pooping. Meanwhile, the compost is forced to the bottom of the bin.

A few times a week, we harvest our compost using a metal blade attached to a hydraulic winch and an automated conveyor belt. Reams of compost pour out of the bottom of the bed. Bagging close to one thousand bags of worm compost a month, our small artisanal dirt shop began to look more like Worm Power's Dominican cousin. Though still not able to process 100 percent of Grupo Puntacana's organic waste, we crank out some forty-two tons of humus a year, worth roughly $42,000 in sales.

Grupo Puntacana is still not Zero Waste, yet. The project had demonstrated that companies have the capacity to provide solutions to challenges normally solved by governments. Ted Kheel's concept of conflict resolution was a key part of our strategy. We took a complex, seemingly intractable problem and separated it, quite literally, into its component parts. Dividing up the materials, Grupo Puntacana no longer produced mountains of "waste." It possessed distinct material types that could be valuable. Plastic, glass, cardboard, and aluminum became recyclables. Food and yard scraps became worm poop fertilizer. Zero Waste's combination of recycling and composting permitted Grupo Puntacana to divert roughly 60 percent of its waste from the local dump, despite yearly increases in volume as the resort grows.

Julio incorporated our organic compost into his golf course maintenance. Instead of relying exclusively on imported chemical inputs, he can save money and reduce the course's environmental footprint by buying local. More importantly, the success of Zero Waste earned us enough credibility within Grupo Puntacana to propose fresh offbeat ideas to confront ever-changing challenges facing the resort.

THE CERTIFICATION BOOM

Over the years I have watched a proliferation of new, eco-friendly programs in the hotel industry. Towel reuse programs encourage guests to hang their towels back on the rack to avoid excessive water use in laundering. Virtually all hotels tout their anti-plastic credentials, with restaurants and bars offering paper instead of plastic straws and cutting single-use plastics. Hotel rooms feature key-controlled lighting and air conditioning systems that shut down automatically to save energy. LED lighting and energy efficient appliances in hotel kitchens save energy. Eco-chic has arrived in the hospitality industry.

The push to make hotels greener has also led to a glut of sustainability certifications. Today there are a half-dozen or more hotel certifications: Rainforest Alliance, Green Key, Blue Flag, Green Globe, Travelife, and Earth Check, among others. Meant to simplify the evaluation of a hotel's programs according to industry-wide best practices, certifications help standardize the way properties measure their social and environmental impact. They also make it easier for customers to determine whether a hotel is a good corporate citizen. After a quick look at a hotel's website featuring the logo of a certification, customers can book with some degree of certainty that the hotel is a responsible company.

Undoubtedly, certifications can produce benefits for a hotel operation. They can help save water and energy, provide a PR boost, and offer a point of entry for hotels without a background in sustainability. Certifications also simplify the ability of customers to make informed choices. There is even data, though not conclusive, that certified hotels are favored by guests. As a result, they do better financially than non-certified locations.

However, while a good start, certifications are a limited tool. Trying to make a cookie-cutter process to evaluate different properties is a good idea but much harder than it would seem in practice. As a result, certifications are not a universal remedy for hotel sustainability.

First, certifications and their fees can be costly. An annual certification is only part of the cost. In addition to regular audits and site visits, the hotel must implement operational changes to comply with certification requirements. Blue Flag, for example, insists on specific standards for health, safety, and public environmental education for beaches and marinas. It requires beach lifeguards, expansive water quality testing, and infrastructure investments to make the beach more accessible to the public. All are admirable goals, but they cost money.

Certifications also require staff time. Larger properties often assign the responsibility to a specific person or department. They may even hire someone or contract an external consultant solely to maintain their certification, and costs continue adding up.

Despite the significant investment required, certifications don't guarantee a solution to all the sustainability challenges a particular property may face. This means they may end up competing with other important programs for funding. Ironically, by dedicating staff and resources to certifications, hotels may have to sacrifice resources for other important sustainability programs.

At Grupo Puntacana, for example, certifying the Westin Hotel likely would have meant sacrificing other key environmental initiatives. Would it make sense to abandon Zero Waste, a company-wide initiative, to certify a single hotel property?

In spite of the cost, the payoff is supposed to come from increased numbers of hotel guests. The theory goes that customers will be willing to book a vacation, or even pay more, if the hotel is a certified, responsible operator. As a result, certified hotels should maintain a consistently higher occupation and a better room rate than non-certified properties.

Yet it is difficult to correlate bookings with a specific certification program and even harder to put a revenue value on a specific program. A notoriously data-driven crowd, many hoteliers are skeptical and hotel managers are dubious that certifications truly make their property more competitive. As a result, given the choice of investing their limited annual budget in a certification or changing the cushions in the lobby, I know more than a few hotel managers would buy the cushions.

This points to a significant challenge that certifiers themselves face. Creating standards to evaluate different hotels can be tricky business. The hotel business is constantly changing and evolving. Properties vary in size, design, business model, and location. Products, goods, and services common in one place may be unavailable in another. While recycling, for example, may be a given in some cities, in other regions it may not be possible at all. Given the vast diversity of hotel types, designing a coherent certification that applies to a wide variety of properties is a complex challenge.

As a result, the applicability of different certifications varies wildly. Green Key may work for a small twenty-room hotel in Maine but be irrelevant to a 1,500-room all-inclusive property in Jamaica. This partially explains the proliferation of different certification programs. There needs to be many models of certifications to match the diversity of hotels.

In the minds of customers, this can dilute the value and meaning of each one. If guests are not familiar with the certification a hotel possesses, it is unlikely it would influence their booking decision. In other words, if they don't know the difference between Green Globe and Rainforest Alliance, the certification may be meaningless to consumers.

Certifying is not only costly for hotels; it can be costly for the certifying organization. To stay in business, certifiers need to generate revenue to cover staff, conduct audits, update standards, and publish results. They must keep after slacking properties to keep them from falling out of compliance, and must market their product to new hotels and generate revenue. This pressure to produce can lead to potential conflicts of interest.

This is not meant to bash certifications. They have a place in the sustainability toolbox, but they are not a complete solution. In the end, the key question is whether guests actually care. A study by Tripadvisor.com may support some hoteliers' pessimism about certifications.

TRIPADVISOR'S GREEN REVIEWS

TripAdvisor, the omnipresent website that allows travelers to generate their own reviews and publicly rate travel experiences, has become a powerhouse in the tourism industry. It is so influential that nearly all hotels have a person designated to read and respond to reviews, both positive and negative. A hotel, excursion, or restaurant's reputation can be built up or torn down on TripAdvisor and similar websites.

Curious about customer perceptions of different sustainability initiatives, TripAdvisor allowed researchers to mine their massive database of so-called "green reviews" to examine customer perceptions. The researchers sought to identify the types of initiatives customers favored. Could towel reuse, for example, affect guest ratings? Are certifications key to customers preferences? What programs were regularly mentioned in guest reviews?

Perhaps somewhat predictably, guests were generally happy that the hotel had good social and environmental practices. User-generated reviews commented positively on many of the usual suspects, like energy-saving programs and recycling. Similarly, customers mentioned towel and linen reuse programs.

Even with hotels that offered a wide variety of sustainability programs, guests tended to comment on the more common initiatives they were familiar with.

However, none of these programs inspired TripAdvisor reviewers to improve their rating of the property. As long as the initiative didn't negatively impact their stay, visitors appreciate efficiency measures. But they are not game changers. This makes sense. The greatest beneficiary of most efficiency programs is the hotel itself, since it, not the guest, saves money.

The few programs that did move the needle on reviews were those that directly impact the guests' experience. For example, a hotel's green review could be improved by as much as half a star based on unique food options: organic, locally sourced or sustainable foods. (A half star may not sound like much, but TripAdvisor's highest rating is five stars. A half star is very significant.) Reviewers also liked programs they could participate in directly, like volunteering options or educational programs for their kids. If they could unload their little ones for a few hours to learn about sea turtles, that was impactful.

While on the one hand these findings can be depressing (i.e., humans are so selfish we only care about the planet if it's good for us individually), it is valuable information for hotel operators. If providing local or more sustainable food options also improves a hotel's rating, that is actually a very big win. (If only our hotels knew this when we tried to convince them to serve lionfish.)

If hotels can become more competitive by creating ecological guest experiences that guests want, it serves as a powerful motivator. They can target high impact sustainability programs that differentiate them and satisfy what their customers are looking for. This doesn't mean efficiency and certifications don't have a place in hotels, but that the justification for them is not necessarily customer satisfaction. Keep the towel program but serve some local veggies too.

Food, as it turns out, is often a critical piece of the sustainability puzzle. Modern agriculture has a massive impact on the planet. It uses enormous quantities of water, land, and fertilizers. Agriculture is one of the largest contributors to climate change, representing a sizeable portion of the global carbon footprint. A hotel's impact on climate is increased when you consider agriculture and transportation, especially on islands where much of food is imported. Providing options for sustainably farmed food can represent a profoundly positive environmental outcome for the tourism industry.

Customer preference for locally sourced or organic products could have important implications for improving the livelihoods of local farmers, as well. The transformation of small farms into large-scale agro-business or real estate can destroy livelihoods and devastate small communities. If tourism prioritizes supporting local agriculture, it can translate into positive gains for farmers and the planet. Grupo Puntacana was oblivious to TripAdvisor's findings when we began a modest vegetable garden in the early 2000's.

LOCAL FOOD ON THE BEACH

Punta Cana is not exactly the agricultural breadbasket of the Dominican Republic. Intense sunshine, while perfect for sun-starved vacationers, is generally too harsh for growing crops. The region boasts a minuscule amount of topsoil, with only a thin layer of dirt covering the limestone rock found throughout the region.

The rainfall also favors tourists more than fruits and vegetables. Rain is sporadic and limited most of the year. When it does rain, the downpours are so intense that often it comes down sideways. There are no rivers to supply fresh water for irrigation and large-scale agriculture is generally unheard of in Punta Cana.

However, Punta Cana does have a few advantages for *small-scale* agriculture. In particular, the region boasts a huge number of restaurants and hotels with a near insatiable demand for fresh produce. Likewise, local residents and foreigners with second homes tend to be just the types of clients looking for local, healthy food to add that perfect touch to their beach vacation. For Grupo Puntacana, the lack of topsoil may present less of an obstacle. Our foundation is already mass-producing worm compost from food waste.

Grupo Puntacana Foundation's farm started small. We planted a few simple rows of herbs and vegetables in some store-bought soil. The idea was to encourage resort-goers to visit the new garden. Before we knew it, a daily procession of homeowners in golf carts began showing up to buy produce. We expanded, incrementally at first, but faster as demand grew.

Grupo Puntacana promotes sustainable agriculture for its visitors

Soon the Foundation was supplying a few of the resort's restaurants. The chefs brought us seeds of herbs, greens, and vegetables they wanted to incorporate in their menus. The

"Foundation Salad" became a staple item around the resort. We added a delivery service, and stacks of plastic crates filled with basil, lettuce, and other herbs cluttered the entrance of the Foundation. Twice a day we made the rounds of local kitchens, dropping off fresh produce.

In 2010, the Dominican government donated a specialized "tunnel" greenhouse designed for the tropics, featuring a water-saving drip irrigation system. The tropical tunnel produces regular bumper crops of tomatoes and peppers. Rather than a few scraggly plants, the system pumps out hundreds of pounds of veggies.

Over the last ten years, our quaint little garden has pumped out a steady supply of food for the resort. It covers almost an acre of land, with a shaded nursery, a forested stand of plantains and bananas, and a recently planted fruit tree orchard. We have a dozen different herbs and vegetables—arugula, lettuce, cucumbers, eggplants, peppermint, basil, pumpkin, passionfruit and papaya, among others.

Today the Foundation's farm supplies locally grown produce to all of the resort's restaurants, including an industrial-scale employee kitchen at the airport. Though still unable to fulfill all of the resort's demand, the farm is the largest of its kind in the entire region. Our clients have extended beyond the resort to other communities. We even set up a Farmer's Market, inviting other nearby farmers, artisans, and fishermen to join us in selling their products.

As the farm grew, though, we discovered an important downside to our success. The farm generates revenue, fresh food, and a good feeling for the resort community. However, the growing demand for fresh produce became increasingly water intensive. We needed to think strategically about the use of local fresh water. I set out to find a better way to grow.

FISH + HERBS = AQUAPONICS

Growing plants in hot weather means heavy watering to keep the soil and leaves moist. What if we could grow plants *in* water, instead? I began studying hydroponics, a production system in which crops have their roots in water, rather than planted in soil. The system uses less water for irrigation, since the plants float above the water buoyed by foam containers. Their roots dangle below, soaking up nutrients. Able to avoid pests normally found in soil, the plants grow quickly.

However, the water by itself doesn't contain all the nutrients and minerals the plants need to grow. In hydroponic systems, farmers add water-soluble synthetic fertilizers for the crops to absorb through their roots. This means that hydroponics is a highly efficient and productive approach to growing vegetables, but not necessarily an organic, chemical-free one.

We were on the right track, but a hydroponic system not only meant using synthetic nutrients, it meant having to *purchase* these inputs, driving up the cost of the project. We might be able to grow more, but it would be more expensive and depend on imported products.

Grupo Puntacana uses aquaponics to expand its agricultural production while saving water

While exploring new ways to farm, we also thought about growing different kinds of food. Aquaculture, the farming of fish, shrimp, and other aquatic creatures in controlled environments, has been proposed as a more sustainable solution for producing fish and seafood. With a growing global demand for seafood, many wild fish stocks are in deep trouble; we have already seen how overfishing impacts parrotfish. Aquaculture, with a promise to alleviate pressures on wild populations, has undeniably become a player in modern food production.

Large-scale aquaculture, though, is not without its critics. Salmon and shrimp farming in particular have gotten a bad rep for polluting local environments, accidentally releasing non-native species into coastal ecosystems and destroying marine habitats such as mangrove swamps. Aquaculture often also demands fish-based food, meaning it continues contributing to overfishing.

Yet not all aquaculture is created equal. There are certainly systems that cause limited negative repercussions. If done right, we thought aquaculture might have a place in Punta Cana.

Instead of deciding between hydroponics or aquaculture, we decided to do both. Aquaponics is a hybrid that combines the two systems. With roots in ancient China and Aztec Mexico, aquaponics is a mashup of aquaculture and hydroponics in a single closed-loop system that grows fish and produce simultaneously.

First, you grow fish in large tanks. As you feed them, they generate organic waste. The fish tanks are connected to a bio-filter, which treats the nutrient-laden water to make it safe for plants. The treated water is then pumped into the plant beds. The plants, like a traditional hydroponic system, float in the water where they suck up the nutrients they need through their roots. In aquaponics, the plants derive their nutrition from fish poop instead of chemical fertilizers. Water from the plants circulates back to the fish tanks. From start to finish, aquaponics uses the same amount of water. Only a small portion of it is lost to evaporation.

Aquaponics not only uses precious little water, but also produces 100 percent organic fish and vegetables. Adding pesticides or herbicides to the plants, as in most modern agriculture, would be lethal to the fish. This was the type of local, sustainable solution we were after.

Modern aquaponics, while derived from an ancient technique, is still in its infancy. When we got started in 2015, there were a few basic handbooks and some scattered aquaponics experimenters toying with their own systems. But I didn't find much else for guidance.

Susanne, the Foundation's project manager, has a background in large-scale shrimp aquaculture but she was nervous about experimenting with live fish in a new system, and had never attempted to grow vegetables. It took months of encouraging her (and the not-so-subtle hints of dropping an aquaponics book on her desk), but eventually she capitulated.

As usual, we started through trial and error. To avoid importing costly equipment from aquaponics suppliers, we designed our system using local materials. We had a local boat builder fabricate two 500-gallon fiberglass tanks that could hold roughly 150 fish. We selected tilapia, a grayish, large-lipped freshwater species that are hardy and fast-growing, as our starter fish. Tilapia doesn't taste too fishy, produces white-meat filet with few spines, and turns out to be an ideal food for unadventurous travelers.

From the fish tanks, the wastewater had to be treated to be made palatable for the plants. The fish water flows to the biofilter, the heart of the aquaponic system. It sounds sophisticated, but in reality a bio-filter is little more than a box filled with different materials that the water passes through. In our case, rather than expensive volcanic rocks or imported substrates, we used plastic bottle caps and leftover window screens. These recycled materials provide surface area for beneficial microorganisms to hide in and reproduce. By encouraging the proliferation of microorganisms, the biofilter breaks down ammonia in the fish wastewater. With a healthy population of good bugs, the water is cleaned up naturally.

Once treated, the ammonia-free wastewater flows into a series of homemade concrete beds filled with floating plants. The plants are fitted neatly into floating foam containers (also recycled material) with their roots hanging below in the nutrient-rich water. Our aquaponics system grows basil, mint, lettuce, and watercress. If a guest orders a mojito at our resort, it is made with fish-powered aquaponic mint.

Our aquaponics project continues to grow. We have expanded to seven 500-gallon tanks, a half-dozen plant beds and even hired a full-time aquaponics staff person. We also diversified to include ornamental koi, in addition to tilapia, for local fishponds. It turns out that selling alive koi is more profitable than tilapia filets.

For Grupo Puntacana, aquaponics has turned out to be what development experts call an "appropriate technology." Our community wanted fresh fish and vegetables and we needed a water-friendly method to grow them. By adapting an ancient agricultural practice to our local conditions, we made our farm more efficient and ultimately organic. Fish waste is a natural fertilizer for our vegetables. Once again, we had managed to take an animal's poop and turn it into sustainability gold.

THE ACCIDENTAL BEEKEEPERS

Living and working in an island resort, you sometimes get some strange requests. One day I got a call from Oscar de la Renta, the legendary Dominican fashion designer and an early investor in Grupo Puntacana. Oscar had a problem. He had bees in his bathroom and needed me to help get them out. A bee colony had infiltrated a duct in his air conditioner unit and built a hive there. Each time he turned on the air, swarms of honeybees rode a wave of cold air straight into his bathroom.

These types of calls had become increasingly common, not from renowned fashion icons, but from resort restaurants and homeowners. A few times a month, the Foundation would get requests to remove or fumigate bees from a roof, a nearby tree, or anywhere else a few thousand bees could squeeze their way in. What was going on?

Honeybees, though not native to the Dominican Republic, have become a common and mostly welcome resident. Prized for the pollination services they provide for flowers, trees, and other crops, honeybees are actively incorporated into larger agricultural projects in the DR. In fact, the Dominican countryside is dotted with subsistence beekeepers that produce honey and offer their bees to pollinate different crops. Punta Cana also has its share of other beekeepers, mostly informal hobbyists making extra cash when not working in tourism. Bees can be a good side hustle, offering a valuable secondary source of income.

The spread of bees throughout our resort had a scientific explanation. It was part of the natural progression of a bee colony. Beehives are a caste system, headed by one queen bee. Sitting at the top of the hive hierarchy, the queen is pampered and protected by drones and worker bees that do the heavy lifting to keep the hive humming. Eventually, though, the queen gets old and the hive selects one of her progenies to replace her. Led by the spry, younger queen bee, the hive exiles the old queen.

The ousted queen gathers part of her former colony and takes off in search of a new home. It's highly dangerous to be a homeless hive, since they are susceptible to birds and other predators. Often the castaway colony settles in the first available site—a cavity in a tree drilled open by a woodpecker, a hole in the roof of a restaurant, or Oscar de la Renta's bathroom air conditioner.

Oscar was conscious of the bees' role in our local ecosystem. He refused to fumigate them; instead, he recruited us to deal with the problem. With no knowledge of beekeeping, we hired a local beekeeper to collect the intruding hives and move the errant colonies to his place. As we got more and more bee removal calls, though, it became clear this quick fix wasn't going to work. The beekeeper got paid, kept the hives and sold the honey. We were the honey middleman working for free. It was a bad deal. We needed to put the bees to work for us.

The Foundation bought a handful of yellow, wooden bee

boxes, gathered five exiled colonies and set our sights on becoming beekeepers. One day I invited a former Foundation employee and passionate beekeeper to stop by to have a look at our hives. Pedro Julio, aka Rubio, was mortified by what he saw. Our hives were infested with Varroa mites that were crippling the colony with disease. Our bee populations were sick, keeping the hive populations too low to produce excess honey. Rubio spent the rest of the afternoon with us, cleaning up the hives and cursing our incompetence. He stuck around for a few days to help us get our act together.

Eventually we struck a deal; Rubio would go into business with us. The Foundation would provide land, boxes, and bee-keeping equipment. Rubio would handle the bees. Instead of paying him, we would split the honey we produced. For the first few years, it seemed like poor Rubio had been swindled. He hustled day in and out, but we only had a half-dozen colonies. We produced a meager, though delicious, trickle of honey.

Yet Rubio had a vision and he stuck with it. He expanded the hives. Five hives became fifty. We worked with Rubio to replace existing landscaping with bee-friendly, melliferous plants. We combated the Varroa mites with natural remedies and learned how to split the colonies before the old queen was banished. We set up a bee removal service in Punta Cana and began actively pursuing new colonies.

From the beginning, Rubio insisted on keeping our honey pure, refusing to mix honey varieties or cut it with other addi-tives. He was adamant that we would have healthier hives and get a better price if we built our reputation on producing pure, unadulterated honey.

Rubio's intuition proved correct. We now have over 450 hives dispersed throughout the resort. Our bees produce between one thousand to two thousand gallons of honey a season, depending on the weather and available flowers. The Foundation has its own award-winning honey brand, Puntacana Forest Honey, as well as selling new products like pollen and royal jelly.

As our honey production increased, the one-time pest became a profitable business. The Foundation worked out deals with local gift shops, supermarkets, and even the airport, to sell Puntacana Forest Honey. We "export" our honey to departing travelers through sales at the airport without having to pay customs or importation duties. Beekeeping even became a tourist attraction, bringing visitors and students from local and visiting schools for tours of the honey production process.

Bees started out as a headache for us. Through an unusual partnership with Rubio the beekeeper, that nuisance has become an asset. Our beekeeping has blended seamlessly with our sustainable agriculture, providing many of the same benefits. Clients that want to eat healthy, fresh produce typically also like the wholesome benefits of consuming high-quality honey. Beekeeping has also become a profitable and unexpected marketing tool, giving us a unique way to communicate our sustainability programs to our guests. For many of our guests, a tour with a local beekeeper and tasting fresh Dominican honey is a far more memorable experience than reusing a dirty bathroom towel.

CHAPTER FIVE

FILLING THE VOID: COMPANIES AS SUSTAINABILITY PARTNERS

IT HAD TAKEN A FEW YEARS, BUT I HAD FINALLY CON-vinced my college buddy, Discovery Channel host, and noted architect Danny Forster to visit Punta Cana. As a favor, he had brought along a Discovery cameraman to shoot a short pro-motional video of our sustainability programs.

Standing in front of a nondescript cement block building with a shaded but steamy-hot waiting room full of patients, Danny tried to make sense of what he was seeing. A government-run health clinic that was jointly operated with a luxury resort. It was odd, to say the least.

"Why is a beach resort running a community medical clinic?" Danny asked.

Earlier in the day, we had toured the golf courses and white-sand beaches of the resort. I took him to our recycling plant and even got him to dig his fingers into some worm compost. Though eccentric, most of our sustainability projects were directly connected to the business of running a resort. But healthcare for the community? Danny rightly noted it was odd.

Grupo Puntacana's relationship with the clinic started in 2006, when my colleague Paul and I gave a neighborhood kid a boost over a chain-link fence to get into the abandoned Verón Rural Clinic. It was clear it had been deserted for years. The building was in total disarray, with boarded-shut windows and untamed vegetation creeping up the walls.

In the Dominican Republic, a large part of the population depends on rural clinics like this one. Most people either can't afford private healthcare or they live too far away to reach a decent hospital. Their only option is what the government has to offer. To meet this need, the Dominican government created a patchwork of 1,500 rural primary care health clinics spread throughout the country's small towns and villages. The conditions of each clinic and the quality of care they provide vary widely. Some communities are more fortunate and have better facilities than others. The Verón Clinic, despite being adjacent to the one of the most economically active regions in the country, was decidedly unlucky.

PRIVATE PUSHES PUBLIC SECTOR

The Verón Rural Clinic operated briefly in the 1990s but was shut down in the early 2000s. Only its cracked and crumbling skeleton remained. The clinic was originally built to provide service for a rapidly growing community, at the time estimated to have thirty thousand residents. Once shuttered, the clinic had no doctors, no equipment, and no patients. Until Paul and I broke in.

I didn't know anything about the clinic or its ill-fated past until the Via College of Osteopathic Medicine (VCOM), a medical college associated with Virginia Tech, approached us with a unique proposal. VCOM offered to build and staff a free medical facility for the local community.

VCOM planned to run the facility with hired doctors and their medical students. The school had a unique philosophy. They wanted to graduate not only future doctors, but also responsible "global citizens." VCOM proposed hiring a Dominican doctor to direct the clinic, supervise students and attend to patients. The students would gain a real-world opportunity to care for patients in Verón, while opening their eyes to the reality of practicing medicine in a developing country. The school would leverage the clinic to gather donated equipment and medicine, as well as recruiting volunteer doctors to conduct periodic medical missions.

It was an offer we could hardly refuse, but there was a problem. Grupo Puntacana didn't own the existing clinic in Verón, nor did we have the authority to open and operate a new health clinic even if we wanted to. To reopen the Verón Clinic, we would need to broker a deal with the Dominican Ministry of Public Health, a task more difficult than it might sound.

In the DR, government services can become politicized. When it comes to helping citizens, who are also voters, resources controlled by government bureaucrats tend to gravitate to communities where they are politically advantageous. The Minister of Public Health, a political appointee, was unenthusiastic about dedicating resources to Verón, a community with relatively few registered voters. He also didn't see value in sharing the goodwill of a functioning hospital with a private corporation and some well-intentioned gringos. The government would just as soon keep the Verón Clinic inoperable.

After months of insistence and a healthy dose of political pressure from Frank, we eventually signed a three-way deal to refurbish and open the clinic. VCOM and the Ministry agreed to staff and jointly manage the clinic with doctors and medical students. Grupo Puntacana Foundation, on behalf of Grupo Puntacana, would run interference to smooth out misunderstandings between the foreign university and the DR government. The Foundation also provided seed capital for the remodel and committed to fundraising for the clinic into the future. GPC's engineering department oversaw the reconstruction.

Using Grupo Puntacana's corporate relations, we convinced the local electric utility, CEPM, to donate electricity. The phone company, Claro, donated internet and phone service. A few additional companies chipped in with funds and supplies to get the clinic off the ground. Donations continued to filter in, including air conditioning for the entire facility, an X-ray machine, and other specialized equipment. The local community chipped in with manual labor during renovation.

Less than a year later, the newly refurbished Verón Rural Clinic officially reopened with a fancy ribbon-cutting ceremony and the presence of the once-skeptical Minister of Public Health. Initially, the community's response to free medical care was tepid. After seeing the decrepit clinic closed for over a decade, they were understandably suspicious about the care being offered.

Eventually, though, the clinic began to gain the community's trust and the waiting area filled up. After a year, nearly 150 patients a day arrived for a range of services including prenatal, primary and emergency care. The clinic had been fully incorporated into the national health care system and was bustling.

Since its modest beginning, the clinic has been operating without interruption for well over a decade, providing medical care to tens of thousands of patients. The Via Medical College has rotated hundreds of students through the facility and directed hundreds of thousands of dollars in donated medicine, equipment, and supplies to the facility. The Dominican government has been a steady partner through it all, maintaining the clinic staff and sharing costs. Verón's clinic went from a ruin to a success story. All it took was for the private sector to insist the public sector do its job.

A HEALTHY HELLO

As Danny pointed out, the marriage between a beach resort and a health clinic is unusual. More often than not, the most thought hotel managers give to public health is to worry about a bad case of diarrhea making the rounds among hotel guests. Hotels don't typically dedicate much time contemplating the health of the local community.

There is, however, a strong connection between community health and tourism. Frank once summarized this linkage. "We got involved in the Verón Rural Clinic to ensure we have healthy employees so they can do a good job for us. It's just good business."

When visitors arrive to Punta Cana, who are the first people they interact with? It's not the hotel general manager or the CEO. Visitors' first contact is usually with reception staff, a bellman, a bartender, or wait staff. These positions serve as ambassadors for the resort. As the first line of interaction, hotel staff greet guests and makes them feel safe and welcome. This warmth is part of the Dominican charm that has made Punta Cana such a popular destination.

However, many of our employees live in Verón, where living and sanitary conditions can be precarious. If our employees get sick, it could affect their job performance. It's hard to be outgoing and hospitable when you feel like crap or you are worried about a sick family member at home. Likewise, if hotel employees need to spend their salary on medicine or health-care for their family, that leaves less money to buy food or pay for their kids' school. That type of stress can make them less effective in their work. Worse, if they miss work because of sickness, it directly impacts the hotel's effectiveness. As a result, the health and wellbeing of our staff has become a key part of our business.

The spread of infectious diseases has increasingly become a concern for tourist destinations. A number of neighboring destinations have been impacted by infectious diseases like cholera, malaria, zika, and dengue. The coronavirus (COVID-19) famously wreaked havoc globally on the world economy, with particularly devastating consequences for the travel industry. This has led the entire industry to rethink check-in, cleaning, and hygiene to keep guests and staff safe. Large-scale disease outbreaks can scare potential visitors and stop tourism in its tracks.

The Verón Rural Clinic has become a critical point of first detection in the case of an emerging disease outbreak. This allows Grupo Puntacana and the appropriate authorities to form fast responses and take preventative measures to developing health issues *before* they transform into crises. The clinic is like a finger on the pulse of community health in Punta Cana.

More than a charitable program, the Verón Rural Clinic is yet another example of Grupo Puntacana practicing enlightened self-interest. The government-backed facility treats patients from all over Verón. In fact, only a small percentage of GPC employees, who possess health insurance, use it at all. The clinic is an efficient way to help our employees *and* the community, requiring relatively little investment compared to its outsized impact.

Indeed, an investment in the health of the local community is in investment in our own business interest. Once again, it comes back to the airport. If we want the region to continue to prosper and the airport to continue to grow, we need healthy working people in our region. The Verón Rural Clinic helps make the region a safer place to live, work, and visit. It's good for Verón, but it's also good for Grupo Puntacana.

The clinic provides an equally important lesson: It demonstrates that the private sector can be a valuable sustainability partner, even collaborating with the government. Rather than a donor, our company became both broker and dealmaker in providing free, effective health services for Verón. Grupo Puntacana did put up money, but far more important was how the company used its convening power and reputation to bring together diverse partners to improve public health.

In this case, a unique partnership was formed between a US university, the Dominican government, the local community and a tourism resort. Grupo Puntacana helped channel the partners' different talents and resources towards getting the clinic operational. The company lent its name, reputation, and connections to give the project credibility and to attract other companies to contribute. Frankly, it's likely the clinic would still be boarded up if Grupo Puntacana hadn't taken the initiative and prodded the government to open it.

Waking the Sleeping Giant means realizing there are many ways companies can help make the world a better place. Money is sometimes the *least* important contribution a company can make. Serving as a credible and consistent partner is often far more impactful than a donation. Uncovering unique partners, pushing the government, and leveraging relationships are common in the business world, but can be transformative in sustainability.

Companies also possess the clout to elevate small initiatives far beyond the limited scope of the usual sustainability players. Not-for-profit foundations, philanthropists, and even international donors may have less access to the resources and people of influence capable of scaling small projects into expansive programs with greater impact. Combining the know-how of not-for-profits with the influence of well-connected companies can create a multiplier effect for sustainability programs like the clinic.

Becoming sustainability partners frequently requires companies to fulfill new and sometimes uncomfortable roles. The Verón Rural Clinic clearly demonstrated for Grupo Puntacana that the reward far outweighed the risk. With each success, GPC has been encouraged to continually challenge itself to become immersed in new projects, taking on functions not normally associated with a typical beach resort. We even learned that a resort can function as a national park.

THE PEREGRINE FUND

In 1965, a group of biologists studying peregrine falcon populations concluded the birds were headed off a cliff. The falcons are known for their speed; they are the fastest species in the animal kingdom. When hunting, peregrines dive-bomb their prey, reaching velocities in excess of two hundred miles per hour. Once they select a target, they compact their body into a ball and descend full speed, colliding with unsuspecting birds in flight. Their prey explodes into a cloud of feathers upon impact and the falcons grab the carcass midflight. A successful peregrine hunt rivals the sight of a cheetah hunting on the African plains.

Once widespread, peregrine populations declined in the 1950s, principally caused by pervasive use of DDT. The chemical pesticide weakened their eggshells and crippled the birth of offspring. Despite being listed as an endangered species, coupled with a nationwide ban on the sale of DDT in the US in the 1970s, a group of scientists decided more was needed to be done to save the bird.

Cornell University professor Tom Cade kickstarted peregrine conservation by developing creative methods of breeding the falcons in captivity, and then successfully releasing them in the wild. He later helped found The Peregrine Fund (TPF), a foundation dedicated to saving the peregrine falcon. From 1974 to 1997, the organization released four thousand falcons into the wild.

By 1999, the group had successfully reversed the fortunes of the peregrine and it was removed from the endangered species list. It was one of the world's most successful conservation efforts of a critically endangered species. In the process of conserving peregrine falcons, TPF realized they had a unique talent for saving birds of prey. Instead of shutting down the organization, they expanded their mission to protect more than one hundred raptor species around the world.

The Peregrine Fund made another important discovery in their early work with peregrine falcons: birds are highly adaptable to new environments. If they can find food and nesting sites, they can inhabit spaces not traditionally associated with bird wildlife.

For example, one of the most successful release sites for peregrine falcons was none other than New York City. The city's skyscrapers, bridges, and parks became new hunting territory for the falcons. They fed on rats, pigeons, and other urban pests. TPF concluded you often have to take what you can get in bird conservation. It turns out cities can work just as well as pristine environments to save a species from the brink of extinction.

In the early 2000s, The Peregrine Fund turned their attention to the Ridgway's hawk, an endemic raptor species found only in the Dominican Republic. Habitat loss and human persecution (an unfortunately common refrain in Nature) had reduced the Ridgway's numbers to just two hundred to three hundred individuals. The Ridgway's hawk was one of the most critically endangered species in the world. The surviving population was concentrated in the poorly protected Los Haitises National Park. It was unclear how the hawks, whose range traditionally spread throughout the island, had become limited to such a small area. Yet it was clear they would be wiped off the face of the earth if something wasn't done soon.

One of the primary challenges the hawks faced were rural farmers living in and around the park. The Dominican Republic is chicken country. Raising chickens is as natural as breathing air. Dominican families, both in urban and rural areas, keep chickens for food, fighting, egg-laying, and general companionship. Even in big cities, you might see chickens next to a large shopping mall or stylish new restaurant. Pass through a small town on almost any weekend and you will find hordes of men holding their prized chickens, petting them and readying them for battle in cockfighting rings, one of Latin America's most popular pastimes.

Unfortunately, Ridgway's hawks occasionally run afoul of the beloved chicken. The hawks typically stick to a steady diet of rats, snakes, small birds, and large lizards. They don't eat adult chickens, which are too big to carry off in their talons. Ridgway's hawks will, however, pick off the occasional baby chick. This set them up for conflict with the Dominican farmers living in the community of Los Limones, adjacent to Los Haitises. The farmers, tired of losing their brood to birds of prey common around the park, had set their sights, and their rifles, on the Ridgway's hawk.

The Peregrine Fund biologists spent close to a decade documenting the hawks' island-wide decline. They studied the remaining population, their nesting and feeding habits, and the assorted risks that threatened the hawks. The foundation documented human persecution of the hawk population. It worked with local people to understand their attitude towards the animals, allay their concerns, and try to persuade them to stop shooting birds. The Peregrine Fund quietly toiled away in a remote corner of the national park, with the majority of Dominicans entirely unaware of the hawks' plight.

Around this time, I got an email from Frank Rainieri. He had seen a presentation about the hawks' precarious situation. He had never actually seen one of the hawks personally, but he had an idea to help them. Frank proposed bringing a few hawks to Punta Cana, where people made their living in tourism, rather than tending chickens. No one would think to shoot them in Punta Cana, much less within our property. Our resort could serve as a sort of wildlife refuge.

I was doubtful. I assumed their low population was a product of their demanding ecological needs. Surely the hawks had obscure eating requirements or only nested in a rare tree. Maybe they bred too infrequently to recover their low numbers. Reintroducing the hawks to Punta Cana sounded good, but I was fairly certain it wouldn't be feasible. Nonetheless, I dutifully investigated.

To my surprise, The Peregrine Fund was in fact looking for new sites to reintroduce the hawks. They had pieced together a historical record of the hawks on the island. They aimed to reestablish hawk populations in the sites they once inhabited, which were hopefully safer today than when they disappeared. Nonetheless, the new sites would be at least as safe as the Los Haitises National Park. TPF informed us the hawks were once found in Punta Cana. We invited The Peregrine Fund for a site visit, where they confirmed our resort had the both the habitat and prey the hawks required. Compared to the rest of the country, the property was virtually chicken-free. Our resort could be suitable hawk habitat.

The endangered Ridgway's hawk becomes a welcome addition to the resort

HACKING A NEW HOME FOR HAWKS

We made a deal with The Peregrine Fund: Grupo Puntacana Foundation would make a small donation to reintroduce some baby hawks on a pilot scale and provide TPF researchers room and board. If the experiment worked, we would help continue to support their researchers, recruit new partners, fundraise, and support Ridgway's hawk conservation in Punta Cana. The hawk experts from TPF would do the rest.

In 2009, researchers spent the early months of the breeding season monitoring mating hawks in Los Haitises National Park. After careful observation of the nests, they selected a few pairs that could spare a nestling for the new experiment in Punta Cana. The project manager, Thomas Hayes, donned climbing gear with a rope harness and a hardhat, scaling each palm tree to lower the chicks down. Meanwhile, the parent hawks dive-bombed Thomas to drive him off. At thirty-five to sixty feet off the ground, it was hazardous work.

Thomas cuts a striking figure as a hawk conservationist. He

is a hunter, a carpenter, and in the offseason hunts elk in Idaho with a bow and arrow. But he got his start in conservation as a falconer, learning to train falcons, hawks, and eagles to hunt and bring their prey back to him. His wife Christine is equal parts badass. During the hawk breeding seasons, they camped for months in the rustic shacks of local villagers near Los Haitises with their infant daughter, monitoring the hawk nests and working with community members. When I decided to get into conservation, the image I had of my future profession was someone like Thomas Hayes.

The first year, Thomas and his hawk team transferred three baby hawks from Los Haitises to Punta Cana in his pickup truck. Each hawk was fitted with a metal ring on its leg that described its sex, the year it was introduced, and where it was born. A thin radio antenna was latched onto the hawks' backs so the researchers could track them with telemetry equipment.

Once in Punta Cana, the hawks began a process known as "hacking." The newly outfitted chicks were carefully placed in a special "hack box" perched on a wooden tower. Far from the chicks' parents, Thomas and his staff imitated them, bringing the chicks thawed lab rats for several months and meticulously tracking the chicks' progress. The chicks rarely saw Thomas or his team, which ensured they would not become habituated to humans.

Eventually, the hawks learned to fly and fledged from the hack box, returning daily for several weeks to sleep and score free food. In a few more weeks they learned to hunt on their own, before finally abandoning the hack box and the rat buffet in search of new territory. The hawks were free to roam their new home in Punta Cana.

Each year we reintroduced a few more chicks to the resort. The third year, we had a breakthrough. A pair of hawks built a nest and hatched the first baby Ridgway's hawk in Punta Cana.

The breeding pair confirmed that the trial was a success. If the hawks reproduced in Punta Cana, they were adapted to the habitat. Encouraged by this initial success, Thomas and company intensified their efforts, bringing even more hawks from Los Haitises. More breeding pairs formed. By year five, we had jumpstarted the local hawk population within the resort.

Ten years later, the Ridgway's hawk has become a fixture in Punta Cana. The resort is now home to some 120 hawks, including more than a dozen mating pairs. Hawk couples stick together for life, leading to as many as twenty chicks born in Punta Cana each year. We have made enough generational leaps that many of the new adult pairs were both born in Punta Cana. The population within our resort has become saturated enough that a handful of hawk pairs have moved on to neighboring resorts and hotels.

OPENING THE CORPORATE TOOLBOX

While The Peregrine Fund are the hawk specialists, Grupo Puntacana has not been a silent partner. In fact, Grupo Puntacana offered different departments of the company as a toolbox for hawk conservation.

Using the strength of our public relations department, we have directed all kinds of media attention to the hawks: press visits, television programs, radio spots, articles, videos, and even a national awareness campaign. Our PR department publicized the hawks' dire situation with the same zeal as if it were a selling golf packages at the Westin. The Grupo Puntacana Foundation now offers bird-watching tours for our hotel guests and homeowners. Working with our legal department, we submitted legislation to the Dominican Congress to create a National Ridgway's Hawk Day.

The project continues to evolve. We involved our electric

utility in protecting hawks. The raptors adapted extraordinarily well to our resort, residing on our golf courses, hotels, and high-end residential neighborhoods. However, they also regularly perch on the power lines around the property. In Los Haitises, there is no electricity. The hawks never saw power lines and never associated them with a threat. Within the resort, electric lines represented a hazard that could potentially electrocute unsuspecting hawks.

In the United States, strict federal laws protect raptors from human threats, including dangerous power lines. Electric companies are required to retrofit older lines and ensure new lines are designed to be raptor safe. In the rest of the world, including the Dominican Republic, raptors are on their own. Electric wires may be the silent killer of thousands of raptors a year, but no one is counting.

After investigating solutions, we imported specialized plastic sleeves to cover "hot" wires and prevent electrocutions. We mapped the most dangerous power lines and Grupo Puntacana's electric company installed the equipment on 150 poles, safeguarding the hawks. Our electric company has become an enthusiastic provider of hawk-friendly electricity. It even lends its ladder extension truck so Thomas and his crew don't need to scale the palm trees with climbing gear.

In fact, our entire resort community has become a hawk social network. Our foundation now gets regular phone calls, texts, and emails reporting injured hawks and alerting the hawkologists to new nests. Some offer donations. The Puntacana International School sports teams are now named the Hawks and a giant flying hawk logo looks down at the school's field.

HAWK CHANGEMAKERS

The Ridgway's Hawk Conservation Project has been an overwhelming success. Though the hawks are not entirely out of danger, their situation has drastically improved. Their prospects are brighter than at any point in the last fifty years.

When we got started, however, no one had heard of the vanishing Ridgway's hawk. Now there is growing nationwide awareness of the need to protect them. It all began with the Punta Cana experiment. New partners have come on board, including the National Zoo and other corporate foundations, helping to increase resources for hawk conservation. With a strong and growing population in Punta Cana, The Peregrine Fund has discontinued hawk reintroductions to Punta Cana. Now they have a new hacking site in another location in the Dominican central mountains. A few hawks were also discovered in Haiti, launching a new hawk conservation locale.

What do Ridgway's hawks tell us about the role of companies as sustainability partners? The project demonstrates that there are many ways companies can make sustainability work. Corporations can fulfill unique and previously unexplored niches, such as forming partnerships with organizations like The Peregrine Fund, even if the work has little relation to a company's core business.

Grupo Puntacana is not a conservation organization. Yet with very little investment, our partnership with The Peregrine Fund leveraged the strengths of our company to help save a species. Like the clinic, the initial seed funding we provided was probably the *least* important contribution we made to the project. Far more importantly, we offered to let TPF transform our resort into an unofficial, private national park. Grupo Puntacana opened its doors to raptor conservation and the hawks responded.

The truth is that few companies imagine themselves as potential change-makers. They assume their role in sustainability is limited to cleaning up their own act by polluting less or fulfilling some generic prescribed goals set out by the United Nations. Companies often throw money at charities and launch new eco-friendly products. Their primary goal, however, is to generate goodwill or marketing benefit for the company, not to specifically solve some intractable social or environmental problem.

What many companies are missing is the profound (and practically effortless) contribution they can make to sustainability simply by putting their weight behind worthwhile causes. Rather than asking how a particular project can benefit the company, sometimes companies need to apply an adaptation of John F. Kennedy's famous phrase: Ask not what the hawks can do for your company, but what your company can do for the hawks. Grupo Puntacana never expected that saving an endangered species would impact our bottom line. We never anticipated a return on our investment. Frank hadn't given any thought to the potential PR benefit of the project. We did it because we thought we could be useful in the struggle to save the hawks.

Corporations continue to have ever greater power and influence across the planet. The least they can do is consider supporting the occasional eccentric cause with unconventional partners *for no other reason* than their capacity to make a difference. Sustainability can deliver real tangible value to a company. Other times, companies can harness their expertise, position, size, and marketing capacity to do good, regardless of whether the initiative has anything to do with making money. In fact, it may not require money at all, as long as the company is imaginative enough, it can help generate change.

A THINK TANK FOR SUSTAINABILITY

Ted Kheel listened in fascination as distinguished Cornell University professor Dr. Eloy Rodríguez described the journey it took to get his students to the Peruvian jungle. Ted was participating in an alumni weekend at Cornell and Dr. Rodriguez had been assigned as his prominent host.

A self-described Indiana Jones of medicinal plant research, Dr. Rodriguez described how his students took a commercial flight from upstate New York to the capital of Peru and then transferred to smaller planes to reach remote jungle towns. Later they switched to motorboats and eventually canoes before eventually hiking into a rudimentary jungle lodge, where they spent weeks exploring the forest.

"Why in the world would you go to such trouble to sleep in the jungle?" Ted asked.

In Peru, Dr. Rodriguez's students interviewed local shamans and villagers about the medicinal uses of different tropical plants. They conducted experiments on extracts of the plants in a makeshift laboratory to determine each plant's potential medicinal properties. The jungle was loaded with unexplored chemicals and the program, funded by the National Institutes of Health, provided unique research opportunities for students to learn about "bioprospecting," the search for potentially profitable drugs and natural products.

Ted, however, was as struck by their complicated travel plans as the research itself. At lunch, he proposed that Dr. Rodriguez bring his students to Punta Cana, instead. "We have our own airport with direct flights from New York. We can put your students up at our hotel. They can study the plants of the Dominican Republic." Always the pragmatist, Ted pointed out, "It will take much less time to get there and be cheaper, too."

Besides simplifying the professor's travel plans, Ted had another motive. He recognized that the research for natural products would provide further justification to protect the Dominican Republic's unique flora and fauna. If the forest, or maybe even the coral reef, held nature's secrets to making medicine, there was even more reason to protect these threatened ecosystems. Beyond the potential drugs, Ted was drawn to the idea of attracting academic partners to study other challenges affecting the tourism industry. Luring Cornell to his Caribbean resort was a way to get his foot in the door with the university. By forming a partnership, he could engage the university's brainpower in developing solutions to other sustainability challenges.

Eventually Grupo Puntacana and Cornell agreed on an ambitious approach. GPC would build a permanent research and education facility with dorms, laboratories, classrooms, conference space, experimental gardens, and offices. GPC put up the land and Ted's family foundation covered construction costs. The Dominican government would supervise the research and provide local knowledge through the National Botanical Garden. Cornell would provide professors and students, using Punta Cana as a learning laboratory.

The new facility, called the Puntacana Center for Sustainability, was inaugurated in 2001. It was a think tank for sustainability, but once again was an oddball partnership made up of uncommon partners: a prestigious US university, the Dominican government, and a tropical resort. Dr. Rodriguez brought his students each summer and gradually Cornell's presence expanded beyond medicinal plants, just as Ted had hoped. Cornell launched new programs with other international universities in ornithology (the study of birds), hotel and hospitality management, and even distance learning,

Sensing the potential of his novel idea, Ted began aggressively recruiting other universities. Eventually he caught up with the "Godfather of Biodiversity," eminent Harvard professor E.O. Wilson. Winner of multiple Pulitzer Prizes, Wilson has authored some of the most influential conservation books in history and invented the scientific discipline of socio-biology. E.O. Wilson is like Elvis to environmentalists.

When Ted approached him, Wilson and his Harvard colleague, Dr. Brian Farrell, had dreamed up an ambitious new concept but they needed a place to test it out. The idea was to create the "Encyclopedia of Life," a digital compendium of all the species on the planet, complete with high resolution photos, videos, sounds, graphics, DNA barcodes, descriptions, and collection data. The Harvard team argued that conserving Earth's biological diversity was complicated by how little we know about the planet in the first place. If we wanted to conserve species, it was critical to create a collaborative, living encyclopedia where experts could share what we know about the planet's flora and fauna and fill in the gaps of what we don't know. The Encyclopedia of Life was the first step to truly understand what needed saving.

The Puntacana Center for Sustainability attracts prestigious partners, including EO Wilson from Harvard University

Ted pitched them on the idea of attempting one of the first chapters of the encyclopedia in the Dominican Republic. Dr. Farrell has a long history with the country (his wife is Dominican), but beyond that he found the country biologically intriguing. As he noted, the DR is "big enough to be interesting, but small enough to be doable." In other words, though the DR has loads of endemic species (plants and animals found only on the island), it is a relatively small space. Cataloguing the country's biodiversity would be far more manageable than taking on the entire Amazon basin, for example. (It was, incidentally, also easier to get to.) Punta Cana could serve as a launching pad for the Encyclopedia of Life.

THE SMALL MAJORITY

In 2004, Wilson and Dr. Farrell visited the Puntacana Center for Sustainability and brought a team of students to begin their inventory of local species. They first targeted one of the largest, least studied and most diverse groups: insects. Ironically, insects dominate the animal kingdom, especially in the tropics, forming the physically smallest majority on the planet. Combined, they have the largest biomass of all terrestrial animals. At any time, it is estimated that there are some 10 quintillion (10,000,000,000,000,000,000) individual insects alive. Harvard students and researchers set out to collect as many insects as they could find in Punta Cana.

To collect them, researchers spread out giant tarps on the ground, sprayed a pesticide cloud into a forest (that only affects insects), and spent the night scooping up everything that fell out of the trees. On other nights, the Harvard crew set up white sheets and shined black lights on them, attracting bugs from near and far. They grabbed everything that landed on the sheet and stuffed them into glass vials filled with alcohol.

Once they had a few thousand specimens, they set up fancy microscopes rigged with digital cameras to take high-resolution 3D photos of the specimens for the online encyclopedia. They then pinned the insect specimens into specialized cabinets, grouping each genus into a different drawer—beetles, moths, ants, butterflies, and so on. At the end they created a museum-grade collection of local insects for scientific purposes, as well as for showing tourist visitors.

Simultaneously, the team combed local natural history museums to digitize existing collections. They found a surprising number of private insect collections in the Dominican Republic that had never been catalogued or photographed, filled with some species that hadn't been seen for decades. They also worked with the Botanical Garden to digitize the plants.

The project quickly grew and attracted new funding, allowing Harvard to train a small army of local students and scientists to continue the work year-round. They set up a small-scale research laboratory at the national university in Santo Domingo. The Puntacana Center for Sustainability housed a satellite laboratory to continue the laborious work of databasing the island's biodiversity.

The Dominican Republic chapter of the Encyclopedia of Life project has carried on for close to two decades, training dozens of students and compiling hundreds of thousands of entries into the database. The project has expanded to new countries, new forests, and involved hundreds of new scientists and researchers.

At a distance, this was yet another peculiar match. The preeminent research university on the planet partnering with a Caribbean resort to study insects. Yet this is exactly what attracted Harvard to Punta Cana in the first place: a bizarrely unique but highly productive partnership. Punta Cana, though blessed with unique coastal habitats and remaining tropical forests, is not even the most biologically diverse part of the DR. But it has other important advantages. The Center for Sustainability gave the researchers a convenient field station to get research done and the airport made it a quick trip from Cambridge. Grupo Puntacana's eagerness to collaborate helped encourage Harvard's efforts, giving them a turnkey facility to get started.

In this case, Grupo Puntacana's role was more of enthusiastic cheerleader than generator of scientific knowledge. As a result of the partnership, we learned a tremendous amount about our local insects and plants, finding ways to share the information with our guests. Harvard produced guides, posters, and interpretative materials we used with our visitors.

More than anything, the partnership with Harvard sent a powerful signal that the Center for Sustainability was not just a PR stunt. Admittedly, I was star-struck by the opportunity to enlist E.O. Wilson and Harvard to work with our company. But I also knew it immediately lent credibility to our efforts. Far from a program without substance, it showed our commitment to supporting serious scientific endeavors, even if they were not directly aligned with the business of operating a resort. Our budding relationship with Harvard later evolved into collaboration in a field that is deeply connected to our resort: sustainable architecture.

THE MODERN, THE VERNACULAR, THE SUSTAINABLE

During his visit to Punta Cana, Danny Forster mentioned off-hand that the Harvard Graduate School of Design (GSD) was looking for student projects. The GSD, one of the world's preeminent architecture schools, offers a three-year degree comprised of two grueling years of academics and a third year "studio." The studios take different shapes and forms, but often the students are paired with businesses, museums, governments, and architecture firms to work on real-world projects. As a recent grad, Danny proposed pitching a design project for Grupo Puntacana to the GSD.

Working over lunch, Danny and I whipped together a proposal for a semester-long course around students designing a master plan for an undeveloped piece of beachfront within the resort. The lot, known as Playa Serena, was the jewel of the Grupo Puntacana property. For years Ted and Frank had wavered on how best to develop this mile-long stretch of white-sand beach and palm trees. We tasked the aspiring Harvard architects to inject fresh ideas and insight into developing Playa Serena.

The students were assigned a unique challenge: craft a real estate plan that did *not* depend on having a golf course. Grupo Puntacana's real estate team had become convinced the Caribbean was over-saturated with golf course communities. With designer golf courses piling up, it was becoming hard to distinguish one resort from another. GPC wanted to diversify its residential communities beyond golf. We thought Harvard could help us out. More than a new master plan, we needed some out-of-the-box thinking.

Before they could suggest new ideas, the students needed to understand how our resort functions. During winter break, a dozen Harvard grad students descended on Punta Cana for a weeklong indoctrination. The future architects held design charettes with multiple departments of Grupo Puntacana: real estate, engineering, airport operations, architecture, and sustainability. They toured existing golf course homes with local builders, picking the brains of experienced Dominican architects regarding what construction materials they used and why, how to design for a tropical climate, and the market preferences in Punta Cana. The students even spent an afternoon learning different techniques of weaving a Dominican thatch roof. Finally, the students pored over the resort's existing master plan with Frank Rainieri, both the one on paper and the one in Frank's head. He explained why Playa Serena was so special. It was a total immersion in Punta Cana architecture.

The course, titled "The Modern, the Vernacular, the Sustainable," was an attempt to marry Grupo Puntacana's environmental ethos with modern architectural concepts, all while respecting an indigenous architectural language. The Harvard students would need to blend these different ingredients to produce singular recipes tailored for Playa Serena.

With a sunny visit to the Caribbean behind them, the students spent a dreary winter in Cambridge dreaming up designs for Playa Serena. They logged months conducting planning exercises, building digital and physical models, and debating the best use of the land for selling real estate. They employed cutting-edge software to determine the best orientation of buildings to take advantage of breezes for natural cooling, while avoiding direct sunlight to minimize the need for air conditioning.

In the spring, a delegation of Grupo Puntacana executives and Dominican architects (including Oscar Imbert, the architect of the original Punta Cana Airport) traveled to Harvard for the final critique. We spent eight intense hours in a classroom listening to their proposals, questioning their ideas, and analyzing their designs. The students had built 3-D models, digital renderings, and reams of posters and design sketches. We got some bizarre ideas and some more down-to-earth proposals. At the end of the day, Frank summed up the experience.

"I am used to getting building designs on a paper napkin! It's obvious the tremendous effort the students put into these projects. Some are amazingly creative but would be impossible to execute in Punta Cana. Others have elements we could use. But more than anything, you helped us look at our property with fresh eyes. This can help us rethink the way we plan our entire community."

By partnering with an architecture school, Grupo Puntacana got a low-cost but cutting-edge injection of new ideas. Many of the designs turned out to be completely impractical for our resort. It didn't matter. The partnership was easy to justify. GPC would never hire a traditional master planning firm and give them this much latitude to propose such courageously original ideas. Professional firms are simply too expensive to risk paying a lot of money for outlandish but unfeasible designs.

The Harvard students, on the other hand, were unencumbered. They could propose unusual plans that pushed the envelope of our thinking. It was a partnership that enriched our development planning and gave the students an opportunity to test their thinking with an actual client.

Since the Harvard course, we have run similar architecture programs with University of Syracuse and Roger Williams University, each exploring new ideas for different parts of our resort. During these exercises, students reconceived the airport's thatch-roofed buildings as modern spaceships blanketed with living green walls. Inspired by Nature's own design of limestone coral, they conceived a condo and mixed community center for the Hacienda residential neighborhood as a giant structure that looked like Swiss cheese sitting on an island in the middle of a man-made lake. In their designs, entire residential neighborhoods were organized around color schemes of different flowers and shrubs.

Some of the ideas have made their way onto our property, others remained beautiful yet conceptual renderings. Later, one of our university partners inspired a structure based on their class that actually got built.

TECH MEETS WATER

"Where do you get your drinking water?" I was sitting in a Virginia Tech (VT) classroom on my first visit to campus, responding to questions from a group of civil and environmental engineering undergraduate students. The visit involved a crammed schedule, meeting with potential academic partners from the various colleges and departments of the university. Laser focused on engineering challenges, the VT students wanted to understand how water works in the Dominican Republic.

I patiently explained how in Punta Cana each resort digs its own drinking water well and distribution systems to provide the hotel with potable water. Each resort also builds its own water treatment plant to treat its sewage. Often this sewage is reused for irrigation around the resort grounds.

The students, however, were interested in the communities *around* the resorts. Rather than the hotels, the budding engineers peppered me with questions about Verón. Where does it get its water? Is there a centralized water system? Who distributes water in Verón? What happens to the sewage? Do the users pay for water? The students were intent to learn more about real-world public sanitation. The Punta Cana region and its surrounding communities was an intriguing classroom.

The history of water in the Punta Cana region is closely aligned with the boom in hotels. New resorts generated jobs that attracted people from all over the island looking to help build, landscape, and find work in tourism. For the last thirty years, jobseekers have streamed into Verón, contributing to explosive population growth. Today Verón is a peri-urban city with an estimated eighty thousand inhabitants.

With virtually non-existent unemployment, Verón has become one of the most economically vibrant towns on the island, bursting with entrepreneurs hustling, buying, and selling.

Verón probably has more commerce per square foot than even the most successful shopping mall. On one street, you can find car mechanics, discount clothes shops, fruit vendors, Chinese food, carwashes, and discotheques. Verón crams a city's worth of services into one small community.

Despite its hyperactive informal economy, there is a serious downside to Verón's growth. Neither the hoteliers nor the Dominican government were fully prepared for the pace of development. In fact, the community's rapid expansion has consistently exceeded the meager infrastructure investments made by the DR government. Unlike the region's hotels, Verón has grown without a plan.

The resorts were all designed, planned, and built by professional firms. In the absence of public facilities, hotels built their own water distribution systems and water treatment plants. They were constructed according to master plans following strict building codes, so the hotels have reliable water. When the water quality isn't up to par, they can filter it.

Verón, on the other hand, evolved with no master plan, no public infrastructure and no local government. As the number of hotels expanded, the community grew, though not in anything resembling the orderly paradise within the resorts. It more closely resembles the disorganized *favela* slums of Brazil in its haphazard layout. Verón's water system is as muddled and disorganized as the community itself.

WATER DETECTIVES

Despite its rough appearance, Verón shares a critically important feature with the hotels. Both depend on the same source of drinking water: the freshwater aquifer. The community, like the hotels, taps into this large subterranean water source through an assortment of private wells, loosely supervised by the local government and the national water authority. There is no centralized water system for the hotels or the community.

However, unlike the hotels' privately built systems that pipe fresh water to their doorstep, Verón's residents get their household water from an informal mosaic of water delivery: leaky supply trucks; five-gallon bottled jugs; and, if they are lucky, private wells with filling stations. Occasionally, residents have water piped to their homes, but water is not always available to all residents. There is also a significant disparity in the quality of water when comparing the resorts to the local community. As the students would discover in their research, water quality in Verón is typically inadequate at best.

Similarly, Verón has no central sewer system and private septic tanks are uncommon. Instead, wastewater is piped out of homes, motels, and stores through makeshift plumbing and discharged directly into the ground. Instead of going to a water treatment plant, raw sewage is pumped underground and out of sight, most often into cracks and fissures in the limestone rock, filtering to underground caves. In other words, the rapidly growing community of Verón is dumping its sewer water underground, where eventually it seeps into the region's only source of potable water. This is a very bad idea.

In 2010, Virginia Tech's engineering students partnered with us to fill in the many gaps in information about the community's water. For several weeks, the students roamed Verón, interviewing community leaders and neighborhood associations to dig into the water issue.

They took water samples from cisterns, taps, and water tanks to test community water quality. The students mapped all of the private wells that had been dug in different neighborhoods and plotted their findings in mapping software. After weeks of field work, they went back to campus and slogged through the data. This type of boots-on-the-ground research had never been undertaken before. Like detectives trying to crack a mystery, the students produced the first-ever state-of-the-water report in Verón. The results were terrifying.

Virginia Tech students survey water in the local community in collaboration with Grupo Puntacana

Virginia Tech's data confirmed our suspicions: Verón had disturbingly tainted drinking water. The vast majority of water tested in local homes and rooftop storage tanks was contaminated and unsuited for consumption or use in bathing, cooking, or cleaning.

The research also linked the tainted water to community health. An alarming number of people in Verón suffer from skin, stomach, and intestinal infections, causing missed workdays and medical expenses. In addition to diarrhea and hygiene-related skin diseases, dirty water increased the likelihood of water-borne illnesses, such as cholera, dysentery, hepatitis A, and typhoid. Poor water quality was keeping the little Verón Clinic quite busy.

Not only are local people at risk from contaminated water, but so is the hotel industry. Access to fresh water is as integral to Caribbean tourism as white-sand beaches and piña coladas. You need water for showers, kitchens, pools, landscaping, and a dozen other activities in a resort. Without clean water, there would be no tourism in Punta Cana. Led by a group of Virginia Tech undergraduates, we confirmed that sewage was a hidden threat with the potential to upend Dominican tourism. Verón's water problem is also Punta Cana's water problem, and it's a ticking time bomb.

SMART WATER

Water *quality* isn't the only problem. Permission to dig a new well is authorized by the local government with a small permitting fee. The municipality, unfortunately, lacks the technical capacity (or scruples) to determine a safe number of private wells to guarantee the future availability of water.

As a result, the Virginia Tech research showed a proliferation of private wells in Verón. In fact, the students recorded close to one thousand private wells in the town. A few small, but dense, neighborhoods had as many as sixty to seventy private wells. Each well is operated like a small business, with the owners selling water to residents who don't have plumbing at home.

This sprawling assortment of wells translates into many separate straws sucking from the same aquifer. As more and more private wells are dug in close proximity to one another, the concentrated extraction causes a decreasing water level in the aquifer. The subsequent vacuum of newly unoccupied space invites coastal saltwater to fill the void. Like a boat that springs a leak and takes on unwanted seawater, the aquifer has new holes for saltwater to enter. This phenomenon is known as saltwater intrusion. The continued and concentrated pressure on Punta Cana's aquifer, especially from the large number of unplanned individual wells in Verón, has made the threat of saltwater intrusion real.

Ironically, much of what we know about one of the most critical issues facing the region has been revealed by a couple of teams of undergraduate students. Though water issues have been studied by international experts, consultants, and government agencies, few have given us as much practical information as Virginia Tech. Unpaid undergraduates helped document the impending water crisis unfolding outside the boundaries of our resort at a fraction of the cost of expensive water consultants.

Our partnership with a university not only informed our understanding of the problem, it encouraged us to take a shot at a solution. Armed with the research results, we presented our findings at meetings with a half-dozen neighborhood associations in Verón. The community's reaction ranged from disbelief to disinterest.

In the neighborhood of Domingo Maíz, however, the residents were shocked by how polluted their water was. They wanted action. Unlike other neighborhoods, however, Domingo Maíz didn't plan on waiting around for the government to fix the problem. "You just told us our drinking water is contaminated. What can we do about it right now?"

Unfortunately, there is no easy answer. The cost and complexity of building a massive, centralized sewage treatment facility for Verón is prohibitive. Politically, similar to the conundrum of the health clinic, the Dominican government has little enthusiasm for investing in water treatment, especially in a region with relatively few registered voters. If the hotels are so worried about water, the government reasoned, they should pay to solve the problem in Verón. Besides, most of the country operates without water treatment, anyway. Why would the government invest in cleaning up sewage for the tourism industry instead of a larger city with equally complicated sanitation issues?

For their part, most of the hotels have already paid for their own water treatment facilities. They not only don't have the resources to pay for an expensive centralized sewage system that includes the local community, they believe it's the government's job. Isn't that why the tourism industry pays so much money in taxes, precisely so the government can resolve this type of issue? Water treatment falls squarely within the government's responsibilities.

Verón's sanitation also presents technical challenges. More than a traditional grid, Verón is a sprawling clutter of buildings and construction. It looks like the houses were sprayed randomly across the map like pellets from a shotgun blast. Forget about building codes or urban planning. Houses are dispersed in all angles and directions. Getting plumbing to each individual house would require seriously creative engineering.

While the public and private sector sat on the sidelines, the Grupo Puntacana Foundation team huddled with Virginia Tech, the US Peace Corps, and Grupo Puntacana's engineering department to debate different alternatives. Ultimately, we decided to design a small-scale demonstration project for the 150 or so houses in Domingo Maíz. Rather than a traditional water treatment plant for all of Verón, we could break the problem down into manageable chunks by designing a decentralized system. This would also allow us to test experimental water treatment methods. The project would give us the opportunity to learn from our mistakes *without* spending tens of millions of dollars. Most important, we didn't have to wait around for someone else to get it started.

A CONSTRUCTED WETLAND

After considerable brainstorming, our team settled on a "constructed wetland" for Domingo Maíz. This system is a man-made habitat that imitates the functions of a natural wetland to treat wastewater. Just as natural wetlands filter excess nutrients and pollutants in rain and runoff, a constructed wetland uses a pond system and plants to remove harmful contaminants from sewage, while trapping organic matter and sediments. The sewage passes through a biological filter rather than a chemical process.

We kept the design simple. Dirty water was piped from each house to the wetland by gravity, avoiding costly pumps and electricity. In the first phase of treatment, sewage flows to two large cisterns where solids settle out and separate from the water.

The partially cleaned water then passes to the second phase of purification: a large gravel-lined pond seeded with special, nutrient-absorbing plants. Just like a natural wetland, the pond is home to millions of microorganisms living in the gravel and plant roots. The man-made ecosystem sucks up the remaining sludge and after passing through the wetland, purified water is safely returned underground.

The wetland was truly a collaborative effort. It took us three years to design, fundraise, and eventually build Domingo Maíz's constructed wetland. The neighborhood association convinced the municipal government to donate the land. Grupo Puntacana strong-armed several local contractors to pitch in with low-cost use of heavy equipment, pipes, and plants. The Peace Corps, Virginia Tech students, and Grupo Puntacana's engineers drew up plans to build the system.

For more than a month, we dug up most of Domingo Maíz to plumb the neighborhood and create the wetland. The entire neighborhood was transformed into a construction site, complete with backhoes, compressors, drainage ditches, and piles of rock and dirt. I worried that if we failed, we would never be able to put Domingo Maíz back together again.

After a few weeks, Domingo Maíz was reassembled with one important change: Its sewage was being transformed into a lush, verdant wetland on the outskirts of town. The experimental system functioned as designed, improving local water quality. We had successfully built the first functioning constructed wetland in the country and the neighborhood association inaugurated the facility with a festive ribbon-cutting ceremony.

The constructed wetland on the outskirts of Domingo Maíz attempted to solve a local water problem, but dirty water is not limited to Verón. Pollution from sewage is a concern in cities and towns throughout the Dominican Republic. Soon our wetland attracted development organizations, local governments, and foundations to see it firsthand. Within a couple of years, several Dominican companies had formed partnerships and funded similar wetland systems. Our constructed wetland concept had been replicated in other regions in an effort to clean up different rivers and waterways.

In Domingo Maíz, our think-tank for sustainability had moved from theory to action, taking an academic exercise and transforming it into a low-cost, functioning water treatment plant. Though we had not solved all of Domingo Maíz's water issues, we had empowered the community to take action to improve sanitation. By partnering with the private sector, the community had tapped into resources, technical expertise, and financing. It had also found leverage to approach the municipal government to secure land for the project.

As Verón and Punta Cana continue to grow, water issues are not going away. Attempting several decentralized, but low-cost experiments in other neighborhoods like Domingo Maíz, may be one way to approach solving the issue. Small-scale treatment plants have the potential to protect groundwater, and to create momentum for more large-scale investment in a regional solution. Domingo Maíz is already providing lessons of what worked and what didn't, which can inform future decision-making. Ultimately, it is likely more partnerships including the private sector will be necessary to confront Punta Cana's emerging water crisis.

FROM HITCHHIKERS TO ELECTRICIANS

In the Dominican Republic, it's not uncommon to see people standing by the side of the road with their thumb out, trying to flag down a ride. Hitchhiking, known as getting a "*bola*," is as common as dancing merengue or playing sandlot baseball. Less common is seeing dozens of children in blue uniforms lined up along the road with their thumbs out. In 2003, this was the case in Verón. The uniformed kids were high school students looking for a free ride instead of waiting for a public bus to take them to school.

Among its deficiencies, Verón had no public high school. In order to attend school, Verón's teenagers were forced to pay for public transportation to make the hour and a half trek to Higuey. Before a modern highway was built, the road to Higuey was treacherous, producing dozens of monthly accidents. Once there, the classrooms were overcrowded with students from Higuey, not to mention the overflow of kids from Verón. It was a hard road just to get through high school.

Kids unable to afford bus fare or unwilling to put up with the aggravating trip ended up working, or worse. Many try their hand at the kind of low-paying, informal work that doesn't require a diploma. The public education system in the Dominican Republic has its problems, but young people are far better off graduating from high school. Non-graduates have a much tougher time getting a decent job. In Punta Cana, the best paying hotel jobs are filled by better qualified candidates from Santo Domingo or other cities. Without a high school, local kids have little chance of getting ahead.

Similarly, local businesses have fewer qualified candidates to fill vacant positions. Forced to hire transplant candidates from far away, businesses often pay above-market wages, moving costs, and even housing. The lack of local talent has made labor costs for many Punta Cana businesses higher than they would be if there was a nearby source of skilled candidates.

The negative impact of no high school goes beyond the classroom, spilling into the local community. A growing city of young people with idle time, little money, and dim prospects leads to other concerns: delinquency, drugs, teenage pregnancy, and crime. In tourism, few things tarnish a place's reputation faster than lawlessness. There is no shortage of examples of thriving destinations that quickly bottomed out when they become too seedy or unsafe for tourists. In Punta Cana, the lack of a local high school was yet another indirect risk to the tourism industry. If the local youth had no future, Punta Cana could become more dangerous and less attractive.

Concealed within this problem was an opportunity. Punta Cana has a massive demand for workers with technical training: mechanics, electricians, plumbers and maintenance staff. The region has close to fifty thousand hotel rooms. A two thousand-room hotel has hundreds of air conditioning units, small fleets of vehicles and miles of plumbing. If local candidates were trained with the right skills, they could find job opportunities. Training a cadre of young people would facilitate trained technical staff in the hotels, filling a significant void.

Besides vocational jobs, hotels can always use more bilingual staff. If you have ever struggled to get extra toilet paper in a foreign country because of language barriers, you know the feeling of relief when someone understands what you are asking for.

Bilingual bartenders, waiters, receptionists, and housekeepers are prized finds in Dominican tourism. Beyond creating life-changing opportunities for an underserved population, a new high school could help make the region, and its hotels, more appealing.

As usual, there was a catch. The Dominican government had no plans to build a new school in Verón. Existing schools in the region were already underfunded, understaffed, and overcrowded; the government hardly wanted the expense and headache of a new school.

A PRIVATELY-RUN PUBLIC SCHOOL

Frank and Ted of course saw the big picture. The region needed a new high school, and fast. They saw the risk for the region *and* Grupo Puntacana's bottom-line. By now the company had the know-how to operate a school. GPC was already managing a private school for the children of employees, called the Puntacana International School.

But they had learned the hard way that overseeing a school is a big responsibility, has a steep learning curve, and requires a serious financial commitment. GPC had its hands full with over three hundred students at the Puntacana International School and was not in a position to open a free public school. We recognized the need for a public high school in Verón, but the only way to build it would be to find a partner. Or two.

Ultimately, Grupo Puntacana brokered a deal with the Dominican Ministry of Education and the Catholic Church. GPC agreed to pay for the building and subsidize the school. We would also support it in the future. The Dominican Ministry of Education would incorporate it into the national school system and provide teachers (though eventually GPC had to subsidize their meager salaries). The Catholic Church was recruited to run the new high school, installing a priest as director. The partners formed a board of directors with representatives from the three institutions, as well as members of the community.

In 2004, Grupo Puntacana inaugurated the Ann and Ted Kheel Polytechnic High School in Verón, making it the only public high school within fifty square miles of the Puntacana International Airport. Unlike other public schools, however, the Polytechnic was not free. Embedded with the private sector ethos of "there is no free lunch," each student pays a nominal tuition to attend. The actual amount is the equivalent of a large bottle of beer a week, a pricing concept Frank himself devised. He calculated that if a family could afford to drink beer, they could certainly pay for their kids' education.

The Polytechnic offers a basic high school curriculum but also provides technical training in the afternoons. The students, and later adults from the community, have access to technical workshops, practice bars and kitchens, a computer laboratory, and English language classes. The workshops are managed with an expanding array of partners from different foundations, government agencies, and international donors.

Initially the Polytechnic taught one hundred students. Today it comprises more than three hundred kids and has graduated close to one thousand. More than nine thousand students in total have been certified in technical training. Grupo Puntacana now operates a yearly internship program for students to work in different departments of the company. This has led to dozens of Polytechnic graduates working for the company, one of the original objectives when the project started. Open now for nearly two decades, the Polytechnic School continues to adapt to changing needs in the industry. Computer skills and digital capabilities are becoming key components of teaching at the school.

The Ann and Ted Kheel Polytechnic High School holds a

special significance for Grupo Puntacana, and not just because it bears the name of one of its founders. The high school is a resource that keeps giving, adding more value to Punta Cana with each graduate. Providing future employees with better and more relevant skills allows them to contribute to the tourist destination. Young people that find good jobs and more opportunities are more likely to stay out of trouble and build a better future for themselves. It may sound simplistic, but in developing countries, training someone to become a plumber or a mechanic can be the difference between getting ahead and a future of poverty or crime.

Once again, the Polytechnic demonstrated that an unusual alliance led by the private sector can overcome government inertia. Working with the church and the government, Grupo Puntacana devised a cost-effective shortcut to build a high school. Rather than waiting for the public sector to confront the problem, GPC had dragged it into participating in the solution.

The Polytechnic School achieved far more than that. Providing skills training to local people contributes to better service. Better service leads to better guest experiences and higher occupancy rates. With fewer kids at risk on the streets and less potential for crime, the reputation of the Punta Cana destination remains positive and can continue to compete internationally. All told, the Polytechnic School is a solid investment in a competitive destination.

HIGH RETURN ON LOW INVESTMENT

A private company running a public high school and free medical clinic? Endangered wildlife cozying up on a golf course? Universities sending their students to a luxury resort to study sewage?

Grupo Puntacana's diverse partnerships seem peculiar when

taken out of context. If it was a publicly held company, stockholders might be inclined to wonder what any of this has to do with the business of landing planes, booking reservations, and selling real estate. Isn't a company's job to make money and produce value for its stockholders? Do companies really have an obligation to give anything back to society?

At Grupo Puntacana, we generally avoid the philosophical debate about the role of corporations in society. We don't normally use the term "corporate social responsibility" because it sounds like we are being forced to do it. Upholding some unspoken moral obligation to society is simply not relevant to our decision-making. While we enjoy the heartfelt satisfaction of helping people and Nature, that's not the primary reason we do it. Sustainability is not random acts of kindness; it is part of a strategic approach to keeping our business competitive.

Partnerships are an efficient and cost-effective investment in solving threats to our business, whether the risk is the availability of clean drinking water or a lack of electricians. Our partners deliver skills, resources, and expertise we don't have, complementing our weaknesses with their strengths. By building lasting partnerships, we can get out in front of potential threats in real time before they explode into full-blown crises. Working with atypical partners and investing time, energy, and money in seemingly idiosyncratic programs, we are betting we get a far better rate of return, solving potential problems before they become catastrophes.

CHAPTER SIX

A FOUNDATION HEART WITH AN MBA BRAIN

AFTER A FEW YEARS IN PUNTA CANA, I WAS ASKED TO serve on the board of directors of a small foundation dedicated to bird conservation. Founded by a group of hardcore birders complete with convertible khaki pant-shorts, binoculars, and bird checklists, the foundation was created to protect local birds through guided tours and environmental education programs. Secretly a birder myself (minus the khaki zipper pants), I was excited to help. At the board meetings, we talked shop about our favorite birding locations, reviewed the progress of different projects, and bandied about ideas to strengthen the foundation's efforts. The foundation was small and specific but filled a useful role.

THE DONKEY PROBLEM

During one meeting, the foundation's newly hired director (we'll call him George), presented us with an exciting new development. George enthusiastically told us how he had obtained funds to eradicate donkeys from an island in the middle of a lake in the southern Dominican Republic. The board members exchanged looks of confusion.

"What do donkeys have to do with birds?" we asked.

He responded that donkeys had been introduced to the island by farmers. The invasive species were wreaking havoc on the island's natural vegetation and wildlife. The donkeys ate all the local plants, making it hard for the birds to find seeds and food. A negative chain reaction caused by an introduced species was cascading down to the local birds. If the donkeys were removed, however, native habitat would recover and the birds' population would recuperate. Getting rid of donkeys meant helping birds indirectly. "More importantly," George added, "we need the funds to pay our salaries."

It was not exactly the foundation's mission, but we reluctantly signed off on the donkey scheme. However, shortly thereafter he presented another new project: studying rare, native mammal species. The solendonte and the hutia are enigmatic animals found only in the Dominican Republic. The hutia looks like an oversized rodent with weirder habits. They live in underground caves but come out at night, climbing trees to feed on leaves and forest vegetation. This combination of cave-dwelling and tree-climbing is odd for land mammals. The hutia also makes a high-pitched shrieking noise when startled, an unpleasant nails-on-chalkboard sound I have experienced.

The solendon is similarly strange. It is a prehistoric, shrew-like creature left over from the dinosaur days, complete with a primitive-sounding name. About the size of a small cat with a long, pointed mouth, solendons can inject venom through their hollow bottom teeth. They also live in underground caves, coming out at night to forage for insects on the forest floor.

Both mammals were thought to be highly endangered, but no one knew enough about them to be sure. An international conservation organization had offered funds to investigate their respective populations and recommend ways to protect them. Unless more research was done on the habits, population, and threats to these two mysterious mammals, it would be impossible to conserve them.

George had successfully applied for the funding. Once again, we were told that researching the mammals would indirectly save bird habitat. The new funds, not coincidentally, would also help offset budget shortages.

In time, as the foundation continued to tack in new directions in pursuit of funding, it no longer resembled the bird conservation organization the board members had originally agreed to help. The foundation became a shapeshifter, an instant specialist in any Nature-related endeavor, as long as it meant funds deposited in its bank account. Rather than pursuing new ways to help save birds, the foundation hunted money.

The bird foundation grew. It had new staff, new vehicles, and the projects expanded throughout the country, even to places with few birds. Free guided bird walks, which didn't generate revenue, were abandoned. The organization signed an agreement to help the Dominican government manage a national park. It launched an ambitious ecotourism project and offered to consult on climate change projects. Soon, it was recruiting corporate sponsors to support its wide-ranging efforts. Where funding opportunities arose, the foundation was there. It was cash-obsessed and off mission.

Eventually, George legally renamed the foundation to accommodate its ever-widening mission, effectively erasing its bird-centric beginnings. It replaced a focus on birds to become an all-encompassing environmental foundation, whose primary mission became "conservation" (and fundraising). Most of the original board of directors, including myself, resigned. We had nothing against being a conservation generalist, but we no longer felt passionate about the work the foundation was doing. Specifically, we weren't interested in dedicating our time to help raise money for the director's salary.

MISSION DRIFT

There is no doubt that running a foundation is not easy. If you have ever been around one, you could be forgiven for thinking that foundations exist exclusively to raise money. Or as my great uncle Ted used to say about universities, another species of money-hungry not-for-profits: "They exist to do three things: Teach, conduct research, and fundraise. In reverse order of importance." Universities, Ted joked, spend as much time pursuing money as they do educating students.

This relentless pursuit of money pervades the vast majority of environmental foundations (and many not-for-profits, in general). Rarely in a position to generate revenue from sales of goods or services, foundations fundraise. Besides covering staff salaries, they pursue money for everything from vehicles to airplane tickets to staplers. Cash keeps the good work humming and without it, even the best-intentioned foundations don't stand a chance of making an impact. While understandable, it can also be a missed opportunity.

Mission drift (also "mission creep") refers to the gradual departure of an organization from its original objective. Whether it is attempting to grow, following the director's personal impulses, or simply keeping the lights on, mission drift causes an organization to gradually abandon the specific area or niche where it has expertise, instead taking on a wider range of activities, often in areas where it has none.

In the case of the bird foundation, George gave up its focus on birds. At the same time, however, it lost its principal constituents—bird enthusiasts. Now the foundation had few genuine supporters that could vouch for its work and know-how. The tight-knit and proactive community of birders that launched the organization no longer identified with it. Instead of the voluntary support of birding enthusiasts, the foundation's primary allies became the donors that gave it funding.

Foundation donors, for their part, have a vested interest in ensuring that the programs they fund are a success, or at least appear to be. Foundations deliver on a checklist of grant requirements by filling out forms and reports. Provided a project can jump through a gauntlet of administrative hoops, it can be deemed successful, regardless of the actual conservation results. Donors use the paperwork to justify how the resources have been deployed.

In this way, foundations set themselves up for future funding, using each completed grant to demonstrate to new prospective donors their capability at managing project money. Like a good card player, clever foundations can parlay one grant into successive grants.

At the bird foundation, this process had little to do with saving birds. Instead, it became an illusory game intended to please donors and create a bridge from one grant to the next. There was, of course, a significant downside to the foundation throwing its hat into the fundraising ring. By giving up its focus on birds, the foundation subtly transformed into just another small environmental organization in an already crowded space. In the environmental field, every grant proposal, no matter how small or insignificant, attracts an army of foundations elbowing each other out of the way to get at the funds. (Which, incidentally, explains why so few environmental organizations collaborate together. They are too busy fighting each other to get funding!)

Now the bird foundation was forced to compete with bigger, more experienced foundations with expertise in a wider range of fields and a more established track record managing funded projects. Pitted against other larger foundations, the former bird foundation looked exactly like every other environmental foundation on the block, but less qualified. It became much harder to get new funds.

LESSONS FROM THE PRIVATE SECTOR

Stanford Graduate School of Business lecturers Kim Jonker and William Meehan observe the bizarre lack of focus of foundations in their article, "Curbing Mission Creep," in the *Stanford Social Innovation Review*.* Their study shows that private companies, unlike foundations, seldom overstep their core competencies beyond their definitive brand of products or services.

The researchers conclude that just like private industry, foundations need a strong mission that addresses an unmet public need. They should use their unique skills to address that need and stay focused on their mission, learning to say no to funding opportunities that stray from their objectives. Foundations must also continue to inspire their stakeholders and board of directors.

Finding the money to pull this off is no small feat. The not-for-profit cash conundrum is real. How does a foundation remain true to its mission while expanding its resource base? In other words, how does a foundation founded to save birds avoid chasing down invasive donkeys and prehistoric mammals instead?

Up to this point, this book has concentrated on the ability of *companies* to achieve powerful societal impact. We have pri-

---

* Kim Jonker and William F. Meehan III, "Curbing Mission Creep," *Stanford Social Innovation Review*, Vol. 6, Issue 1 (Winter 2008), Pages 60-65

marily explored the role of for-profit companies in sustainability. Not-for-profit foundations are, however, key players, too. They fulfill a crucial role in sustainability: providing passionate professionals and specialists that work full-time on solving social and environmental challenges.

Governments and companies have full plates already. It's not enough that they commit a part of their resources and ingenuity to confronting global challenges. Even so-called "triple-bottom-line" companies and B-corporations (companies with sustainability literally embedded in their charter), have their hands full just running a business. Evolving social and environmental issues need someone with their eye on the ball full-time. Foundations fill this role.

Yet there is significant room for improvement in the way that not-for-profit foundations currently operate. In particular, the relationship between foundations and companies could use some rethinking. If we expect to make a dent in ever increasing global challenges, we can't continue business as usual, whether it's for profit or not-for-profit.

This chapter explores ways foundations can act more like businesses, operating with the heart of a charity but the brain of a business. Equally important, we'll discover strategies companies can employ in their relationships with not-for-profits to produce better and more lasting results. Companies may indeed hold the key to enabling foundations to spend less time chasing cash and more time building a better planet.

DIVERSIFY YOUR PORTFOLIO

In the late 1980s, Grupo Puntacana made what many developers would consider a peculiar decision. The company voluntarily set aside 1,500 acres of property as an Ecological Reserve. With much of the land still undeveloped, the entire property was still more of a reserve than a resort. But Ted Kheel and Frank Rainieri didn't plan to keep it that way. They dreamed of one day filling the void with hotels, golf courses, and residences. With that in mind, the duo set aside a portion as protected land long before it needed protecting. The new reserve immediately became the largest privately-owned protected area in the eastern Dominican Republic. The company eventually donated the land to the Grupo Puntacana Foundation.

The Ecological Reserve is habitat for much of the region's original flora and fauna—orchids, hardwood trees, lizards, frogs, snakes, crabs, iguanas, and birds. Lately, it has become a magnet for researchers and wildlife enthusiasts. For two decades, scientists from this region and abroad have studied all aspects of the reserve, from population dynamics to invasive species to medicinal properties of plants to the grooming habits of ants. As the Punta Cana region has grown and primary forest has slowly been replaced with human development, the Reserve has become essential habitat for many species.

Beyond its function as a biodiversity refuge, the Reserve performs another important role. Within the larger Reserve is a forty-five-acre forested area with twelve freshwater lagoons and a network of trails. Named the "Indigenous Eyes Ecological Reserve," after the Taino Indian custom of calling freshwater pools "eyes," the Reserve is an important tourist attraction. In fact, it is one of TripAdvisor's highest-ranking activities in all of Punta Cana. The freshwater lagoons are different shapes and sizes, crystal clear and filled with turtles and fish. Diving into one of the chilly lagoons is often compared to entering the fountain of youth (or at least a really good remedy to a hangover).

Equally important, Indigenous Eyes has become part of a portfolio of activities providing significant income to the Grupo Puntacana Foundation. And it happened naturally. As the attraction became more popular, the foundation created entrance gates for safety purposes. Soon, we detected a growing number of tourists and locals visiting and we had to staff the entrances to regulate visitor traffic.

The Puntacana Ecological Reserve is one of the most important attractions in the Punta Cana region

Eventually, we began to charge minimal access fees to reduce overcrowding and mitigate environmental impact. Ironically, the entrance fees only served to make the Reserve more popular. Apparently when forced to pay, people realize that something is valuable. Or they suffer from FOMO (fear of missing out) and want to visit even more.

Today, Grupo Puntacana Foundation generates a six-figure yearly income through user fees from Indigenous Eyes. It invests those resources in improving trails, hiring staff, and offering new guided programs. The funds support the Ecological Reserve and also support the Foundation's existing and new projects. Whether they know it or not, each visitor helps protect hawks, feed worms, care for bees, and restore corals reefs.

OUTSOURCING FUN

With a steady flow of incoming tourists, a for-profit excursion company approached the foundation with a proposal for a new eco-tour. We agreed on a concession contract to promote low-impact tours in and around Indigenous Eyes. Maintaining a priority on providing wildlife habitat, the foundation limited the types of activities and the number of monthly visitors in the reserve. Outside of Indigenous Eyes, we limited excursions to battery powered Segways, bicycle rides, and guided walking tours. Visitors can only access a small portion of the trails, avoiding sensitive areas, to limit the impact of overcrowding.

The excursion company, meanwhile, assumes all costs and risks associated with the business: insurance, marketing, staffing, transportation, equipment, and commissions to salespeople, among others. They confront complaining customers, fix broken equipment, and conduct hand-to-hand business combat with dozens of other excursion companies in a highly competitive market.

The business of having fun in Punta Cana is no joke. Rather than taking on these headaches directly, Grupo Puntacana Foundation outsources the work in exchange for fees. Through the concession contract, the foundation generates funding to protect the Reserve, allowing it to concentrate on the types of programs it does best. We took one of our most attractive assets and used it, carefully, to generate a unique source of revenue.

Obviously, not all foundations have a potential revenue source like the Indigenous Eyes Ecological Reserve, nor a captive market of tourists nearby willing to pay for admission. Our Ecological Reserve is undoubtedly a unique resource, both natural and financial. The overarching point, however, is that foundations need to behave more like businesses, diversifying their sources of revenue and sticking to their core competencies. Successful businesses don't generally stray far from what they are good at. Businesses focus on what they do well. Foundations would benefit from thinking the same way.

If we return to the bird foundation briefly, it certainly had the expertise to develop paid, guided bird tours in protected areas. The foundation was highly qualified to take advantage of this revenue stream. Though the tours might not have solved all of its financial problems, it would have been a consistent source of income. Instead, the foundation concentrated all of its efforts on fundraising from grants.

Commercial excursions within the Ecological Reserve is part of Grupo Puntacana Foundation's "all-of-the-above" philosophy. We generate resources from a range of sources. The foundation sells honey, worm compost, vegetables, tilapia filets, and entrance fees to Indigenous Eyes. It also seeks private donations, grants, and large-scale projects with multilateral donors. We partner with other organizations that bring their own expertise, funding, and experience that complement our work.

Of course, the foundation also receives annual financial support from Grupo Puntacana, the parent company. These guaranteed resources give us an advantage over other smaller foundations that don't have a corporate benefactor. But rather than live exclusively off the company's largesse, we proactively leverage those resources to expand and diversify our income stream. The Grupo Puntacana Foundation operates like a for-profit not-for-profit with the same entrepreneurial spirit as the corporation.

Our solid financial base affords a luxury many cash-strapped foundations don't have. Instead of spending valuable time and energy competing with other organizations to get at limited donor funding, we can actively partner with them. Grupo Puntacana Foundation collaborates with foundations, companies, and government agencies, accessing their funding, expertise, and resources to complement our work. The foundation competes for grants, but our diverse revenue stream means we can avoid investing our time and money in projects that take us off-mission. Avoiding mission drift takes discipline, but it also requires financial stability.

LEVERAGING COMPANIES

I often get questions about our unique funding structure. Our success has made other organizations curious about how we operate and how we are funded. Specifically, many want to know whether the contribution Grupo Puntacana makes to the foundation is directly related to the number of passengers at the airport or the number of guests at our hotels. This is usually followed by a well-intentioned suggestion that we should implement a tax on each guest's hotel bill or on each arriving passenger at the airport. "With the growth you have in the region, just imagine how much money you would bring in by simply adding a dollar to each of the millions of arriving passengers."

At first glance, charging customers a seemingly innocuous fee seems like a great idea to fund sustainability programs. However, this type of transactional thinking only makes sense when times are good. What happens when there is a down year at the hotel? Or fewer passengers at the airport? (Or a global pandemic like COVID-19 that strangles all revenue.) If the resources the foundation received from Grupo Puntacana were based solely on the company's short-term financial results, the foundation would go belly-up the minute there was a downturn. As such, there is no such fee on passengers or hotel guests, nor would we want one.

The reason Grupo Puntacana invests in the Foundation is because the Foundation produces *value* for the company, in good times and bad. If the company felt the need to tap its customers to foot the bill for its sustainability programs, that would be the first indication that the programs don't generate a return on investment. Far more important than charging per customer, Grupo Puntacana provides the Foundation something much more valuable: its consistent and unwavering support. Instead of serving as the sole source of funding, GPC's annual contribution serves as a platform to cultivate all kinds of new sources of revenue, most of which have little relationship to hotel occupation. The company supports the Foundation's annual budget and covers basic operating costs *regardless* of whether business is good. This has allowed the Grupo Puntacana Foundation to grow steadily for twenty-five years, even in the wake of the coronavirus pandemic, the 9/11 terrorism attacks, and the 2008 financial meltdown. We have survived in spite of events that have slashed tourism revenue.

Additionally, the company provides massive in-kind support. For example, the Foundation utilizes Grupo Puntacana's legal, human resources, public relations, accounting, finance, auditing, budgeting, engineering, and architecture departments. This translates to thousands of dollars of free services through the corporation, the equivalent of massive savings in administrative costs. While GPC's annual donation to the Foundation is critical, its unrestricted access to its corporate infrastructure and human resources is equally valuable. Using Grupo Puntacana's bureaucracy, the Foundation avoids creating one of its own.

The point is not that every foundation can or needs to find a Grupo Puntacana to underwrite its basic overhead (though it does make life easier). The point is that far too many foundations rely exclusively on a traditional donation and grant-seeking funding strategy. They close themselves off to partnerships and more creative financing. Regardless of whether they have a corporate patron, foundations should consider expanding their resource base and spend less time exclusively chasing funds.

Grupo Puntacana Foundation is certainly not the only organization that came to this realization.

RETURN ON CHARITABLE INVESTMENT

One afternoon, I found myself bouncing along a pockmarked dirt road near Bonao in the central mountains of the DR. As we got farther from the highway, the landscape went from farms and rural villages to small clusters of simple houses. As the houses thinned, we came upon something unexpected: manicured lawns, bucolic buildings, and what looked like a college campus in the middle of nowhere: The Cigar Family Campus.

The Cigar Family Charitable Foundation is a small not-for-profit dedicated to health care, education, and sustainable employment in the Dominican Republic. It was founded by the A. Fuente & Company cigar manufacturers with their industry partners and the Dominican Institute for Integrated Development (IDDI). The Fuente brand is world renowned for their award-winning cigars but they are less known for their work in Bonao.

This small community is critically important to the Fuente business, a relationship the family started when it established a cigar rolling facility in the area decades ago. Fuente doesn't mass-produce cigars with industrial cigar-rolling machines. Their cigars are hand-rolled in small towns near Bonao, where it is by far the largest employer.

Being the biggest company around meant that Fuente was usually the first stop when villagers needed money to solve different community problems. Through the years, Fuente received a near-constant barrage of donation requests from employees, community members, and neighborhood organizations: uniforms for the local baseball team, sheets of metal for a roof damaged by a storm, even money for a coffin for a relative's funeral. The company met as many requests as they could, but they were frustrated that no matter how much they gave, it only increased the number of requests they got. Instead of putting out small fires, each donation seemed to fan the flames of more requests. Without a formal giving strategy, Fuente was like a rudderless ship, giving away money in all directions with no way of gauging if they were headed in the right direction.

AVOIDING THE DAO

In Latin America, there exists a long tradition of the "*dao*," a term which refers to a giveaway or gift to disadvantaged people. For decades, strong-armed dictators used the *dao* as part of a strategy to pacify resistance against the government. If the people were given money, food, televisions, and free electricity, they were less likely to rebel to overthrow bad leaders.

Today a different kind of *dao* has taken hold, usually promoted by politicians looking for votes, well-intentioned companies, and corporate foundations. The corporate *dao* is less a tool of political control than the result of a lack of know-how in making effective donations. Most companies seem to think giving away money doesn't require expertise. They start giving without a plan or based on the whims of the CEO. As a result, corporate charities often struggle to effectively deploy their resources or measure the results of their giving.

This is not a trivial amount of money. Large companies wield significant sums for donations, often enhanced by tax benefits and incentives for corporate giving. Well-meaning government incentive programs encourage charitable giving but give little guidance on how to do it well. With the bar set exceedingly low, companies struggle to make a difference with their donations, much like the Fuente & Company cigar manufacturers funding random funerals.

Determined to stop the trickle of donation appeals and get more positive bang for their charitable buck, Fuente approached the Institute for Integrated Development (IDDI) for some direction. IDDI is a seasoned foundation with decades of experience in poverty alleviation in the DR and Haiti. Together they devised the Cigar Family Charitable Foundation, a proactive strategy to improve the impact of their giving. They decided that all donations should be measured against indicators in the local communities. Rather than a shotgun spray of small gifts, their efforts would be laser-focused on solving specific, clearly defined issues affecting the towns near their rolling facility.

IDDI did some research in the region and concluded that the area's most pressing issue was a lack of educational opportunities for local children. Kids had to travel long distances to reach underequipped rural schools. The hassle and transportation costs meant local school abandonment levels were high. Predictably, testing and aptitude scores in the region were low. Parents were disengaged from their kids' literacy and education, having little formal connection to the existing schools. Lacking skills and education, graduates from local schools rarely attended university and likewise had trouble accessing good jobs.

Cigar Family made a bold decision to commit nearly all of its charitable resources to launching a new local school to serve five rural communities near Bonao. Instead of building the infrastructure alone and handing the school off to the government, they committed to making the school's ongoing growth and improvement a core charitable objective. They started with a basic school, but once it was built, it rapidly expanded to kindergarten through high school.

The Cigar Family Charitable Foundation then added health education, sports, arts, and music programs for over 450 students. The campus continued to expand to include an events pavilion, baseball stadium, computer centers, and campus-wide

Wi-Fi. Graduates increasingly began attending university, often with financial support from Cigar Family. This was the college-esque campus I visited.

The school actively engaged local parents by creating adult education programs and hiring them at the school. Parents were encouraged to get involved through a newly created association, and local adults were able to take advantage of the facilities for training and ongoing education opportunities after school. The school became a part of the fabric of the local community, not just an isolated space for kids alone.

As the school became a central part of the community, random requests for money slowed considerably. Not only was it obvious that Cigar Family had a plan, it was equally clear it was making an impact. The school also gave the company a coherent and simple response to the scattered donation requests that did come in. As a policy, the foundation didn't make small individual gifts. The school and its related activities were the foundation's primary focus and highest priority. Small, isolated donations would only detract from the critical work it was already doing. Ultimately, the community could see for itself that Cigar Family was fulfilling this mission.

A TOAST ACROSS AMERICA

The Cigar Family Charitable Foundation's "business" model uses a unique formula to fund its activities without relying exclusively on the Fuente corporation's generosity. The partners believed they could convert their giving into a powerful sales and marketing tool for the Fuente brand while encouraging their customers, distributors, and associates to get involved. Cigar Family would become a platform for generating ongoing charitable funds.

First, the foundation is incorporated in the United States

as a tax-deductible entity (the technical term is a 501(c)3 foundation). Individuals and corporations in the United States can make donations to the foundation and deduct the contributions from their US taxes. This vehicle encourages US citizens to support the charitable work of Cigar Family in the Dominican Republic, a significant advantage for fundraising.

The Fuente corporation makes an annual contribution which covers salaries and basic operating costs. This means the foundation staff don't have to constantly fundraise. Cigar Family, further, is structured as a membership organization, relying on contributions from supporters beyond Fuente. Rather than one-time gifts, it recruits its customers and vendors to become ongoing members.

Membership infers certain "benefits," such as special trips to visit the Cigar Family campus, as well as opportunities to interact with Carlito Fuente himself. Carlito is a celebrity in cigar-smoking circles. While I was on campus for their annual graduation, there was a riveted group of visitors admiring the school, enjoying the Dominican countryside, and fawning over their cigar idol, Carlito. Most of the visitors were members that had donated either cash or equipment to the foundation.

Importantly, membership also gives vendors access to the product. Fuente cigars are ranked as some of the best in the world. Since they are hand-rolled, they are relatively scarce in international markets. Low availability increases already high demand, meaning only privileged retailers can get their hands on Fuente cigars. The company astutely leverages the scarcity of their product, making the cigars more exclusive but also generating contributions to the Cigar Family foundation.

The Toast Across America program offers specialty cigars that can only be purchased and sold by foundation members. Cigar Family describes The Toast as a "unique opportunity for cigar retailers, customers, and employees nationwide to unite for one cause while enjoying specially made cigars. Held each fall, it is the largest fundraiser for the Cigar Family Charitable Foundation, using special cigar packs to raise money for children and families living in the cigar-producing region of the Dominican Republic."

In this case, the strategy brings in much needed money for the foundation and also helps grow their customer base. It asks retailers to give to a worthy cause, thus earning the privilege to sell their product. This is an impressive piece of philanthropic jujitsu and its success is quantifiable. In Bonao, the program's success is measured through graduation rates, aptitude tests, and the number of graduates that enter into university. Internally, the company can measure new business and revenue.

Today, most companies engage in some sort of charitable activity. Unfortunately, few are good at it. Worse, being a mediocre or terribly inefficient charity seems to be perfectly acceptable. The amount of money that a company gives away seems to overshadow whether it generates any measurable impact. That should not be the case.

Companies should seek to maximize the value-creation of their philanthropic activities just like they do their corporate ones. Ironically, when companies analyze their business operations they continually evaluate performance. Rarely would a successful company invest in a new product or new market without fully analyzing the potential for that new business line to succeed. Companies constantly self-evaluate for efficiency, return on investment, and potential for growth in the future. This gets lost when it comes to corporate philanthropy. It's a missed opportunity and one that could help solve chronically underfunded social and environmental challenges.

Cigar Family is managed much like a firm, including measuring its return on investment (ROI). In this case, it measures its "return on charitable investment." Rather than having to react to random requests that show up on its doorstep, Cigar Family can be strategic and concentrate on solving specific challenges in the communities they depend on.

IDDI, the not-for-profit partner, recognized that it could support its long-standing mission to reduce poverty by partnering with a company and creating an innovative revenue-generating structure for community development. This is exactly the type of mutually beneficial partnership between foundations and corporations that needs further exploration.

My visit to Cigar Family was not coincidental. I had heard about their unique structure and thought we could pick their brains about how to set-up a "Punta Cana Family." If Cigar Family had developed a formula for fundraising that also helped their brand, it might also work for us.

This is another point often lost on not-for-profit foundations. When something works for one organization, why not share the experience with others? Imitation is the highest form of flattery. I wasn't too proud to recognize that Cigar Family had devised a successful strategy that our foundation could learn from and potentially take advantage of.

FAIL AND SHARE

In his Ted Talk "Shut Up and Listen," author and consultant Ernesto Sirolli recounts how, as a young aid worker, he and his Italian colleagues set about teaching Zambians to grow their own food. They had been surprised to learn that the Africans had no agriculture, despite possessing terrific soil and ideal growing conditions.

Determined to help the Zambians, Sirolli and his team brought in Italian agricultural experts and bags of tomato seeds. In short order they had planted crops along the fertile banks of the Zambezi River. As expected, they produced a bumper crop of vegetables. "Look how easy it is to grow tomatoes here," they boasted to the Zambians. "This is what you need to do to get out of poverty."

However, just as the tomatoes became red, ripe, and ready to harvest, two hundred hippopotamuses emerged from the river and ate the entire crop. The project was ruined. The Italians were horrified. The amused Zambians explained, "That's why we don't have agriculture here. The hippos." The stunned aid workers questioned why they hadn't warned them. "Because you never asked us," they responded.

Undoubtedly the Zambians knew the hippos would gorge on the Italians' crops before they ever planted them. The moral of the story according to Sirolli: "Shut up and listen." Foundations repeatedly commit blunders in developing countries for one simple reason: they don't listen to the local people. Local knowledge, though seeming unsophisticated, is frequently the key ingredient to pulling off successful projects. According to Sirolli's experience, the simplest way to solve global challenges is to ask questions and listen to people.

However, this story hints at another weakness that routinely affects well-meaning foundations: they don't share their failures. The Italians were unlikely the first group to come to Zambia to help pull the villagers out of poverty. They probably weren't even the first well-intentioned foreigners to try to grow crops on the fertile, but hippo-lined, banks of the Zambezi. What makes Sirolli's story unique is his willingness to share what went wrong in the hopes that other organizations avoid the same mistakes, achieving better results going forward. In fact, he wrote a book about his many mistakes in Africa: *Ripples from the Zambezi*. Instead of papering over his flops, he made a virtue out of sharing them.

For not-for-profits, sharing failure is not the norm. Because so many foundations survive on a steady diet of donor funding, they are hesitant, or even downright resistant, to admit to short-comings in their work. If an organization proposes a project and it doesn't work out as predicted, there is a justifiable fear that donors won't fund their proposals in the future. So foundations typically keep quiet when they fail.

The unintended consequence is that organizations knowingly propose flawed ideas, which have likely failed many times before, to unknowing donors. Despite having already been proven unsuccessful in practice, a proposal can still seem plausible on paper. Unfortunately, one silent failure can become a domino of ongoing failures into the future.

KAYAKS RUN AGROUND

In 2010 I got a call from a colleague (I'll call him Gary), leading an ecotourism project in the Dominican Republic. The goal was to promote different modalities of tourism in the DR besides sun and sand beach tourism. His organization had observed that the DR possessed a wealth of natural and cultural attractions, on par with the ecotourism magnet Costa Rica. Yet besides the beach, these Dominican gems were undervalued and under-visited. Gary proposed that, with proper guidance, these sites could be transformed into nature-based ecotourism, producing new jobs and economic opportunities for communities previously untouched by tourism.

In Punta Cana, Gary proposed a new kayak excursion at the nearby Bavaro Lagoon. The lagoon is a large wetland surrounded by mangroves, providing habitat for loads of birds and aquatic life. There are a handful of hotels nearby, but most consider the lagoon a mosquito-infested swamp, not a tourist attraction. The kayak excursion would, in theory, rehabilitate the lagoon's unpleasant appearance and make it an ecotourism magnet.

After receiving funding from an international donor, Gary's team pushed ahead, buying a dozen kayaks, paddles, and life jackets. They convinced a handful of community members to become guides and dutifully trained them in identifying waterfowl and aquatic plants. They took staged photos of tourists observing birds and wildlife, which they printed into posters and brochures.

Then Gary and company waited for the tourists to show up for the excursion.

They never did. The scheme was sound conceptually, but it had a fatal flaw: Gary had ignored how fiercely competitive the excursion market in Punta Cana is. Selling tours is one of the most brutally cutthroat segments in the tourism industry. Though there are millions of visitors a year, the market is saturated with excursion operators offering every kind of tour imaginable. Swim with the dolphins, catamaran booze-cruises, sugarcane jeep safaris, zip-lines, snorkeling, Segways, even a trip that involves dipping your toes into a bucket of feet-cleaning fish.

The excursion operators rely on established tour operators to book their clients. With so many options, it is vital to curry favor and set up commission arrangements with the tour operators. Unless you possess your own marketing team, there is little chance anyone will come on your kayak tours without a tour operator. Even then, the tour operators will do their best to send their clients only to excursions where they reap a profit.

Gary is an environmental education specialist. He can identify a snowy egret from a football field distance. He can explain the fascinating natural history of a mangrove swamp and he is a charismatic and likeable guy. But he has no idea how to run a kayak business, much less compete with established excursions with decades of experience in Punta Cana. His organization had written the kayak proposal but had no plan to sell it. As the saying goes, a goal without a plan is a wish. Gary assumed that if he bought the kayaks and trained the guides, eager ecotourists would line up on their own.

What was more shocking was that Gary's organization had already attempted the kayak scheme in other Dominican communities with the same results! In addition to Bavaro Lagoon, Gary's kayak scheme had failed everywhere it was tried. Each community was left with a pile of unused kayaks and trained (but still unemployed) guides. Besides a ribbon-cutting ceremony to launch operations, there have been few, if any, paid kayak excursions since the project began ten years earlier.

Using kayaks to pull local people out of poverty and into the tourism economy is a perfectly sensible idea. It might have actually worked if Gary had taken Sirolli's advice and asked for the input of local people. Unfortunately, Gary's plan was pre-packaged. He never asked the locals if Bavaro Lagoon or the other towns had their own hippos.

PIVOT POINT

In start-up businesses, admitting when something isn't working and adapting the existing business model is known as a "pivot." If the original plan stumbles, the company consciously recognizes the need to adjust to the realities of the market. In fact, having the courage and wherewithal to pivot before it is too late is considered a virtue for a young CEO.

Not so for foundations. Foundations are often unwilling, or even prohibited, from pivoting. Donors can be inflexible about allowing changes to a project, even when it's clear it's not working. Foundations tend to blur the lines, chalking up clear failures as successes to avoid impacting future funding. When they do knowingly fail, they avoid talking about it; it's just business as usual.

Despite failure in community after community, Gary kept buying more kayaks, betting the scheme would eventually work somewhere. The project's success was measured by the number of people trained and the number of kayaks purchased, not the number of customers, new jobs, or revenue generated.

There were plenty of questions Gary could have asked to improve the chance of succeeding. Were there other *successful* kayak excursions around and what were the conditions that made those excursions work? Was it the outgoing and fun-loving guides? Was it the incredible wildlife viewing? Was there an Instagram-able attraction where visitors just had to get selfies? Maybe stand-up paddle boards had become more fashionable than kayaks and he should think about changing equipment. Whatever the case, the easiest way to find answers is to talk to local people.

If the DR didn't have examples, he could have looked for functioning examples in similar places. In Fajardo, Puerto Rico, for example, there is a night kayak excursion where guests paddle through a mangrove swamp to an open saltwater lagoon. The lagoon is filled with bioluminescent bacteria that make the water glow like a swarm of fireflies. Visitors paddle out at dusk, gliding through the mangroves as it gets dark. Once in the lagoons, the kayakers splash their paddles in the water, causing it to light up like liquid fireworks. The tour attracts thousands of visitors and has created the type of nature-based ecotourism economy Gary was after. Did the DR have a similar attraction that could be promoted?

Gary should have simply admitted that it wasn't working as he originally planned and made changes. Instead, there are piles of unused kayaks scattered around the DR collecting dust.

EMBRACE YOUR ENEMY

In the seminal book *Encounters with the Archdruid*, author John McPhee attempts to understand some of the deep-seated distrust between environmentalists and developers. He takes the militant environmentalist, David Brower, on a series of field trips to commune with three ideological foes: a geologist that helps develop mines, a US politician responsible for many of the dams in the American West, and a real estate developer. Charles Fraser, the resort developer, coined the term "druids" for environmentalists, characterizing them as "religious figures who sacrifice people and worship trees."

One of the most thought-provoking books in the ecological genre, McPhee's work explores the philosophical divide that separates a hardline environmentalist from men with profoundly diverging ideas about land use, exploitation of natural resources, and man's relation to Nature. Only by bringing these philosophical adversaries into intimately close contact is it possible to reveal the nuances of each side's argument. Ultimately, the adversaries grow to respect one another's viewpoint. McPhee seems to argue that these competing factions would do well to listen to each other more often.

What if McPhee introduced David Brower to the CEO of Walmart? Walmart is one of the world's largest and most powerful department stores, as well as the largest grocer in the United States. Their single-minded focus on delivering low-cost goods has made Walmart a driver of consumerism in the US. It has also led to labor issues, accusations of mistreatment of employees, and cutthroat practices with goods providers. The company's carbon footprint equals that of entire countries. For most of its history, Walmart was not a player in sustainability. Peter Seligman, a modern-day druid, changed that.

ROB WALTON GOES DIVING

Peter Seligman is the founder and then-CEO of the influential environmental organization, Conservation International (CI). As legend has it, one day Seligman convinced Walmart chairman Rob Walton to join him scuba diving. (Walton also sat in on a CI Board meeting and learned about the issues firsthand from the organization's leaders.)

Seligman challenged Walton, a conservation neophyte, to do more. Why not wield Walmart's biggest negative impact on the environment, its size, to produce positive results? The sway the company commands is so massive, Seligman reasoned, that its every purchasing decision has worldwide impact. When Walmart does something, it produces a global chain reaction amongst suppliers, competitors, and customers. Couldn't Walmart use its vast commercial power to protect the planet? Seligman dared Walton to overcome his corporate timidity about environmental issues and utilize his company as a sustainability change agent.

In the ensuing years, Walmart has developed a far-reaching sustainability agenda with dramatic results. Walmart used its focus on providing low-cost products to innovate new cost-saving strategies in its entire global operation, simultaneously reducing its energy consumption and carbon footprint. The company modernized its shipping and transportation operations, implementing cutting-edge tracking technologies to save money and fuel. It invested in renewable energy and energy efficiency in all of its stores, reducing operating costs. All told, Walmart was able to eliminate millions of metric tons of greenhouse gas emissions while staying entirely with its mission "to save people money so they can live better."

Beyond improving its energy performance, Walmart is one of the largest supermarkets and consumer goods stores on Earth. The products and goods it sells can literally reshape consumer preferences, as well as what its competitors sell. In particular, Walmart has the capacity to expand the market for sustainable products.

For example, Walmart raised its standards for its seafood providers, heavily endorsing Marine Stewardship Council (MSC) certified brands in its grocery department. Offering a "blue fish label," MSC certifies seafood products, allowing consumers to verify that their purchases are sustainably sourced. This means the products are caught from the wild (rather than produced in damaging methods of aquaculture), don't contribute to overfishing, and utilize sustainable practices that avoid non-target species such as dolphins and turtles. MSC is the most reliable and widely recognized sustainable certification for seafood.

With the volume of seafood Walmart sells, its competitors, including many large grocers in America, had to learn, at the very least, what MSC meant. Many incorporated the certification into their sales. Suppliers had to research where to get certified brands. A fringe certification program suddenly became commonplace in many large grocers. Walmart helped MSC achieve the type of scalability other sustainable certifications struggle to achieve.

Walmart also prioritized the sale of more eco-friendly products. It placed energy efficient light bulbs on the shelves of high-traffic areas of their stores, giving them a sales boost over more damaging bulbs. Eventually it phased out the sale of inefficient light bulbs entirely. Walmart prioritized the sale of organic milk and in a very short time became one of the largest providers of organic milk on the planet. Organic milk became a mainstream product, not just one you could find in a health food store. If you were a dairy farmer or milk producer, you had to figure out how to make it organic, and fast.

Walmart worked with suppliers to transform product

packaging, reducing the amount of fuel they consumed in transportation of goods, while decreasing the amount of garbage each product generated. For example, they convinced a detergent manufacturer to reduce the packaging size of their product by offering concentrated detergents in smaller packages. In exchange, Walmart would place the detergent in prime real estate in its stores or produce specials to get the product in front of customers.

By achieving reduced packaging on this single product, Walmart saved on shipping and stocking, and freed up shelf space for new products. Walmart actually saved money by simply convincing suppliers to redesign their packaging, at almost no cost to themselves. By leveraging its global influence within a single product category, Walmart single-handedly forced a sweeping change among all detergent suppliers.

THE WALMART EFFECT

In his book, *The Walmart Effect*, Charles Fishman uses the phrase title of his book as shorthand for the range of both positive and negative impacts resulting from the way Walmart does business. He outlines the many negative ways that Walmart's business model hurts communities, ecosystems, and small businesses. Yet its single-minded focus on achieving savings is well-suited to saving energy, reducing waste, transforming products, and making environmentally friendly products more affordable. Walmart has discovered how sustainability can be harnessed in support of its mission and continue to be profitable.

This is just one example of how a giant company, generally seen as a blight on the environment, is capable of enforcing its will, in a positive way, to support the environment. By no means is Walmart the perfect citizen. Good behavior in environmental practices doesn't absolve the company from other shortcomings.

There is still much criticism of the brand (and more recently, its prime competitor in consumerism, Amazon). Many argue no matter what it does to reduce its footprint, Walmart will always represent a net negative on society.

However, it is undeniable that harnessing the size, power, and efficiency of global brands like Walmart offers huge potential to make environmental gains. Walmart is capable of influencing consumers, competition, and ultimately global markets. Environmental organizations must be willing to take the risk to engage them, challenge them to do better, and help them figure out how to get there. Conservation International took a big risk engaging with Walmart. They put their credibility on the line, but the results were significant.

This approach is becoming increasingly common. The Nature Conservancy, the world's largest environmental foundation, spent close to a decade headed by a former investment banker from Goldman Sachs, Mark Tercek. In his book, *Nature's Fortune*, Tercek makes the argument that companies can benefit financially from environmentally based decisions that ultimately reduce costs, increase revenue, and enhance return on investment.

Tercek's point of view is more in keeping with a corporate CEO, rather than a typical foundation leader. Not only is The Nature Conservancy run more like a business, it is forming partnerships with some of the largest corporations in the world to achieve more substantial environmental commitments. It might not be too late for the druids to learn from their nemeses.

THE SLEEPING GIANT WITHIN

GRUPO PUNTACANA'S UNIQUE HISTORY SERVES AS A CASE study in sustainability. However, GPC's experience is by no means an instruction manual for other companies. For one, the challenges the company faces in the tourism industry are constantly evolving, as are the solutions needed to confront them. Today's COVID-19 or seaweed invasion will likely be something different in the future.

Likewise, specific actions that have worked in Punta Cana can only serve as a rough guide for how other businesses can approach sustainability. They are not a blueprint. The exact solutions that worked for GPC may not be replicable in other tourism companies, much less companies in other industries. However, that doesn't mean they aren't valuable.

By sharing the experiences of Grupo Puntacana, my aim is to provide a unique perspective on how to get sustainability done and, more importantly, to inspire other companies to get started looking for creative solutions to their problems. Often sustainability is a matter of perspective. Getting a peek behind the curtains of how one company got into it can help business leaders relate, demystifying what is often presented as an overly complicated subject. Sustainability is not easy, but it doesn't have to be complex, either.

In the final chapter, we'll look at several key takeaways from different examples of companies that have unlocked the extraordinary power businesses possess to both improve their fortunes, as well as make the world a better place.

Before that, though, let me start with a little cautionary tale of a hard-learned lesson from getting it wrong.

NATURE'S DIVERSITY LESSONS

Some ideas seem just too good to be true. PlayPumps was an eye-catching technology that fused two admirable objectives: children playing and the production of clean drinking water for poor communities. Bursting onto the development scene in the late 1990s, PlayPumps harnessed the energy produced by children spinning on a merry-go-round to pump drinking water from a well up to an elevated storage tank. It was a simple yet brilliant idea. Drinking water would be continuously pumped by joyfully playing children, providing consistent water for the community. The village women would no longer have to walk far and wide to fetch water, saving them from the exhausting and time-consuming effort. All the while, the PlayPumps would improve community health.

PlayPumps seemingly solved a problem that was common throughout the developing world: lack of easily accessible water and massive time and effort required to find it. The concept caught on quickly. In 2000, PlayPumps won the World Bank Development Marketplace Award before attracting support from then-First Lady Laura Bush. In 2006, Pepfar, the US President's Emergency Plan for AIDS Relief, announced the establishment of a public-private partnership with Play-Pumps worth an estimated $60 million, with $10 million to come directly from the US government. PlayPumps International announced an ambitious global campaign to deploy four thousand PlayPumps across thousands of villages throughout sub-Saharan Africa, providing clean drinking water to ten million people by 2010. PlayPumps received expansive media coverage and attracted financial support from prominent philanthropic charities.

Playpump's global rollout quickly ran into problems. The first issue was price. It turned out that individual PlayPumps cost $14,000 to build and install, about the same amount as *several* conventional (and less sexy) hand pumps. Despite the robust fundraising prowess of PlayPump's promoters, they would be able to provide far fewer total pumps than more established (and less expensive) pumps for the same money.

PlayPump's design created other drawbacks. In order to match the water output of a traditional handpump, it required an absurd number of hours of energy, in the form of children playing, to meet a small village's minimum water requirements. By some estimates, PlayPumps required as many as twenty-four hours of non-stop playing on the merry-go-round to meet local water demand. This raised the moral question of whether this constituted child labor as opposed to child's play.

Because it required more energy to operate than originally calculated, in many cases it didn't solve the problem it had set out to. Instead of children blissfully spinning, many PlayPumps were operated by teams of village women drudgingly pushing the wheel to produce water. The new technology simply replaced the long trek to retrieve water in plastic "jerry" cans with hours manually forcing PlayPumps to fill a cistern.

Finally, as many experts pointed out, PlayPumps provided a solution to the wrong problem. The primary water issues in many African villages are water *scarcity* and water *quality*. Many villages simply don't have enough potable groundwater close enough to the surface to tap into. Nearby water is often too contaminated, silty, or salty to use for drinking water. The reason villagers have to walk far and wide to fill their jerry cans is the lack of clean water nearby. PlayPumps do not disinfect dirty water and as such contributed little to solve this problem.

Similarly, if the locally available water supply doesn't meet current demand, PlayPumps don't increase local water supply. They don't access new sources of water; they simply pump from existing sources. In many cases, by increasing the draw on already scarce water resources, Playpumps may have caused wells to dry even faster.

Under growing scrutiny, in 2010, PlayPumps International shuttered its operations and donated its remaining inventory to Water for People (WfP). Water for People would deploy the pumps as one tool in a more diversified strategy to address water issues on a village by village basis, depending on their specific challenges.

A SUSTAINABILITY TOOLBOX

An article titled "The PlayPump: What Went Wrong," by Daniel Stellar of the Columbia University Water Center, emphasizes that water supply itself is the most critical factor in the challenge of accessing potable water in any given community.* Water issues are multifaceted and particular to each case; therefore, no one-size-fits-all solution, such as PlayPumps, could adequately address water concerns on a global basis.

The story of PlayPumps proved, the hard way, that water

---

* Daniel Stellar, "The PlayPump: What Went Wrong," *State of the Planet*, News from the Earth Institute, Columbia University, July 1, 2010, https://blogs.ei.columbia. edu/2010/07/01/the-playpump-what-went-wrong.

issues are sensitive to local conditions. PlayPumps hit on an ingenious idea that was terrifically suited to certain situations, but in the end, it failed in many others. What works in one village in Africa can't always be replicated somewhere else, even in another nearby village. More often than not, more than a single solution, complex problems like water demand a toolbox of solutions.

To their credit, many of the project's donors and foundations admitted PlayPumps' failure to meet its much-hyped objectives. Importantly, they decided that failure *was* an option. Rather than pressing on or covering up PlayPumps' shortcomings, they made it a virtue to cut their losses on a global roll-out and give the pumps to experts that could deploy them sensibly. They also wrote about the experience, sharing what did and didn't work so that others could learn from them.

Sustainability practitioners can learn a lot from the Play-Pumps of the world. New breakthrough ideas and technological inventions have long over-promised on their ability to solve complicated global issues, while under-delivering when actually attempted at any reasonable scale. This was a particularly high-profile example.

The truth is that the social and environmental challenges we face across the globe are overwhelmingly complex. Local conditions are diverse. The need to deploy a diversity of solutions is an obvious takeaway. There is rarely a cure-all that works everywhere. Claiming so is not only disingenuous, but often leads to wasting precious resources on untested technologies and ideas. This is an uncomfortable fact for many development organizations and donors, especially when they come across a sexy new idea that impresses donors and boosts their funding. Yet banking on trendy concepts has led to countless reprises of the failed PlayPumps experience.

If there is one single lesson this book hopes to impart, it's that sustainability requires an adherence to that old environmental adage, "Think Global, Act Local." While the scale of the adversity we face requires us to think big, more often than not, long-lasting solutions demand that we start small.

Like Nature itself, sustainability must be designed to respond to *local* conditions. A healthy ecosystem bursts with myriad species that have been forced to develop unique survival strategies designed for that specific place. Each species has evolved to thrive and compete in its particular environment, but those strategies will likely fail in new locations if not adapted to new conditions. Sustainability too, needs to be able to adapt to local situations. We must first understand the problem in its proper context and then design appropriate, custom solutions.

Likewise, Nature has evolved to favor diversity. In agriculture, a monoculture of a single species, like corn or wheat, is far more susceptible to disease, changes in climate, or pests than a more varied cropping system. A diverse agro-ecosystem is more resilient to change and able to withstand different stressors.

The same concept applies to sustainability. There is no single, one-off solution for the diversity of challenges we face. Play-Pumps alone couldn't solve a global water crisis, but perhaps they can form part of a larger array of solutions that can be mixed and matched to suit different circumstances. As the Columbia Water Center accurately pointed out, there is no panacea. Global problems are complex, coming in a "multitude of flavors." Successfully attaining a goal of sustainability calls for solutions of many flavors.

SAVE ONE PLACE AT A TIME

In 1997, Julia "Butterfly" Hill ascended 180 feet up an emblematic redwood tree (later named "Luna") in Humboldt County, California. The act was meant to stave off the Pacific Lumber

Company from clear-cutting the nearby redwood forest. For over two years (738 days exactly), Butterfly lived on two six-by-six-foot platforms in Luna. She called in to radio interviews with a solar-powered cell phone, hosted television crews to protest old-growth clear-cutting, and even became an "in-tree" news correspondent for a cable station. Her presence in the tree generated international media coverage, infuriated loggers, and started a national conversation about the role of environmental activism. Julia was my generation's Greta Thunberg.

In 1999, redwood activists and the Pacific Lumber Company came to an agreement to preserve Luna and a two hundred-foot buffer zone of nearby trees. After a long but ultimately successful battle, Butterfly finally came down from Luna.

Julia Butterfly Hill is the embodiment (albeit an extreme one) of "acting local." It doesn't get more local than using yourself as a human shield for two years to protect one redwood tree. She effectively transformed her crusade to save a larger tract of forest into a fight over a single tree. While not all environmental conservation needs to take such a confrontational approach, Butterfly makes a strong case for an idea that *is* fundamental to achieving sustainability goals: choosing to defend one place relentlessly and without distraction.

Unfortunately, this is not always the case with sustainability practitioners. In fact, a significant challenge facing the field of sustainability is the short attention span of many of its acolytes. International organizations and activists are famous for continuously bouncing around to save new places, like bees pollinating new flowers. In the field of environmental protection, the resume of many prominent conservationists looks more like that of a travel blogger than someone defending a specific ecosystem. From Africa, to Latin America, to the Pacific, environmentalists are planet-saving globetrotters, rarely sticking around to defend just one place.

Scientists are not much better. They migrate from old to new study sites, following their curiosity and available research funding, before moving on to new subjects, hypotheses, and new locations. The most prominent researchers appear to spend their careers on airplanes, dropping in and out of new communities and ecosystems, testing out new ideas along the way. This constant migration makes for a colorful career, but how effective is it in actually saving the environment?

Measuring environmental change, good or bad, requires decades. Yet environmentalists seem to be attempting to save the planet on their own abbreviated travel schedules. With so little continuity, it is not surprising to see the spotty record of results and mixed progress in conservation. Driven in part by the ever-changing priorities of donors and large organizations, this constant migration is exacerbated by the restlessness of people working in sustainability. If we don't have the patience and perseverance to stick around one specific place over a long period of time, can we really expect to wage a successful battle to defend it?

A BORN-AGAIN CONSERVATIONIST

University of Pennsylvania professor Dan Janzen makes a powerful argument for the importance of continuity in one site. Janzen spent the better part of his distinguished career as a tropical ecologist and evolutionary biologist with a single-minded focus on producing scholarship. Finding new places to study meant mimicking the planet-spanning travel of many researchers. Janzen published hundreds of journal articles from tropical forests around the world, including Mexico, Africa, India, Southeast Asia, Australia, and Costa Rica. His prolific scientific output helped him rack up some of science's most prestigious awards.

Often this single-minded focus led him to ignore the quickly degrading conditions of the habitats he was studying. He believed his job was "to study forests, not save them—the latter is the conservationist's task." Scientists weren't activists, according to Janzen, they should remain detached from the forces disturbing forests and concentrate on understanding the complex web of relationships found there.

Eventually though, the reality of rapidly declining forest health became too obvious to overlook. If Janzen didn't do something to stop the destruction of his research subjects, he wouldn't have anything left to study. With that, Janzen became a "born-again conservationist." With his expansive knowledge of the worlds' most diverse tropical forests, Janzen easily could have become another global conservation ambassador. Instead, he dedicated his life's work to protecting a single habitat in a single place: the dry forests of Guanacaste, Costa Rica.

In his book *Green Phoenix*, William Allen describes how Janzen used his considerable clout as a scientist, and most of his ongoing research, to spearhead conservation efforts in Guanacaste. Rather than dedicating his limited time to save *all* tropical forests, he hitched his expertise to Costa Rica. Building a vast coalition and working closely with local politicians, scientists, and communities, Janzen helped form an alliance that successfully reversed the fortunes of highly impacted dry forest. The Guanacaste team expanded the small, underfunded and barely managed Guanacaste National Park in northwestern Costa Rica into a 300,000-acre reserve: the Guanacaste Conservation Area, or ACG.

Along the way, Janzen converted his intimate understanding of the myriad issues facing the ACG into a one-stop shop for policymaking, fundraising, publicity, and scientific research. His deep familiarity with local conditions provided a critical lesson: What works in one place may not work in Guanacaste. "One shirt does not fit all, by any means," Janzen commented.

In Costa Rica, he got to know the players and the threats, so he could adapt long-term conservation strategies to changing political realities. Instead of showing up on summer vacation after classes let out, he was engaged with the ACG full time, helping the managers confront a revolving door of fresh challenges: forest fires, rogue cattle ranchers, lack of boots for park guards, and the egos of politicians.

Unfortunately, Janzen's tenacious obsession on a single ecosystem doesn't usually fit the agenda of the largest donors. The big donors, multilaterals, and foundations spread their time and attention across time zones, cultures, and geographies worldwide, meaning limited available financial support for forests like the ACG goes to a larger, more complex not-for-profit industry. Trying to save the entire planet at once helps many of the most prominent conservation organizations' bottom-line, though it doesn't necessarily maximize benefit for any one place.

Guanacaste, however, wasn't tied to any one large organization but to many local stakeholders. It eventually became an example for other tropical countries. Janzen's long-term commitment to the ACG demonstrated an effective way to get conservation done by marrying himself to a site and defending it.

Dan Janzen and Julia Butterfly Hill are my sustainability spirit animals. They chose a single place (or tree) and defended it. I not only admire their tenacious commitment to one place, I have come to emulate it with my work in Punta Cana.

Ironically, I never envisioned betting my career on protecting a single place. When Grupo Puntacana hired me, I figured I would spend a year or two in the DR, add a few bullets to my resume and move on. My dream job was to travel the world, conserving the breathtaking landscapes and the charismatic creatures that were featured on Conservation International calendars and coffee-table books. It never occurred to me I would plant my conservation flag in one country, much less in the comfy confines of a beach resort.

But my experience in Punta Cana has taught me that some of the most important advances in sustainability come from the hardheaded devotees that fight for a single spot until it's future is more secure. Sustainability could use a lot more of this stability.

DON'T DELAY—ACT

The Iberostar Group is a prominent Spanish hotel chain mostly known for its sun-filled beach properties. Part of a sixty-year-old hotel conglomerate, Iberostar has over 120 hotels in nineteen countries. If you want to have a fun-filled all-inclusive vacation in Punta Cana, Iberostar is a good start.

Iberostar has not traditionally been known, however, for its sustainability efforts. Despite a global footprint of more than thirty-seven thousand hotel rooms, thirty-two thousand employees, and serving eight million customers a year (including the Iberostar resort built in Punta Cana in 1993), the company had been pretty timid with its social and environmental programs, especially in the Dominican Republic. Though Iberostar didn't have a bad reputation, it wasn't considered a leader, either.

In 2018, however, Iberostar jumped into the sustainability game with a splash. The company created a global chief sustainability officer position occupied by Gloria Fluxà, who is also vice chairman and fourth generation of the family-owned Iberostar Group. Iberostar used its expansive global network to connect with prominent global experts and launch an aggressive entry into sustainability, even showing up at the World Economic Forum to talk to thought leaders about sustainability.

Most noteworthy, Iberostar launched the Waves of Change

program. The new company-wide initiative sought to "contribute to the conservation of seas and oceans and the sustainability of the resources obtained from them."

Critically, Iberostar kept it simple. It realized that its core business depends primarily on healthy coastlines and beaches. Rather than creating an overly complicated agenda or trying to check every box in the expansive United Nations "Sustainable Development Goals," it zeroed in on three core areas directly relevant to its hotel business: reduce its contribution of ocean plastics, prioritize the purchase of sustainable seafood options, and protect coastal ecosystems.

SAYONARA STRAWS

First, the company banned plastic straws and single-use plastics throughout its resorts. At all-inclusive resorts, the customer generally pays a single rate for food, beverage, and lodging for the entirety of their stay. When Iberostar's customers order a beverage, it is already part of their vacation package, whether or not it includes fruit, ice, or a straw.

By purging plastic straws altogether, the company eliminated ten million straws annually from its supply chain, a savings reflected on its bottom line, but with minimal impact on the guest experience. (Guests typically use each straw for an average of two to three minutes total, so it's doubtful they get very attached to them.)

The same held true for other single-use, disposable products. By making simple changes in its purchasing policies and the way it serves its beverages, Iberostar no longer purchases as many wasteful products. They could either buy more sustainable options or simply stop offering one-and-done materials, like throwaway plastic cups, within their resorts. They achieve savings both in reduced expenses, but also by reducing the overall amount of waste the resort produces, reducing its waste-hauling fees. When you consider the savings the eliminating of disposable products can produce across thirty-seven thousand hotel rooms globally, eliminating straws and single-use products is a program any CFO can get behind.

SOURCING SUSTAINABLE SEAFOOD

Iberostar also dug into sourcing sustainable foods, particularly seafood. In the Caribbean, this can be a lot harder than it sounds. For hotels in cities in the US or Europe, finding sustainable food options is a matter of calling up the right vendor and getting a reasonable price. Nowadays restaurants offer everything from organic and farm-to-table to gluten-free, free-range, and foraged. Even "misfits" foods (imperfect or slightly ugly fruits and vegetables) have earned a place in the lineup. The options for specialty foods are seemingly endless.

On the other hand, many Caribbean islands have limited agricultural production. There are almost no free-range options on speed dial. It can be challenging to find locally produced ingredients, much less certified organic varieties. Much of what the Caribbean consumes, it imports. New and exotic food categories are just starting to show up on Caribbean menus.

Sourcing sustainable seafood options is especially challenging in the Caribbean. This seems counterintuitive because when we think of Caribbean islands, we picture the catch-of-the-day getting hauled fresh off a local fisherman's boat. We imagine a Caribbean Sea stocked full of fresh fish bounty. Yet much like the DR, many Caribbean fisheries are stressed. They don't produce nearly as much seafood as we imagine. Overexploited fisheries reduce available seafood options, or as we have seen, drive fishermen to "fish down the food web" and target critical species.

On top of this, all-inclusive hotels like Iberostar offer expansive food buffets. Finding local seafood at that scale is generally out of the question. It has to be imported from other countries. Though hotels are generally able to import sufficient seafood to stock their restaurants, sourcing *sustainable* seafood adds more work and costs than most hotels are willing to take on.

Nonetheless, Iberostar persisted. As a large resort, Iberostar realized it could use its purchasing power to apply pressure on its seafood vendors to locate new product categories. In particular, they were able to source previously unavailable Marine Stewardship Council (MSC) certified fish and shellfish (just like Walmart). Though imported, they found several sustainably harvested species at a scale they could use at their resort restaurants.

Iberostar got what it wanted from vendors and this benefited other hotels in Punta Cana as well. Grupo Puntacana, with 300 total hotel rooms, is relatively small compared to Iberostar. GPC alone doesn't generate the kind of seafood sales from its vendors that would motivate them to go out of their way to find MSC-certified products. Iberostar, however, was big enough to not only find MSC products, but to buy enough of them to make the price competitive with non-certified products. This meant that Iberostar had unintentionally made MSC products available locally to other resorts like ours. When big resorts dig into sustainability it can have a positive ripple effect on other hotels nearby.

AN ENVIRONMENTAL AWAKENING

Finally, Iberostar turned its attention to protecting coastal ecosystems. In the Dominican Republic, the company hired a Stanford PhD to study corals near its resorts and to begin coral restoration efforts. Iberostar's team met with our Foundation and other coral restoration practitioners in the Caribbean to explore ways to work together. Eventually, Iberostar built a land-based nursery as an exhibition space for their guests to learn about threats to coral reefs. They plan to ramp up restoration efforts in the coming years at all of their properties.

It is entirely reasonable to be skeptical of Iberostar's sudden environmental awakening. After sixty years without paying much mind to the ocean (despite operating a business that depends on beautiful beaches), Iberostar abruptly attained environmental enlightenment. The company committed itself to protecting the sea, surging from non-factor to marine pioneer in the space of a year and a half.

Regardless of why Iberostar got involved or how long it took them, the potential benefit to coral reefs and the ocean is huge. It took decades, but the company eventually made the connection between the sea and its bottom-line. Now it appears to be building a credible, long-term marine conservation program. By any measure, adding a global hotel brand like Iberostar to the fight for the ocean should be considered a victory for the environment.

In fact, Iberostar is exactly the type of Sleeping Giant that we should be trying to recruit to the sustainability movement. The urgency of threats means we simply don't have time to fixate on Iberostar's rationale. There's too much work to do. As long as Iberostar remains committed to protecting the sea in the present and future, it's reasonable to be less concerned with what they did or didn't do in the past.

Ulysses S. Grant, the decorated civil war hero and former president of the United States, once remarked about war-time decision-making, "Anything is better than indecision. We must decide. If I am wrong, we shall soon find out and can do the other thing. But not to decide wastes both time and money and may ruin everything." His point was not to waste time and resources over-thinking every decision, or to hand wring over past choices. You need to act decisively, even if it means making mistakes. Start now.

Iberostar easily could have spent another decade or two dabbling around in assorted marine initiatives while slowly devising a long-term strategy to help protect the ocean. Instead they decided to go big and act right away. Rather than paralysis by analysis, they aggressively pursued a new mission. With the current state of the oceans under such severe threat, Iberostar should be applauded for its boldness.

Similarly, start simple. Iberostar made a strategic decision of where their efforts could do the most good, both for the environment and their company. By focusing on the sea, Iberostar linked the most important natural resource their business relies on to their sustainability efforts. Getting rid of single-use plastics, improving purchasing and protecting local reefs are straightforward, quantifiable goals.

Admittedly, one of Grupo Puntacana's biggest shortcomings as a sustainability pioneer is how few fellow hoteliers in the region have followed our lead. While the hotels in the region respect our commitment, most of us at GPC think of ourselves as an outlier in the industry. Our resort neighbors have long suspected that sustainability is Frank Rainieri's quirky hobby, but not necessarily the key to his business success. The most common excuse is that Grupo Puntacana is not an all-inclusive hotel, so it doesn't face the same challenges the larger hotel chains face. The hoteliers praise our efforts but they don't follow our example.

However, what if Iberostar Group is the first domino to fall, producing a chain reaction amongst other all-inclusive hotel chains in the Punta Cana region? If Iberostar can do it in the DR, why not throughout the Caribbean? There are many hotels that look a lot like Iberostar. If Iberostar is capable of inducing other hoteliers to take up the sustainability cause, it would be a major victory for the tourism industry. Companies like Grupo Puntacana should support companies like Iberostar, even if they are late entries to sustainability.

Though often seen as business *leaders*, CEO's are often business *followers*. By aggressively pursuing a sustainability agenda, Iberostar Group is sending a strong market signal that is difficult for other hoteliers to ignore. Sustainable tourism is a real market tendency, not just the odd behavior of some sustainability "anomalies" like GPC. By acting, however belatedly, companies like Iberostar have the potential to make real waves of change.

AN OUNCE OF PREVENTION

In 2007 the Cisneros Foundation called me to talk trash. I was familiar with Grupo Cisneros, one of the largest and most successful family-owned businesses in Latin America. The company began in Venezuela but had transformed into a global conglomerate. I had also heard of the Cisneros Foundation, having seen artwork from their vast collection in museums. After a quick online search, I learned that the foundation also had expansive education programs. Yet I had no idea what they were up to in the DR, or why they wanted to discuss garbage.

Eventually we set a date for a visit to Punta Cana. We would spend the day touring around our resort and exploring Grupo Puntacana's different projects: schools, health clinic, Center for Sustainability and our recycling center. To my surprise, we were joined not only by the foundation staff but also by Adriana Cisneros, a top executive in the Cisneros company and the daughter of CEO Gustavo Cisneros. (Adriana would later succeed her father as CEO of Grupo Cisneros.) This was serious firepower for a courtesy visit.

As it turned out, Grupo Cisneros had recently completed

the acquisition of an expansive parcel of oceanfront land about an hour north of Punta Cana, just outside the coastal fishing village of Miches. The company was expanding beyond their traditional media and consumer products businesses to develop a high-end luxury resort development. Tropicalia, the name of the new project, would be embedded from day one with a strong emphasis in sustainability, I was told. They came to Punta Cana to glean some ideas to make that happen.

As I learned, Cisneros Foundation has extensive experience implementing education and cultural programs throughout Latin America. Besides a vast art collection with curricula combining art and learning, the foundation had led literacy programs throughout the region. It was clear they wouldn't need a lot of help from us with education programs.

Cisneros Foundation, however, had little experience in sustainable tourism, and even less in waste management. Having heard about Grupo Puntacana's Zero Waste project, they had sought me out to brainstorm ways they could launch a waste management program. The Cisneros team was particularly intrigued by our recycling facility and envisioned building something like it in Miches.

A TRASH MASTERPLAN

At the time, neither Miches nor Tropicalia had a significant garbage problem, though this was likely to change. Tropicalia was still in the planning phase but would create a great deal of trash someday soon. During the construction of the resort, they would inevitably produce leftover cement, concrete, and assorted building detritus. Once built, Tropicalia's future restaurants, homes, and staff would generate garbage that would need to be dealt with. The resort by itself was going to need a plan for its waste.

Nearby communities were also expected to grow with the arrival of jobs. Miches, a small town surrounded by a half dozen even smaller rural villages, is part of the province of El Seibo, one of the least developed regions in the country. However, as Tropicalia grew, it would need employees and contractors to work in the resort. Workers would either come from local Miches villages or move there from farther away, triggering population growth. A larger local population would increase solid waste.

With pristine, undeveloped beaches within striking distance of the Punta Cana airport, Miches was primed for development. Just as we had witnessed firsthand in Punta Cana, growth encourages growth. Tropicalia foresaw that the launch of their resort was likely to stimulate the expansion of other resorts in the region. Impending plans for Tropicalia had already motivated several Miches landowners to speed up plans for building new hotels. Once development begins, there is likely to be a half dozen or more new hotels dotting Miches' white-sand beaches.

By planning ahead and involving the local community, Tropicalia was betting it could head off a garbage problem before it turned into a real threat. Managing garbage gets exponentially more complex as you have more stakeholders, more solid waste, and more environmental risk. Miches' future trash problem would be far easier to plan for than to mitigate.

This brings us to another critical sustainability takeaway: the importance of planning ahead. As US Founding Father Benjamin Franklin is quoted as saying, "An ounce of prevention is worth a pound of cure." In other words, it's cheaper and easier to avoid problems than to try to fix them later. It was going be much harder for Tropicalia to come up with a plan to manage its waste if it was already swimming in piles of trash.

In Punta Cana, we have learned this lesson many times over. Protecting existing drinking water sources is far less expensive than building a desalinization plant later on. Protecting coral reefs is way more economical than trying to rebuild them after they have become degraded. In development projects, it is simply good business to get out in front of emerging threats before they metastasize into intractable problems. Prevention is at the core of sustainability.

The timing of Tropicalia's interest in sustainability was quite different than Grupo Iberostar. Instead of reining in thirty-seven thousand existing hotel rooms worldwide under a sustainability umbrella, Tropicalia hadn't even completed a master plan for its resort, much less begun constructing its first hotel. If all went according to plan, they were at least a few years away from operating a resort. Yet the presence of Adriana Cisneros on the site visit to our place indicated that sustainability was not going to be just a passing fancy. Tropicalia clearly was going to invest in sustainability early and often.

Soon after their visit to Punta Cana, Tropicalia hired a firm to design a recycling facility and create a business plan. The new recycling plant would cost upwards of 2 million dollars to build and operate. In theory, it would not only serve their resort, but also Miches and surrounding villages. Waste would be collected from a dozen or so small communities and transported in trucks to their sorting facility. The materials would be separated and compacted, just as they had seen on our property, and then sold to recyclers. The income from the sale of recyclables would help pay for the project. On paper, it seemed like a no-brainer. Tropicalia asked our Foundation, the area's foremost "garbage-ologists," to visit Miches and see how realistic the plan was.

GARBAGE-OLOGY 101

For one smelly weekend, my team and I ignored Miche's beautiful beaches, instead diving into the town's garbage. We trailed the garbage truck on its collection route, bagging a pre-determined sample of waste from each neighborhood based on its population. At the end of the route, we dumped the day's trash in an open field, where we separated and weighed it. It wasn't pretty, but we were able to quickly characterize and quantify the types and volumes of materials each neighborhood produced. We had a pretty reliable snapshot of Miches' garbage future.

To test the feasibility of the Tropicalia plan, we also needed to understand the cost and logistics of transporting garbage. Next, we timed and measured the exact distance between each neighboring community in Miches relative to the existing dump. If Tropicalia wanted to handle all of the local communities' solid waste, it needed to know what it would cost to move it from one place to another, especially since they planned to bring it to a central sorting facility. The DR has poor roads and sky-high fuel costs. Transportation can make or break a recycling business.

At the end of the weekend, we presented our conclusions to the Cisneros Foundation team. What became clear from our visit was that neither Tropicalia nor Miches needed a recycling plant, at least not in 2007. Unlike Grupo Puntacana, the future resort would not include an international airport, an extensive residential community, or large hotels, all of which would potentially generate large volumes of recyclable material. Tropicalia was slated to be low density and ultra-exclusive, with relatively few hotel rooms. The resort alone was unlikely to produce sufficient volume of material for commercial recyclers to be interested in making the trip to Miches to pick them up.

Likewise, Tropicalia was located in a rural area surrounded by small, isolated agricultural communities. There are no super-markets or department stores in Miches. Most "Micheros" don't spend on store-bought canned goods or soft drinks; they grow their own crops or they buy fresh fruit, vegetables, and grains at weekly markets and small bodegas. Accordingly, most of the waste the community generates is organic material from agricultural waste or food scraps. Miches doesn't produce much recyclable material, at all. More than a recycling plant, they needed worms for composting!

Additionally, each individual community is separated by long distances over terrible roads (at least at that time), making travel slow and inefficient. It would take hours for waste haulers to collect garbage in each village and transfer it to a centralized facility. This type of long-distance waste hauling is prohibitively expensive and there was little chance the government was going to subsidize it. Once sorted and packaged for sale, the recyclable materials would have to be transported again to Santo Domingo, a solid three hours away.

The high cost of waste hauling and the small amount of material made Tropicalia's recycling scheme a bust. Though disappointed, Tropicalia pressed on. They pivoted from recycling, instead deploying their vast expertise in educational programs in the local communities. After incorporating the Tropicalia Foundation in the DR, they delayed investment in a recycling plant, choosing instead to begin remaking grade schools throughout the Miches area. They improved classrooms and school infrastructure while deploying their art and culture education programs in local schools. They promoted gender equality, empowering young girls in Miches with access to new programs and training. Tropicalia Foundation expanded into local organic agricultural production and microlending for women entrepreneurs.

Over the course of a decade, the foundation built up a variety of credible programs and much trust in local communities. These same communities will likely provide staff for their resort, so forming a relationship early on made sense. In 2018, their efforts were recognized as finalists in the prestigious United

Nations World Tourism Organization Award for Innovation in Non-Governmental Organizations.

However, by far the most curious aspect of Tropicalia's sustainability efforts is that they took place without actually having a resort in place. Due to different factors (the 2008 financial collapse, difficulty with government permits, among others), Tropicalia the resort was delayed more than ten years. As of 2020, they still hadn't formally begun construction. Nonetheless, they continued investing their time, energy, and resources in the local community for over a decade, despite not having an operating resort.

This sort of preemptive sustainability is practically unheard of, especially in the tourism industry. Far more common is the opposite: resorts that discover sustainability well after different social and environmental problems are already deep-rooted and hard to solve. Tropicalia, however, embarked on a unique experiment in preparing the local community for tourism development *before* it actually took place.

Time will tell what happens in Miches as tourism takes off, but undoubtedly Grupo Cisnero's foresight produced tangible benefits for their new resort and untold financial savings preventing future problems. This is a critical sustainability lesson. An ounce of prevention in Miches could be worth future gold for Tropicalia.

FAIL FAST FORWARD

On vacation in Argentina, entrepreneur Blake Mycoskie was moved by the sight of children running barefoot on the streets. Diving into the issue, he learned about the direct corollary between unsanitary living conditions, shoeless children, and the spread of infectious diseases. Barefoot kids were exposed to more diseases. Worse, sick children were likely to miss school, creating a vicious cycle that was hard for poor families to get out of.

Mycoskie wracked his brain for a solution to the problem of barefoot kids. He ultimately came up with the start-up TOMS Shoes, a for-profit company that would donate a pair of shoes in developing countries for every pair they sold. The idea was to tie TOMS's sales with preventing children from getting foot-borne diseases. Known as a "One for One" company, TOMS attempted to produce both profit and social impact.

The One for One business model was a fast success. TOMS's business took off, as did its charitable activity. TOMS delivered tens of thousands of shoes to communities and regions in need. The company's commitment to combining good deeds with selling shoes fueled vast press coverage, and Mycoskie became a social entrepreneur rock star. TOMS's shoe donation pro-gram became ubiquitous as a sustainability concept. Mycoskie's model was replicated by other social enterprise companies in everything from women's underwear to reading glasses.

As their efforts became more visible, though, detractors began to question the effectiveness of the shoe giveaways. They doubted how much benefit the free shoes generated for the lucky kids who received them. What about shoemakers and shoe sellers in the communities where TOMS gave away its shoes? Were they hurt by the donated footwear? Besides driving TOMS's bottom-line, did the donations help the communities they intended to? Mycoskie was a "serial entrepreneur" who had started numerous different businesses before TOMS, but a relative novice in solving development issues. He took the criticism to heart.

TOMS contracted an independent study to analyze the impact of their donations around the world. The results from the deep dive on One for One were not encouraging. The research showed that recipients appreciated and used the free shoes, yet there was little evidence that the donation generated any life-changing impact. It was also not clear the donated shoes prevented foot-borne diseases as originally intended. After donating literally hundreds of thousands of shoes (and not coincidentally generating millions of dollars of revenue for TOMS), there was little measurable effect on community health, disease prevention, or schooling. Worse, the shoes seemed to make the communities more dependent on external aid. Not exactly the profound change Mycoskie had in mind.

However, what TOMS did next was not only admirable but provides another key sustainability lesson. Once they had confirmed that the shoe donation program was not having the intended impact, they pivoted. They modified the program until they got it right. Rather than retreat into a public relations bunker and hide from their mistake, they made a virtue out of fixing it. They kept iterating until they got closer to the impact they sought.

TOMS set a new course that allows consumers to support different campaigns in five areas: safe water, ending gun violence, homelessness, mental health, and equality. Just as the company diversified its products beyond shoes, it evolved the "buy one, give one away" dynamic it popularized, offering more options for giving. The purchase of TOMS sunglasses, for example, can support cataract surgery in a community in need, as opposed to a free pair of glasses. You'll support a community-owned water system in an area that lacks clean water when you buy coffee beans from TOMS Roasting Co. They continued to tie community investment to sales but diversified the ways they went about it.

SUSTAINABILITY DISRUPTORS

Researchers that undertook the study of the TOMS donation

program were impressed. In his book, *Randomistas: How Radical Researchers Are Changing Our World*, author Andrew Leigh commends TOMS's commitment to "evidence-based results" and self-evaluation, traits that few organizations and businesses tend to apply in the real world.

TOMS is an example of a company becoming a disruptive agent of change to transform an industry. TOMS deployed its unique business model to confront a serious human health problem. When that model proved to be flawed, they tweaked it until they got it right. Unlike many governments and not-for-profits, successful companies are agile and results-driven. When a product is failing, they have the experience and dexterity to adapt to changing markets. This same skill set can be applied to their investments in sustainability.

There is an important distinction between the failure of TOMS's One for One model and the PlayPumps water systems. TOMS includes the benefit of helping children at no additional cost to the consumer. The more successful the business is, the more children they help. TOMS doesn't need to persuade consumers to give them money to put shoes on kids' feet. Instead, they told consumers to buy their shoes and they would figure out how to help kids.

When the shoe donation program turned out to have problems, they used the same creativity that made their business successful in the first place. It continued to evolve the One for One program without relying on donations. TOMS embodies an experimental mindset that allows it to fail fast forward.

PlayPumps, on the other hand, sold a single technology. This required convincing donors that its transformative solution was something no one else was offering. The funds they received came with the promise that they would build PlayPumps, but they had no plan B and little room to pivot. When it turned out PlayPumps were not all they were cracked up to be, they closed shop altogether.

Like PlayPumps, though, TOMS demonstrated a thick-skinned maturity when they discovered their program had flaws. Instead of growing defensive, they owned the problem, shared it transparently and went about getting it right. Though TOMS's business has run into some trouble recently (creditors took over), it undoubtedly made a lasting impact on business and fashion. It was one of the first brands to imbed a social mission in its operations, making the idea mainstream.

Grupo Puntacana has emulated this experimental mind-set. When our worm compost produced eggplants on the golf course fairway, we went back to the drawing board until we honed in on a seed-free compost. When we couldn't get fisher-men to catch and sell invasive lionfish to our chefs, we trained their wives to make money on stuffed lionfish, and the women put the screws to their husbands to catch lionfish.

We fail repeatedly but try to stay nimble in our approach, constantly evolving until we get it right. Sustainability requires a determined, purpose-driven mindset. Put another way: sus-tainability requires sustainability.

SOWING THE SUSTAINABILITY SPORE

Mr. Wilson's Cabinet of Wonder is an oddball book that chroni-cles the role and history of museums, particular the 16th century custom of creating physical "cabinets of curiosities." One of the central characters in the book is an ant species called the Prong-horned ant. According to the book, Prong-horned ants live in large ant colonies foraging on the forest floor. One day, one of the ants separates from the colony and climbs a nearby tree into the forest canopy. The ant bites into the tree branch and sub-sequently dies. Soon a mushroom grows out of the ant's brain, a fungus horn protruding from its head. Nurtured by the ant's remains, the mushroom matures and subsequently rains spores back down to the forest floor. Once again, an unsuspecting ant inhales the spores and repeats the ritual. The mushroom has ingeniously devised a way to change the ant's behavior in order to achieve its own objectives. In this case the mushroom turns the ants into zombies that assist in mushroom reproduction.

Like much in the book, it's unclear whether the Prong-horned ant is a real species and yet it is a useful sustainability metaphor. Like the mushroom, sustainability practitioners need to uncover creative, and often subversive, ways to change people's attitudes and behavior. In companies, sustainability can become a spore that infects corporate culture, influencing a company's decision-making process, often in imperceptible ways.

The key to achieving this, when you don't have biological weaponry like fungus spores at your disposal, is language. The way we talk to people about sustainability is crucial in gaining new supporters, particularly when it comes to environmental issues. Nature faces many challenges, many of which are confusing or hard to understand. If we want people to support environmental protection, we can't talk to the public using the technical language of scientists or the fundraising spiels of foundations.

This point was made plain to me during a three-day board meeting The Nature Conservancy held in Punta Cana. The Board consists of a dozen or so scientists, philanthropists, and highly successful businesspeople who chip in their time, money and expertise to help protect Nature around the world. At the meeting I had the opportunity to chat with one of board members. His background is taking over large, complex companies in financial trouble and turning them around and he explained to me why environmentalists so often fail to make more headway in the business world.

"When you talk about the environment to a manager at your company, you have to know they have many other problems they are busy with. When the environment guy walks into their office, they are probably thinking, 'What do I need to do to get this guy out of here so I can get on with my day?' What if, instead of trying to tell that person what he or she can do to achieve *your* environmental objectives, you ask them what *their* biggest problem is and offer to help them solve it? Don't you think they would be in less of a hurry to get rid of you?"

His point was simple. Few people are actively looking for ways to make their lives more complicated. They want solutions that make their life and work *easier*. Much like Auden Schendler hanging around the maintenance department, looking for creative ways to solve the machinists' biggest challenges, getting results in a corporation can depend on your approach. If you are part of their solution, you can imperceptibly nudge the solution you provide towards the sustainable alternative.

If we can connect with people through language, we can make our mission that much easier to achieve. All too often, foundations don't speak to the needs of their constituents, instead trying to forcibly change their mind with facts and figures. Sometimes, you don't need to change their mind (or forcibly infect it with a mushroom spore). You need to talk to their kids.

PREACHING TO THE UNCONVERTED

In 2003, our coral restoration project had a problem. At that time, coral restoration was still considered a pseudo-science by many marine scientists. We were having trouble attracting funding to support our work. While our CEO was willing to be patient as the corals grew, his daughter Francesca, who oversees the company's finances, was more skeptical. "When can we stop paying for coral reef restoration?" she wanted to know. It was a reasonable but uncomfortable question.

My experience with GPC's number-crunchers had taught me how hard it is to deploy a purely economic argument to justify restoring ecosystems, especially ones as complex as coral reefs. Coral restoration is a long-term endeavor. If we are really successful, we still expect restoration to take decades to produce real economic impact for the resort. I considered making the argument about the economic value of healthy reefs in mitigating the destruction of storms and hurricanes, an argument that scientists had proven to be true. Protecting reefs is an investment, much like insurance, in protecting human infrastructure.

But that angle requires complicated ecological modeling, which is theoretical and difficult to explain to non-scientists. Besides, the bean counters were better with numbers than I am. My shaky math was likely to get me into trouble trying to calculate reef valuation. Our foundation needed a different angle to change Francesca's mind.

Dr. Austin Bowden-Kerby, the singing Santa of coral restoration, happened to be visiting Punta Cana at that time. I decided to let him do the heavy lifting on behalf of the corals. I invited Francesca and her two young sons snorkeling, where they would meet Austin for a boat-side coral reef class. Francesca was always on the lookout for new experiences for her kids, so she agreed. I was sure she had never met a character like Austin before so at the very least she might find coral restoration entertaining.

Austin met them and gave them one of his animated coral speeches. He broke out a traditional reef song in native Fijian. He told them all about coral reefs and the creatures that inhabit them. He explained how corals are actually two symbiotic organisms and how dead corals go on to form vast reefs throughout the tropics. He explained their role in creating and protecting the nearby beaches. Austin taught them how restoration, though experimental, was important, specifically to beach-based tourism. Bobbing in a floating classroom, the boys were fascinated. Then Austin led them snorkeling so they could see the restored reef firsthand.

The plan worked. Whether it had to do with her kids or she just forgot about coral reefs, I gradually got less questioning from Francesca about coral restoration. I also received less resistance from our finance department. Our coral nursery continued to grow. As coral gardening began popping up around the Caribbean, our foundation became a reference for restoration. We started attracting new funding. Rather than a drain on Grupo Puntacana, coral restoration became a signature sustainability initiative. With new money from donors, Francesca officially became a cheerleader of the project.

This was an important lesson. Sustainability is never a given. Just because your foundation works for a righteous cause, there is no guarantee anyone else cares, even your friends and colleagues. There are always going to be non-believers that don't pray at the environmental altar like you do. Most people don't know what a coral reef is, much less lose sleep at night thinking about how threatened they are. We wanted to protect corals, but first we needed to develop a toolbox of strategies to connect with people, finding a way to win them over. At the very least, we had to keep them from being an obstacle.

Some folks may need to hear a business case for restoring corals, others may need a Fijian folk song. At the end of the day, the argument you use to connect people to your cause is less important than getting them to buy in. Austin taught Francesca's kids about the fascinating world of coral reefs and her kids convinced her they needed to be protected. That was it. I had deployed Austin and he sprinkled the spores, like the fungus directing the Prong-horned ant to climb the tree. In the short term, the return on Grupo Puntacana's investment became less relevant.

SOLUTIONISM

More than thirty years ago, my mom put the hit out on an endangered alligator in our front yard, which launched my career in environmental protection. It started over a simple conflict: the alligator was innocently sunning itself next to our pond. Though minding its own business, to my mom the gator represented a lethal threat to me, my brother, and our dogs. The alligator was a federally protected species. It couldn't be touched. This prompted my mom to recruit our shotgun-toting neighbor to dispatch it instead.

The Endangered Species Act is an incredibly effective law. The American alligator, and many other species, benefited from its protection and eventually recovered. Yet even as a small kid, I recognized that any law that led people to do the opposite of what it intended had weaknesses. Instead of protecting the alligator, we shot it.

Sustainability tries to sort out this exact sort of predicament: How to achieve abundant and healthy Nature while accounting for the ever-expanding footprint of human beings on the planet. In other words, how to protect alligators while providing safe spaces for kids to play. Uncovering better ways for humans to co-exist with animals in the landscape was just the type of messy dilemma that I was looking to decode. Sustainability became my mission.

Sustainability, however, has created another dilemma for me. What do you call those of us working in this new field? Life would be easier if we had a recognized title, like plumber or scientist, but there just doesn't seem to be an easy name for sustainability advocates. Sustainability practitioner?

Sustainability-ist? Sustainable developer? Describing my work is like answering the phone with a mouth full of peanut butter. By the time the person you are talking with understands what you're talking about, they get bored and move on. Not even my mom knows what I do for a living.

One term I try to avoid is "sustainability expert." Tim Ferris, author of *The 4-Hour Workweek*, pokes fun at the idea of the "expert" by outlining a recipe to become one in any subject, in just four weeks. His formula involves reading the three top-selling books on your topic, giving a couple of free seminars at the closest well-known university, and offering to write one or two articles for trade magazines. In just four weeks, you can become knowledgeable enough about any subject to speak competently about it, potentially getting paid to do so. You have become an "expert."

Ferris invoked the wrath of academics, PhDs, and public speakers worldwide for his subtle potshot at the idea of the expert, but he makes a good point. Since no one owns the term, it can be coopted by virtually anyone, regardless of their underlying qualifications.

More to the point, in sustainability it's more useful to be a generalist than an expert anyway. We live in a fast-changing and complicated world. We are barely hanging on by our fingernails in the face of an onslaught of constantly evolving challenges—rising seas, crippling poverty, mass extinctions, inequality, extreme weather, global pandemics.

Sustainability demands constantly immersing ourselves in new and different disciplines and honing the skills needed to confront new challenges. Rather than an unswerving focus on one area alone, sustainability pros need to aspire to be pan-tomaths, people with exceptionally broad knowledge across human learning, experience, and scholarship. Being a specialist or expert in a single discipline is not always useful given the diversity of risks we face.

Another term I tend to avoid is "environmentalist." If I use the term at all, it's only grudgingly as shorthand for someone that cares passionately about the environment, as opposed to a job title. Environmentalist is too much of a limiting term, much like "ecotourism." It weighs heavy on the side of the environment at the expense of people and business. Besides, it's tough to be a hardcore "environmentalist" when you work for a development company.

To confront environmental degradation, it's critical to understand the forces working against Nature. When you work with businesses, it's not helpful to stake your position as the opposition from the outset. Few businesspeople want to hire an environmental extremist. Grupo Puntacana is a for-profit company, not a national park. "Environmentalist" sounds more like the people that would be picketing the gates of our resort than the type of problem-solver willing to work for one.

While I admire the original "druid," David Brower (see chapter 6), the guy who would "sacrifice people and worship trees," I am convinced that environmental militancy alone doesn't work. We certainly need visionaries and extremists like Brower to set the boundaries and demand a purist view of protecting Nature. We need Julia Hill to chain herself to a tree to protect the forest. But we also need solution-minded doers in the weeds, finding areas of compromise.

Getting green done means not only working *against* companies, it requires infiltrating them and changing them from within. This means recruiting more "grunts," like Auden Schendler, to demonstrate to companies how it's good business to protect the planet and give people a better life. Sustainability forces companies to reconcile people, planet, and profit. It's crucial that the environment is in the mix of business decision-making, even if it doesn't always win every argument, as environmentalists would have it.

After years of stumbling around a title for myself, I settled on a term coined by law professor, author, and former dean of the Yale Forestry School Gus Speth. In his book, *The Bridge at the Edge of the World*, Speth defines a "solutionist" as a determined problem-solver committed to taking on complex challenges.

According to Speth, there are different degrees of solutionist, but the underlying principle is a disposition to acknowledge and proactively confront the major social and environmental challenges we face. Solutionists don't deny reality or the science that explains it, nor are they intimidated by the scale of the challenge. They are roll-up-your-shirtsleeves and get to work type of people. Solutionist has become both my title and my worldview.

I identify with the term so much that for ten years I helped organize and co-host the Solutionists Awards (*solutionistas* in Spanish) in the Dominican Republic. The award has recognized different individuals, companies, and organizations that embody the problem-solving ethos Speth espouses.

At first, my Dominican colleagues thought I was mangling my Spanish, since *solutionista* is not a word found in the Spanish dictionary. Over time, though, we recognized more than fifty solutionists. Their achievements made the term's meaning speak for itself. Farmers, photographers, fishermen, supermarket chains, community leaders, electric companies, businessmen, and YouTubers, among others. The awardees brought diverse experiences and skill sets from all parts of Dominican society to solve real problems. Few were environmentalists or sustainability experts. In the end, the award served not only to celebrate the good work of each participant, but also to illustrate an expansive and inclusive approach to sustainability.

THE RED PILL

Though I may not be a grizzled old-timer, even I can remember a time when the general public barely talked about environmental issues. Environmental destruction was generally buried deep in the newspaper or covered on television during catastrophic events, like the Exxon Valdez oil spill in Alaska. You really had to dig around to learn about climate change. For most people, the environment was pretty easy to ignore.

Today, environmental issues have gone mainstream. This is due, in part, to the proliferation of new ways we get information. Besides old-school newspapers and television, we connect to current events through the internet, podcasts, streaming video, and social media, just to name a few. With more ways to absorb information, we are bombarded with content about damage to the environment from seemingly infinite angles, apps, and outlets. The environment would be difficult to ignore even if we wanted to.

Another explanation for this increased public awareness, however, is the newfound immediacy of environmental threats. Natural disasters are no longer distant, theoretical notions that will affect our great-grandchildren someday. Coronaviruses, fires, hurricanes, floods, red tides, and plastic islands are trending topics every day. The frequency and immediacy of these natural and manmade disasters have made environmental issues more tangible and newsworthy.

As public awareness has increased, the public, particularly young people, are becoming more engaged. Studies show that younger generations, such as millennials, are increasingly imbedding social and environmental considerations in their lifestyles, purchasing decisions, and career choices. Environment and sustainability is on their minds at an increasingly early age.

I often get approached by kids and their parents looking for sustainability career advice. Should they study marine biology? Start an eco-friendly business? Retreat to a cave in the mountains?

Seeing young people wade into these challenges, I am reminded of the scene in the Matrix, when Morpheus presents Neo with an existential choice. He can take the blue pill and drift off into a life of tranquility, security, and blissful ignorance of the realities of the world. The blue pill is how we have treated the environment for a long time. We either pretend there is no issue or assume someone else will solve it.

Neo's other option is to take the red pill, becoming fully conscious of our harsh reality. Though our world may not be as dystopian as the Matrix, the state of Nature is not always pretty. Humankind has made amazing progress in many ways, but we have definitely abused the planet and its myriad ecosytems.

Sometimes I think, "Take the blue pill, kid. Forget about marine biology. Stay ignorant."

In the end, though, solutionists are optimists. There are certainly days I want to hide under a blanket with a bottle of rum and forget about the threats facing our planet. Yet I fundamentally believe we are as capable of solving environmental crises as we are at creating them. The more aware younger generations are of the uphill battle we face, the better equipped they will be to unearth solutions. The only chance we have at solving overwhelming issues like climate change is by rolling up our sleeves and getting to work.

Protecting the planet means taking the red pill. But I rarely encourage advice seekers to pursue a career dedicated to sustainability. Instead, I encourage them to embed sustainability in their chosen profession, whatever it is. We need an army of sustainability soldiers that, regardless of their career choice, get sustainability on the agenda of businesses and governments. If you are going to be an engineer, be a sustainable engineer. If you are going to be a banker, consider sustainability in your investments. There is literally no profession today that doesn't have some potential to help people and the planet. Companies will continue to be sleeping giants until they are prodded awake. Whether as an artist, an architect or a café barista, we all possess the power to force companies to become drivers of solutions.

It's not going to be easy. But the planet, even in a severely degraded state, is still worth fighting for. As Albert Camus said, "One must imagine Sisyphus happy. The struggle itself toward the heights is enough to fill a man's heart."

ACKNOWLEDGMENTS

TO MY BEAUTIFUL WIFE KRYSTAL, THANK YOU FOR YOUR counsel, encouragement, and patience; I would not have been able to complete my first book without you. Jacob and Victoria, I hope someday hawks, parrotfish, and other wild creatures inspire you to explore and protect our incredible natural world. To the best big bro, Billy Kheel, and amazing family, Marina, Max, and Mia Kheel, a guy could ask for, thank you for putting up with my adventures in eco-warrioring. Mom, your passion for plants and animals has been one of the main inspirations for my career in environmental protection. Thanks to you and Danny for your support.

To the Rainieri family: Frank, Haydee, Francesca, Paola y Frank Elias, it has been an incredible experience working with and learning from each of you. Sustainable development is not just an idea, it is your life's work. I am honored to have been part of it.

My respect and gratitude to the extended family of Ted and Ann Kheel. To board members Robert and Daniel Kheel; Arnold, Ellen, and Beryl Jacobs; your consistent financial and moral support of sustainability have allowed us to continue

Ted's legacy in Punta Cana. AJ Jacobs, Thanks A Thousand for taking me under your wing and being so supportive and generous with your time. Jane, Rick, and Gabby, your affection for Punta Cana is contagious, I always enjoy our conversations on how best to protect it. Julie, Jasper, Zane, Lucas, David, Allison, Douglas, Connie, Dunya, Kate, Eliyahu, Rachel, Sarah, Rivka, and Marti (RIP), your diverse points of view and ideas add great value to our work in Punta Cana. Valerie Anderson, working side by side with you taught me more than you know.

To the current and former staff of the Grupo Puntacana Foundation, this book is my attempt to glean lessons from our sustainability journey together. Sustainability is a process of experimentation and continual learning; it has been amazing sharing this experience with you. Kelly Robinson de Schaun, Susanne Leib, Paul Beswick, Ben Hulefeld, Alejandro Herrera, Maribel Sanchez, Victor Galvan, Griselda Osorio, Rosemary Capellan, Miguel Betances, Daniel Garcia, Daniel Veras, Antonio Barletta, Noel Heinsohn, Laura del Rio, Ainhoa Zubillaga, Rebecca Garcia, Samantha Mercado, Welinton de la Rosa, Aracelis Jimenez, Pedro Julio de Castillo (Rubio), Enyi Baez, Margarita Pillier, and Hipolito Bera, my gratitude for your hard work and perseverance in making Punta Cana a more sustainable destination.

My colleagues at Grupo Puntacana have treated me like family. The ingenuity, creativity, and commitment of our leadership team (past and present) is one of reasons the company has evolved into a sustainability leader. Over the course of fifteen years, I have received unconditional support from too many people to mention here; here is a much abbreviated list: Adolfo Ramirez, Frank Llibre, Alberto Abreu, Karina Guaba, Augusto Casasnovas, Simon Suarez, Julio Diaz, Vincenzo Calcerano, Luis Migoya, Luis Villanueva, Fernando Soler, Hiram Silfa, Ingrid Herrera, Giovanni Rainieri, Alberto Smith, Walter

Zemialkowski, Yudith Castillo, Ernesto Veloz, Lourdes Montas, Wilson Mejia, Liana Reyes, Manuel Sajour, Jessica Rizek, Francisco Suero, Oscar Gonzalez, Antonio Martorell, Radhames Martinez, and Jose Oliva.

My gratitude and respect to the original Board of Directors of the Grupo Puntacana Foundation: Camilo Suero Marranzini, Oscar Imbert, Bernardo Vega. Eduardo Latorre, Freddy Beras Goico, and Welinton Ramos, may you rest in peace.

Grupo Puntacana has benefitted immeasurably from collaborations with diverse partners, and I have had the good fortune to learn from many of you. Jaime Moreno, you are the original solutionist, connecting me to new ideas, technologies, and mad scientists. Joan Parker, Teresa Crawford, Paola Frohring, Dennis Taylor, Austin Bowden-Kerby, and our partners from Counterpart International, your decades-long support has pushed our coral work to new heights. My respect to our long-term partners at The Peregrine Fund, Peter Jenny, Russell Thorstrom, Rick Watson, Marta Curti, Thomas and Christina Hayes, and Martin Quiroga, helping bring the Ridgway's hawk back from the brink of extinction is one of my proudest accomplishments. My gratitude to Joe Pollock, Francisco Núñez, Ximena Escovar Fadul, Lisa Price, Aldo Croquer, Greg Asner, Dr. David Vaughan, Nicolas Pascal, and The Nature Conservancy for lending your conservation experience and expertise to our efforts in Punta Cana.

Without the financial and technical support of our donors, many of the examples in this book never would have been possible. My thanks to Smeldy Ramirez, Lorena Mejicanos Rios, Miguel Coronado, and Santiago Soler for making a lasting and sustainable investment in sustainable tourism in Punta Cana. Svenja Paulino Rodriguez, Mauricio Solano Fernandez, Lars Gottschalk, and Jose Alberto Garcia, you have been model partners. My gratitude to the Caribbean Biodiversity Fund and the Ecosystem-based Adaptation Facility, Joth Singh, Yabanex Batista, Ulrike Krauss, and Junior Buchanan for supporting the coral reefs of the Dominican Republic. Alberto Sanchez and Noris Araujo from the UNDP Small Grants Programme, your steady support has laid the foundation for many of our sustainability achievements.

The Center for Sustainability was launched when Ted Kheel and Eloy Rodriguez hatched an unusual plan for a premier university to help solve problems at a Caribbean resort. I had the opportunity to work with and mentor under Eloy and Erick Fernandes at Cornell University, and I am grateful for their insights and unwavering support. Among the early pioneers from Cornell in Punta Cana were Dave Stipanik, Andre Dhondt, and Manuel Aregullin, thanks to you the Center has evolved into something truly remarkable.

The Center has since grown, expanded, and been enriched by partnerships with diverse universities. Brian Farrell, I value our friendship and your many contributions to my work and career, you have been a consistent and valued partner. Diego Lirman and his team at University of Miami, I am grateful for your contributions to the protection and restoration of Dominican coral reefs. Don Melnick, I miss our many conversations in the "cone of silence," may you rest in peace. My thanks to our partners from Virginia Tech and the Via College of Osteopathic Medicine for lending your time, research, and students to Punta Cana: Dean Sutphin, Dixie Rawlins, Brian Mihalik, Theo Dillaha, Lisa Kennedy, John Dooley, Mark Widdowson, Tom Tillar, Tom Duetsch, and SK Dedatta. Jocelyn Widmer, our understanding of the local community and its myriad challenges has been enhanced by your research, my gratitude to you and your students. My thanks to our friends and collaborators from Roger Williams University including Lisa Raiola, Andy Rhyne, Sarah Reusche, Ben Greenstein, Amy Berkeley, and Arlene Violet.

To Megan Epler-Wood, Tom Lovejoy, Andy Revkin, Martha Honey, Greg Miller, and Don Hawkins, thank you for your time, thoughts, and comments on this book. My thanks to Francoise Letacanois for reviewing a draft of the book, your contribution to Grupo Puntacana's history may not be widely known, but it was invaluable, nonetheless.

The Dominican Republic is full of quiet heroes working to save the island's incredible natural resources, and I have been lucky to call many of them friends and collaborators. Many thanks to Dra. Pirigua Bonetti de Santana, Eladio Fernandez, Yolanda Leon, Marvin del Cid, Ines Aizpun, Rosanna Rivera, Maribel Lazala, William Phelan, Sofia Perazzo, Rita Sellares, Sésar Rodriguez, Ariel Contreras, Omar Shamir Reynoso, Jose Alejandro Alvarez, Ruben Torres, Ivan Gomez, Gibel Orsini, Miosotis Batista, Yohanan Nuñez, Carlos Sanchez, Paola Tineo, Maria Alicia Urbaneja, and Guillermo Rickart.

I am fortunate to have a diverse group of friends that challenge my thinking, introduce me to new ideas, and have supported my work in Punta Cana in different ways over the years. Danny Forster, I'm proud of our Punta Cana collaborations together and happy to share them here. Kahlil Lozoraitis, from reviewing this manuscript to saving dolphins together, you've been in my corner for a long time and I appreciate it. Ben Selkow, you are a drill sergeant and camp counselor at the same time; I am a better professional for our work together. Archie Kasnet, Julio Cantre, Dan Furlong, Davis Thompson-Moss, Chris Coyle, Nina Kontos, Bobbi Lin, Matt Snyder, Kabir Sen, Dan Lawren, Nate Gordon, Jon Bloom, Keith Witty, Ross Stafford, Dan and Emily Shotz, Josh Harris, Phillip Frank, Johnny Sherman, Steve Culman, Mark Labouchere, Jack Kenworthy, Lizzie Nytray, Warren and Jenny Surcouf, Juan Mejia, Juancho Yepes, and Juan Carlos Castañeda, I appreciate our friendships immensely.

I was fortunate to find Scribe and encouraged to actually write a book by Charlie Hoehn and Freddy Ginebra; thanks guys, it's been awesome. Steve Johnson, you have been part psychologist, part writing partner during fours year of work on this project. I am indebted to your patience and contributions to *Waking the Sleeping Giant*. To the team at Scribe, Tucker Max, Libby Allen, Michael Nagin, Alan Gintzler, and Holly Gorman, thank you for getting this book over the finish line!

ABOUT THE AUTHOR

JAKE KHEEL is an environmental innovator whose efforts in the Dominican Republic with the Grupo Puntacana Foundation have won numerous awards and made the country's tourism more competitive and environmentally sustainable. Jake directs the Center for Sustainability, a think tank partnering with renowned universities to conduct environmental research, and helped pioneer one of the Caribbean's largest coral reef restoration projects. Jake frequently speaks at international conferences, including TEDx Santo Domingo. He's been widely published, including the Huffington Post, *Luxury Hotels* magazine, and Harvard's ReVista. To learn more, visit JakeKheel.com.